# Understanding
# Asian Philosophy

## ALSO AVAILABLE FROM BLOOMSBURY

*Classical Chinese Philosophy*, Manyul Im

*Confucius*, Charlene Tan

*Confucius: A Guide for the Perplexed*, Yong Huang

*Daoism: A Guide for the Perplexed*, Louis Komjathy

*The Bloomsbury Research Handbook to Chinese Philosophy and Gender Studies*, edited by Ann Pang-White

*The Bloomsbury Research Handbook to Indian Aesthetics and the Philosophy of Art*, edited by Arindam Chakrabarti

*The Bloomsbury Research Handbook to Indian Epistemology and Metaphysics*, edited by Joerg Tuske

*The Bloomsbury Research Handbook to Indian Philosophical Theories of Religion*, edited by Pankaj Jain

*The Daoist Tradition: An Introduction*, Louis Komjathy

# Understanding Asian Philosophy

Ethics in the Analects, Zhuangzi, Dhammapada and the Bhagavad Gita

**ALEXUS MCLEOD**

B L O O M S B U R Y
LONDON • NEW DELHI • NEW YORK • SYDNEY

**Bloomsbury Academic**

An imprint of Bloomsbury Publishing Plc

| | |
|---|---|
| 50 Bedford Square | 1385 Broadway |
| London | New York |
| WC1B 3DP | NY 10018 |
| UK | USA |

**www.bloomsbury.com**

**Bloomsbury is a registered trade mark of Bloomsbury Publishing Plc**

First published 2014

© Alexus McLeod 2014

Alexus McLeod has asserted his right under the Copyright, Designs and Patents Act, 1988, to be identified as the Author of this work.

**British Library Cataloguing-in-Publication Data**
A catalogue record for this book is available from the British Library.

ISBN: HB: 978-1-7809-3631-4
PB: 978-1-7809-3573-7
ePDF: 978-1-7809-3770-0
ePub: 978-1-7809-3742-7

**Library of Congress Cataloging-in-Publication Data**
McLeod, Alexus, author.
Understanding Asian philosophy : ethics in the Analects, Zhuangzi, Dhammapada and the Bhagavad Gita / Alexus McLeod.
pages cm
ISBN 978-1-78093-631-4 (hardback)– ISBN 978-1-78093-573-7 (paperback)–
ISBN 978-1-78093-770-0 (ePDF)– ISBN   978-1-78093-742-7 (epub)
1. Philosophy, Asian. 2. Religious ethics–East Asia. 3. Religious ethics–India. I. Title.
B121.M35 2014
181–dc23
2014006390

Typeset by Fakenham Prepress Solutions, Fakenham, Norfolk NR21 8NN
Printed and bound in India

*For Siddhartha and Francis. Never stop learning.*
*There is something more than all of this.*

# Contents

# Introduction: Ethical Philosophy in Asian Traditions

In every philosophical tradition, thinkers have been concerned with the questions of ethics. How should I/we live? What actions are right? What does it mean for something to be good? More importantly, how can I/we do the right thing, and become good? Ethical thought is more than merely lists of moral norms or rules to guide one's life. Ethics aims at understanding what the ideal life is for both the individual and the community, and also, crucially, at helping the individual attain such a life. It is this second part of the ethical pursuit that is often neglected in philosophical study of the topic today, and through much of the western tradition. We will see that this aspect of ethical thought, however, was the primary concern of many of the philosophers of the Chinese and Indian traditions. Many thinkers within these traditions focused on and developed self-cultivational aspects of ethics. It was with the *way* to become ideal persons that the thinkers we will look at were concerned. All of them, though they have sometimes very different ideas about the ideal life, had as their ultimate goal aiding the student to achieve a better life. Just what such a life consists of is for us to consider through our investigation of these four texts and traditions.

One might ask the question: why Asian philosophy? And why these four texts? To the first question, I respond thus: the Asian philosophical traditions have much to teach us, in the west. The western philosophical traditions are often very different, and though they are certainly rich and interesting in themselves, there are many other considerations and important developments in Asian philosophy that were never made in western philosophy (and vice versa). In our attempt to answer the basic questions of ethics and to discover and cultivate the ideal life, it is important to pay attention to the thought of all those who have worked hard to answer these questions. The majority of the people of the world are, and have been, in Asia, and the majority of thinkers are there as well. We thus would do well to listen to and take seriously what philosophers from this area of the world have to say about the questions of ethics.

Another good reason to consider Asian philosophical texts is that they help us to see different ways of thinking, and consider how those ways of thinking might help us to answer or dissolve difficult philosophical problems. One doesn't generally make headway on solving problems by thinking conservatively and using the same patterns of thought again and again. We gain insight by thinking differently about problems, by experimenting, trying new things, by being able to entertain completely unique and unorthodox possibilities. In addition, we come to understand the cultural background of the majority of the world's people, throughout east and south Asia. Especially today, as our lives are lived globally as never before in the history of humanity, it is important to understand features of the culture of such massive parts of the world. The thinkers and texts we focus on here were widely influential, even far outside of the places of their own birth. Confucianism, for example, not only profoundly influenced what is today China, but also Korea, Japan, and much of Southeast Asia. Likewise, the originally Indian tradition of Buddhism had an even farther reach, coming to influence all of the Confucian societies of east Asia, as well as all of south and Southeast Asia (including modern day Afghanistan and Pakistan), and even into the north Asian steppe (Mongolia, Russia), and west into Europe (the modern Russian region of Kalmykia is a majority Buddhist area).

This begins to help answer the question of why I focus on *these* four texts and traditions. The *Analects*, *Zhuangzi*, *Dhammapada*, and *Bhagavad Gita* are each representative of a major and influential school of thought in Asian philosophy that influenced people even beyond its own cultural birthplace. One of the things this shows us is that there is something about these texts that makes them interesting and useful not only to those within the "home culture" of the text, but that is more universal, and speaks to people on a more fundamental level. The *Analects* is not a text for Chinese people, the *Bhagavad Gita* is not a text for Indian people, any more than Shakespeare's plays are for Brits or Don Quixote is for Spaniards. The greatest works speak to universal themes in humanity, and aim to guide all people. The texts I have chosen certainly fit the bill in that regard. And in addition, they are all concerned with thinking about and bringing about the ideal life, for a variety of reasons. We will see that what they have to say about the ideal life and how we can attain it diverge, even while also agreeing on some fundamental points.

# Kinds of philosophy

One difficulty in studying Asian philosophy is that the Asian traditions were not, and are not, continuous with the ancient Greek tradition from which philosophy takes its name and its aims. No one in the periods and places in which the thinkers we consider in this book lived would understand themselves to be doing "philosophy" in the sense in which most of us mean this word. They certainly had no equivalent *term* to the English "philosophy" (from Greek "philosophia"—"love of wisdom"). In modern times, terms have been invented to express this idea, including the modern Chinese term *zhe xue* 哲學, translated to English as "sage studies." In India, the ancient term "*darshan*" has been co-opted for use as a translation of "philosophy," although the original meaning of *darshana* is quite different from what we understand as "philosophy."

In order to understand how we might see the ancient Asian thinkers considered in this book as engaged in philosophy, we should first consider the question of just what *philosophy* is. The way the ancient Greek "creators" of philosophy understood it was as a way of discovering truths, through rational methods, normally having to do with *a priori* reasoning (that is, reasoning that does not have to do with observations or empirical evidence), and involving demonstrations, proofs, and conceptual analysis (that is, expression of definitions linked to concepts and theories). Today, "philosophy" still has these connotations, and has also become known as an academic field, practiced by college and university professors who write articles and books advancing one or other issue considered an aspect of the field. Thought of in this way, philosophy is seen as containing a number of distinct areas, each with their own questions. Ethics is one of these, and some others are metaphysics, epistemology, logic, philosophy of mind, philosophy of science, political philosophy, etc.

Although the traditions we will look at in this book are much different from what we might think of today as philosophy, they are concerned with the same problems as philosophers throughout the western tradition, and attempt to solve these problems in similar ways, most importantly through certain kinds of thought and conceptual analysis. Although the thinkers in each of these traditions do much more than *just* such analysis, and for this reason might be considered more than (only) philosophers, they all do engage in philosophical thought as major components of their projects.

# Ethical theories

If we want to call the thinkers and texts covered in this book *ethical*, we first need to understand just what we mean by "ethical thought," and in what sense the thinkers and texts covered are interested in ethics. It is important to make a distinction between *ethics* and *morality* here, because all the thinkers and texts we will explore are concerned with ethics, but not all of them are concerned with morality. Indeed, the *Zhuangzi* (perhaps our most "unconventional" text) claims that morality is part of the *problem*. So what is ethics, and how does it differ from morality?

Ethics deals with the broadest questions of how the individual or community should live. We more commonly call the questions of individual life ethical, however, as we in the western tradition relegate most questions of communal life to the realm of *political philosophy* or politics in general. There is a great deal of overlap between these two areas, however, even in the west. Some of the thinkers we examine in this book would not accept a distinction between the two in the first place. Especially for Confucius and the authors of the *Bhagavad Gita*, the questions of the ideal individual life are inseparable from those of the ideal communal life. And for Confucius most clearly, ethics *is* politics, for reasons we will discuss in Chapter 1. Thus, we do not see such a distinction made between ethical and political questions in these texts.

Given this, we ought to frame the main question of ethics thus (ambiguously between focus on the individual and the community): "How should we live?" The attempt to answer this question will generally focus on notions such as thriving, happiness, harmony, and order. All ethical theories assume that we should live in ways that lead to realization of the proper values—that is, we ought to strive to attain those things or states that have intrinsic value. What these proper values are is a source of contention stretching back thousands of years. What are the values at which we should aim? Wealth? Power? Virtue? Knowledge? Salvation? This is a consideration of all of the thinkers we will examine.

How, then, does ethics differ from *morality*? One way of thinking about morality is that it has to do specifically with actions, and the value of acts. Morality asks the question: "what makes an act *right*?" Something is moral or immoral insofar as it is a right or wrong action. Many thinkers who are concerned with ethics are also concerned with morality. It might seem to us natural or inevitable that ethical thinkers would have such concerns. After all, how can we possibly answer questions about the ideal life and the values connected to it without taking a position on right and wrong action? We will see that three of the texts we examine do deal with both ethics and morality, but that *Zhuangzi* is an interesting exception in this (as it is in so much else). Not only is Zhuangzi unconcerned with morality, but he thinks that as long as one sees things in terms of "right" and "wrong," and strives to act consistent with one or the other, one can never attain a truly thriving life. For Zhuangzi, we will see, attainment of the ethical ideal requires *rejection* of morality. By this, he doesn't mean rejection of *goodness* (in the way we might say that a villain "rejects morality"), but rejection of the categories of right and wrong, good and bad altogether. One of the interesting things Zhuangzi shows us, then, is that it is possible for ethics and morality to come apart. They truly are distinct.

# Asian traditions

There is a related question about Asian traditions, and the question of the identity of philosophy and religion, and their relationship in Asian thought.

For the traditions and schools we will focus on in this book, self-cultivation is the central, overarching issue behind all philosophical thought. Of course, all of these schools, as well as others in Asian philosophy in general, were interested in much more than just self-cultivation. We find robust metaphysical, epistemological, logical, and physical theories in almost all of the Asian philosophical traditions, for example. In most cases, however, all of the non-ethical components of philosophical thought were ultimately seen as being in the service of the central issue of self-cultivation. This is especially so in the case of the traditions we will look at in this book, Confucianism, Zhuangist Daoism, Buddhism, and Vedantic Brahmanism (known today as "Hinduism"). In these traditions, the questions surrounding the ideal person and self-cultivation are central, and other philosophical pursuits are engaged in only insofar as they help us to understand the path of self-cultivation or help us to follow this path to move toward becoming ideal persons.

For this reason, among others, these traditions are often classified as *religions* rather than as *philosophical schools*. In this book we will be overlooking this key distinction for a number of reasons.

First, in many of the Asian traditions (this is certainly true for much of Chinese and Indian thought), there was not a clear distinction made between religion and philosophy as there often is in the west. There are a number of likely reasons for this. Given that religions in Asia are not always concerned with transcendent divinities and Gods or a God, unlike the western theistic religions, there is no clear division between religion, as concerned with *theology* (study of God or gods) and philosophical theory, concerned with ontology, ethics, etc. Insofar as philosophy is understood as the rational investigation (usually *a priori*) of central questions surrounding existence, the world, and our lives, it generally tends to be thought of as proceeding separately of a consideration of God or gods, at least in contemporary conceptions of philosophy (in medieval Europe, although, philosophy and theology were much less clearly distinguished from one another). This is not to say that philosophy cannot deal with God or issues in theistic religion (indeed, there is an entire area of philosophical thought, often called "philosophy of religion" that deals with such issues), but such issues are not taken, in distinction to theology, as central to or definitive of the philosophical pursuit. Perhaps we can think of *reasoning* or (the vague and diffuse) *rational method* as the central feature of philosophy, in the most familiar conception. Religion, on the other hand, is taken to deal with not only transcendent entities like deities, but to surround doctrine, metaphysical and ethical, not necessarily established on the basis of or considered using rational methods. Thus, in religion we find things like revelation and faith take center stage.

This characterization of the differences between religion and philosophy tend to break down, however, when we consider the systems of thought of classical China and India. Part of the difficulty is that some systems we would otherwise recognize as religions, such as Buddhism, certain forms of Confucianism, and Daoism, have no clearly defined conception of a deity or deities, and in the case of Buddhism are non-theistic or even atheistic (there are even certain schools of "Hinduism" such as Mimamsa that reject the existence of a God or gods). In much of the west, theism and religion go hand in hand almost to the point of identity, and this is a major difference between eastern and western religious culture. In addition, the rational methods at the core of what we know as philosophy are often explicitly cultivated and used in eastern religious traditions, including the ones covered in this book. In the case of each of these traditions, there are aspects of the systems that appear to us religious and other aspects that appear philosophical. And it is also true that the members of these traditions themselves never made an explicit distinction between these two types of pursuit—religion and philosophy. Each of the traditions we consider here has a robust historical catalogue of ceremony and ritual, doctrines aimed at achieving soteriological or salvific purposes, and a class of representatives who maintain doctrinal and ceremonial cohesion, a "priestly" class of sorts. All of these things we would recognize as elements of religions. At the same time, all of the traditions engage in rational methods and argument to establish conclusions supporting doctrinal views, stress the importance and indeed the necessity of the rational and reflective life, and consider formative, foundational questions of existence, the world, and ourselves using the toolbox of human rationality (some focus on rationality more than others). All of these things we would recognize as elements of religion. So perhaps the most accurate thing we can say about these traditions concerning the distinction between religion and philosophy is that such a distinction is ill suited to understanding Asian systems of thought, even if it is somewhat useful in the context of western thought. We should try to avoid, and I will in this book refrain from, using this distinction in connection with the Asian schools of thought we will investigate here.

## Self-cultivation in Asian philosophical traditions—the layout of this book

This brings us to the central issue of this book—a consideration of the positions of these four schools of thought concerning the development of the person and the attainment of the ideal life. All four thinkers and texts we will examine held that it is possible for anyone to attain an ideal life. We need three things in order to do this: 1) an understanding of why we fail to have ideal lives; 2) an understanding of what constitutes an ideal life; and 3) a method for moving ourselves closer to this ideal life. Each of the thinkers and texts examined in this book offer views on all three of these. Our consideration of them, then, surrounds their positions on these three points.

Each chapter is organized such that the first sections consider the relevant views on why people fail to have ideal lives, and the ways to cultivate oneself to attain such a life, and the final sections of each chapter consider what the ideal person according to the thinker or text is like, and then the positions of later thinkers and texts in the relevant tradition on these questions. We will find that they are not always the same—there is sometimes as much variation within traditions as there is *across* traditions. We will also consider some comparisons in each chapter between the Asian thinker and school in question and similar western thinkers and schools.

# PART ONE

# Ethics and Self-Cultivation in Ancient China

| EARLY CHINESE PHILOSOPHY—A TIMELINE | |
|---|---|
| 1600–1050 BCE | Shang Dynasty |
| 1050–771 BCE | Western Zhou |
| tenth–seventh centuries BCE | Book of Songs composed |
| sixth century BCE | Book of Documents composed (ftnt aggregative) |
| 771–256 BCE | Eastern Zhou |
| 771–476 BCE | Spring and Autumn Period |
| 551 BCE | Confucius' birth |
| 498 BCE | Confucius' exile from Lu |
| 479 BCE | Confucius' death |
| 476–221 BCE | Warring States Period |
| 372–289 BCE | Life of Mencius |
| 369–286 BCE | Life of Zhuangzi |
| 313–238 BCE | Life of Xunzi |
| 221 BCE | Conquest of the Warring States by the state of Qin (Qin shi huang di, first emperor of Qin) |
| 206 BCE | Eestablishment of the Han Dynasty by Emperor Gaozu ('great ancestor', Liu Bang) |

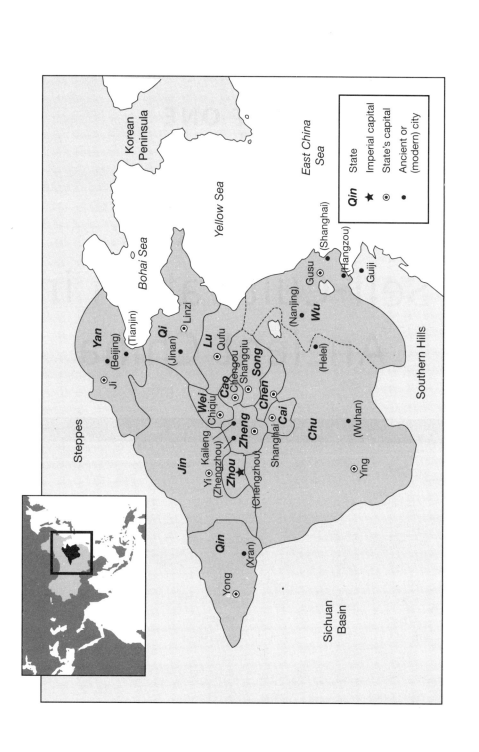

# 1

# The *Analects* of Confucius

Those with wisdom are not confused, those with humanity have no anxieties, and those with moral courage have no fear. *Analects* 9.29

Don't worry about not being known by others, worry that you have no knowledge. *Analects* 1.16[1]

# The life and legacy of Confucius and the *Analects*

We begin with the teachings of one of the central figures of world thought, the ancient Chinese philosopher *Kong Qiu*, better known to the western world as *Confucius* (a Latinization of the honorific *Kong Fuzi*, or "Master Kong"). He was arguably more important to the development of the lives of the majority of the people in the world in the last 2,500 years than any other thinker in history. Confucius lived at a critical point in Chinese history and the history of the world. His teachings and reflections on learning, community, and the path to becoming a better person have had profound influence on both Chinese society and that of the wider global community. There is some justification in calling Confucius *the* foundational figure in the history of Chinese thought, as formative to the culture of China as Jesus Christ and Paul of Tarsus were to the culture of the west. However, the reasons to study and reflect on Confucius' teachings go beyond mere interest in Chinese culture or the attempt to understand the "Chinese mind." The teachings of Confucius are not merely relics of Chinese cultural and philosophical history, fixed indelibly to their own time and culture, which outsiders cannot truly access or appreciate. Rather, they are timeless and universal. In reading and thinking deeply about what is contained in the *Analects* of Confucius, we in the modern west can learn valuable lessons on how to live more compassionate, educated, socially responsible, engaged, and ultimately more satisfying lives.

Although Confucius' teachings are of enormous use to us in the modern world, it is also true that his concerns were very much tied to the social situation of his times. Those times, of course, were not so very much different from our own. The sad negative regularities of human behavior—greed, arrogance, violence, ignorance—all of these were in evidence in Confucius' time as much as they are in our own. It was Confucius' goal to help people overcome these base tendencies. He taught his students how to rise above them and become ideal persons, with dignity, respect, moral authority, and ultimately even a higher level of happiness and thriving as individual and essential members of communities.

Confucius lived during the late years of the declining Zhou dynasty, in the period often referred to as the "Spring and Autumn", which spanned from about 771–476 BCE. This period was one of political and social decay. The earlier luster of the Zhou dynasty, which had triumphed in 1046 BCE over the Shang, began to give way to political conflict between the various vassal states of the Zhou. The central Zhou government lost cohesion, and each of the states went out on their own, breaking away from the central Zhou government and becoming autonomous states. Dukes in control of these states began declaring themselves kings and fought with other states to gain land and resources. Along with this increasing political violence, people began to move away from the standards of conduct that had governed interpersonal interactions and religious ceremonies for many hundreds of years. Selfishness increased, a sense of rootlessness grew, and communities decayed, as people migrated to different areas to avoid war or gain new advantages in more powerful states. Loyalty declined as ministers in the employ of one state often defected and went to another deemed more powerful. There was a growing lack of concern with education and learning of traditional literature. People began to hanker after fame and fortune rather than bettering themselves and their communities, often sacrificing and harming others to do so, leaving families and whole communities in disarray. Status became more important than talent, style more prized than substance. The sense of morality diminished, and suffering increased. Some, such as Confucius, suspected that these changes were not coincidental. We might begin to see parallels between this society and our own.

Kong Qiu (later known as *Kongzi*, or to us *Confucius*), the bookish son of a family of humble status, and scholar of traditional social norms and literature, decided that the social situation of his day was unacceptable and that something needed to be done about it. People had to change, and this change could only be secured through the efforts of individuals such as himself, who prized learning and who were committed to the betterment of human life through morality, virtue, and social harmony.

As a *ru* 儒 scholar of traditional literature, Confucius' services were in demand by the rulers of the various states and principalities, who wished to have their children, especially their heirs, instructed in the ancient Zhou rituals, or *li* 禮, which were still at this point tied to political legitimacy and thought of as required for the proper running of a state. The Zhou rituals and literature were central to political life in the Spring and Autumn period. They were connected with authority, social status, and social control. In this way, we might think of the role of the Zhou rituals in Confucius' society as somewhat similar to the role of the U.S. Constitution, traditional social mores, and "the will of the people" in contemporary American society.

Using his role as ritual scholar to advance his project of bringing virtue to society, creating social harmony, and ultimately improving the quality of people's lives, Confucius took on a number of students, who traveled with him to the courts of different rulers. In instructing the heirs of rulers he emphasized virtue and morality along with his instruction in the traditional Zhou rituals. In fact, as we will see below, he saw the two as inextricably linked—virtue and morality to ritual. He shows us how we might see the social practices and traditions of a culture as tied to the project of attempting to become better and happier people.

How, Confucius must have wondered early on in his career, can we ultimately become better people and bring about social harmony? Do we achieve this through enforcing rules of ethical behavior, or by exhorting others to do more for society? Confucius concluded that neither of these could be the case. The problems in society were not due to lack of controls or good laws, or to the failure of people to make sure that others act properly. Rather, the primary failure of society was in the failure of members of society to look at *themselves*, and their own lives, with critical eyes, to make *themselves* better, more virtuous, more responsible people. Thus Confucius' goal became to instruct and motivate others to focus on themselves and their own actions in community, in order to become better people. Ultimately, Confucius believed, such self-cultivation would lead not only to a better life for the individual, but also to a better shared communal life for all of society. It is possible, although it is difficult, Confucius taught, to achieve the thriving society, in which all of us care for one another, have strong communities and roles in these communities that give meaning to our lives, and are satisfied with our places in the world. It is possible to live ultimately happy, fulfilled, thriving lives. This was Confucius' vision—and it is a vision still possible for us to realize today.

# Social harmony

Living in the humane community is best. If one does not remain in humanity, how can one thereby obtain knowledge? *Analects* 4.1

Confucius taught that one of the keys to improvement of the life of the individual is the improvement of the life of one's community as a whole. Human relationships play a central role in our wellbeing, because being in community and playing meaningful roles in community are essential to what we are as human beings. Just as a human cannot live well without sufficient food and water, a human also cannot live well without meaningful relationships through which to express his or her identity and give him or her a sense of purpose. Confucius attempts to answer questions such as "What is the meaning of life?" He points us to the centrality of the human community. We only discover the meaning of a life, Confucius argues, within a community. Outside of the context of genuine human relationships, there is no real person. One is truly, fully, a person only when one is integrated into community.

This may sound strange at first, but when we think about an assumption that we in the west often make, it becomes much more plausible. In American law, for example, we make a distinction between a full legal agent, who has responsibility for his or her actions, can perform a number of age-restricted activities (such as driving a car, drinking alcohol, voting, etc.), and a less-than-full legal agent, who is under the age required for full legal agency, and who therefore cannot legally vote, drive, drink alcohol, etc. This legal distinction between an adult and a minor is based on an implicit notion of full personhood that makes *rationality* the basis of personhood. One becomes a full legal person upon reaching "the age of reason," we think (an idea we gained thanks to European "Enlightenment" period philosophy). At the age of reason we think a person gains the ability to fully consider and make informed choices about actions, is able to inform himself or herself and choose justifiably between different options. Since, we think, the person can make such informed choices, he or she becomes subject to legal responsibility, and it becomes justified to punish him or her fully for making the wrong decisions. Although here I'm considering the legal implications of our notions of personhood based on rationality, there are also ethical parallels. We generally don't hold people fully morally responsible for particular actions when we deem them to have not been sufficiently rational to make an informed choice. We will often be hesitant to attribute moral failings to children, for example, because we think "He's/She's only a child, and knew no better."

It is important to see that this assumption that one gains full personhood through rationality is not obviously true. Confucius and others had a very different picture of what makes one a full person. Rather than rationality, it is participation in a community that makes one a full person. This might entail that children are not full persons, because they do not play a full role in the community in the sense that they do not yet have a profession, or a spouse and children of their own. But the difference between the Confucian notion of personhood and the Enlightenment notion, even though there is some overlap, is that the *basis* of personhood differs. The Enlightenment notion is that rationality or autonomy is central to the life of the human, whereas the Confucian notion is that thriving relationships or community are central to the life of the human.

Confucius' view is perhaps not as different from our own as it first seems, if we think about what it really entails. It is not simply a relic of a more communalistic culture concerned primarily with social order and hierarchy. Psychologists, anthropologists, and others who study human behavior in our society have long understood that human beings are "social animals," and that it is central to human life to be in community, in relationships with others. Humans gained this sense of community commitment through evolution. We developed as pack animals. A social sense and need formed initially because our early survival in the plains required us to work in packs in order to defend ourselves from much faster and stronger animals more suited for movement in such environments. This is also, according to evolutionary biologists, one of the reasons behind our capacity for abstract thought and intelligence. These were necessary for survival in new and hostile environments. If you can't outmuscle your opponent, you've got to outthink them.

Confucius recognized that relationships are close to the center of human life, and that our ultimate happiness and thriving depends on being part of harmonious and life-affirming communities. Social harmony, Confucius taught, is thus the key to human thriving. Individuals cannot successfully make their way through the world or attain happiness by themselves, abstracted from the context of the most central human communities, such as the family and the village. The family, of course, for Confucius, is the primary, central, first, and most important community in the life of the individual. It is impossible for the individual to truly thrive without a harmonious, thriving family and wider community.

Zaiwo asked, "the three year period of mourning [for parents]—isn't this excessively long? If an exemplary person goes three years without attending to ritual, the ritual will certainly founder. If they go three years without music, music will certainly crumble. The old grain already depleted, and the new grain already established, the season's worth of wood for fire-making drills being completed—isn't this yearlong period enough?" Confucius said, "eating high quality rice, wearing ornate clothes—you would be at ease with this?" Zaiwo answered, "I would." Confucius said, "If you would feel at ease with this, then by all means, do it! The morally exemplary person remains in mourning—for them food has no taste, music brings no enjoyment. He is not at ease staying in this place, therefore he doesn't shorten the mourning period. Now if you are at ease with this, however, then truncate it." After Zaiwo left, Confucius said, "Zaiwo is not humane! When a child is born it is only after three years that it can even leave the arms of its father and mother. The three year mourning period is shared throughout the land. As for Zaiwo, did he have three years of this loving concern from his father and mother?" *Analects* 17.21

That said, it is not advisable, according to Confucius, to sever one's ties with a community if it fails to realize harmony—especially central communities such as the family. For each community, the more central it is to our identity and personhood, the less acceptable it is to "opt out." At the level of the family, one can *never* opt out. One is always, for as long as one lives, a child of person *x*, a parent of person *y*. etc., and the responsibilities that come with these roles attach to the person through biological necessity. Just as I will never, no matter how hard I may try, make it the case that I am *not* the son of my father or the father of my son, I will never be able to extract myself from the familial community containing these people, which is glued together in part by my responsibilities toward them and theirs toward me.

Serving one's father and mother, one should remonstrate with them [when they are doing wrong]. But if one sees that the will of the parents is not to follow [this advice], then one should again become respectful and not oppose/disobey, work hard and not be resentful. *Analects* 4.18

But how, we might ask, does all this help us in the task of self-cultivation, which is our main concern here? How can what Confucius says about the centrality and indissolubility of community help us to learn how to and move toward living live better lives? It might sound, for example, like the kind of social necessity Confucius endorses is more of a burden than a means to better one's life, realize happiness, and attain wellbeing. When we examine just what Confucius means and what his system entails, however, we see that it may not be so implausible after all.

Many in today's world are in what we might call a *crisis of community*. The encouragement we've been given through culture and our historical and philosophical background to make choices, to choose every aspect of our lives, has led to a fracturing of communities. We are given infinite opportunities to "opt out" of given relationships and communities, and are becoming increasingly mobile, such that where we work is most often not where we live, and where we live is becoming increasingly unsettled. A young professional is likely to make many moves, to vastly different areas across the country in the span of his or her career. These days, it is extremely unlikely that a person will end up living their lives in the place of their birth, or that their children will live their lives in the place of their birth. Families are torn apart. Increasingly, divorces lead to separation of children from parents, alienation of family members from each other, and a lack of connection to a family (and certainly a family name). This fracturing of the family can lead to problems dealing with other communities. One finds oneself unable to commit to communities, constantly moving, coming and going, having no real sense of connection to those around one. As professionals trot the globe moving from job to job, their families leave the friends they've made in one area, leave behind familiar surroundings and places and people with whom they have a special connection, to uproot and start anew, knowing no one, having no history in the land or with the people. We are becoming nomads, but not of the classical type. In many nomadic societies of the past, family and clan bonds were even *stronger* than such bonds among non-nomadic people. We see in the Semitic-speaking peoples of the Middle East, for example, the descendants of nomadic groups, a focus on clan and community that rises even to the level of the sacred. This is not a coincidence—there is a very human reason for this. The nomad is, just like any other human, in need of an emotional and spiritual ground. He or she cannot make that connection with the earth, with the people in a given wider community, because he or she is always on the move. But one constant in nomadic life is the family and the wider clan. They move together, support and love each other—family is a source of constancy in a life of change. They serve as the emotional and spiritual ground in a person's life. Without this ground, humans become adrift, getting caught in the blinding change of life, without anchor. We drown in its uncertainties and pains. We cannot truly find meaning in something ephemeral that changes frequently, because with that change will inevitably come loss of meaning, emotional and spiritual ground. Thus, it is key in our search for ways to live better lives that we locate and ground ourselves emotionally and spiritually in a constant source of meaning and joy. Confucius believes that the thriving, harmonious family is the best such source.

The ability to choose, to "opt out" of relationships, is not unquestionably a good thing. The only way to maintain community is to lack a certain amount of choice in determining one's community. There will never be a human community in which there are not abrasive or difficult relations between members of the community. Think of your own family and friends. Have you ever had a relationship in which there has *never* been hardship—no fighting, strained relations, resentment, anger, etc.? Of course not. Every relationship undergoes these difficulties. This is just the way humans are—we get angry, and are often greedy, impatient, and selfish. We are sometimes unfeeling and cruel, even with those close to us. With choice, however, comes a rise in the tendency to dissolve relationships when they hit rough patches. When we reach a rocky point in a relationship with a friend, we can simply terminate the friendship, we can "defriend" them. When the luster has gone out of one's marriage and the relationship hits a rocky patch, one can simply divorce one's spouse and move elsewhere. If we are part of a religious community that says something we do not like, we can simply leave the community and join a different one more in line with our views. Do you begin to see the pattern here? The question arises, how can we ever develop like this? If one quits every time something gets difficult, one never accomplishes a goal. If one stops listening every time another disagrees or offers an alternative viewpoint to one's own, one never learns. If one leaves a relationship every time that relationship becomes difficult, one never develops or maintains meaningful relationships.

Ironically, lacking choice can sometimes make us free. A relationship we might otherwise choose to give up on is strengthened because we find a way to resolve our difficulties and thus come to a deeper understanding and connection with the other. A viewpoint we might otherwise simply ignore or reject becomes something we begin to take seriously as an option (even if we do not come to agree with it), because we have no choice but to listen to its adherents and understand how they think. People who are insufferable to us at first in this way become tolerable, perhaps even endearing to us after time. There is a name for this effect in psychology—the *principle of familiarity*. It says that people will tend to associate with and enjoy, over time, the things and people they are most familiar with. In practice, what this amounts to is the following—if you want to *like* a certain person (or thing), you've got to be around him or her (or it) long enough. Which means that you've got to stick through the inevitable hard parts of a relationship to form the deeper, lasting bonds that make real, meaningful human relationships possible—the kind based on mutual concern and identity, involving willingness to sacrifice for the other. There is simply no way such relationships (and *willingness to sacrifice* is key here) can be built based only contingency, the lack of difficulties, and the "opt out" clause. Just as you can't make a sword without burning the steel in a fire, and you can't win a marathon without months and even years of toil, you also can't form and maintain a meaningful and harmonious relationship without struggling and persisting through difficulties. Human relationships, in this way, are no different from any other human pursuit in the hardships they require. They are, however, much more worth pursuing, Confucius argues, than any other project, because relationships are key to human thriving, to living a good life.

# The "humane" person and the "rites"

Yan Hui asked about humanity. The Master said, "turning away from yourself and returning to the rituals creates humanity. If even for one day you could turn away from yourself and return to ritual, the entire world would become humane. The key to creating humanity lies within *you*—how could it be within others?" Yan Hui replied, "may I ask how to break this down?" The Master said, "if it is not ritually proper don't look at it. If it is not ritually proper don't listen to it. If it is not ritually proper don't say it. If it is not ritually proper don't move with it." Yan Hui said, "even though I am not clever, I ask permission to practice these words." *Analects* 12.1

If the key to living better, more fulfilled lives is to ensure that we are fully integrated members of harmonious communities, how do we go about 1) integrating ourselves properly into meaningful communities, and 2) ensuring those communities are harmonious rather than chaotic or otherwise negative ones? To answer these questions, Confucius uses two very important ethical concepts—*humanity* and *ritual*.

Both humanity (*ren* 仁) and ritual (*li* 禮) are meant to facilitate our integration into communities and help us to make these communities harmonious, in order to ultimately improve our lives. *Ritual*, for Confucius, is a complex ethical concept. It refers to contextual standards of conduct. We all have a notion of standards of conduct proper to certain situations. There are a certain set of rules governing how one acts in court, for example, that are distinct from the rules governing how one acts with friends. Perhaps we don't think that there are rules governing how we act with friends. But consider this carefully—would you bow to a friend when handing over a gift? Would you call him or her "your honor" rather than his or her first name when engaging? Would you slap a friend in the face when you meet them in a hallway or when he or she comes over to your house for dinner? Kiss him or her on the lips? There are most definitely standards of conduct we follow with friends, even though most of the time we do not think about them, but rather only implicitly following them. It becomes clear that there are such standards when someone violates them. If a friend were to come over to your house and slap you in the face seemingly for no reason, the first thing you might think or say is "That's not what friends do!" We implicitly recognize different standards of conduct in different relationships and situations in our lives.

This is, in part, what Confucius meant by ritual. The collected set of standards of conduct that are fixed by situation, role, and community, play a crucial role in the process of building and maintaining harmonious communities. How can we build and maintain a harmonious friendship, for example, if we fail to respect and adhere to the standards of conduct associated with friendship, such as familiarity or informality in speech, refraining from slapping our friends, etc.? In order to build and maintain thriving communities, we need to have ground rules specifying the actions appropriate to each member of the community, relative to their role in the community. For example, in order to have a thriving and harmonious family, we need to know the standards for being a good *father, mother, son, daughter,* etc. The standards one must adhere to within a community in order to ensure that the community thrives are necessarily relative to one's role. If one is a father in a small family, there will be certain standards he must follow, while there will be different standards for a daughter in that same family. In order for the family to be thriving and harmonious, each member of the family will have to adhere to the standards of conduct appropriate to his or her role.

But there is more than just this. Along with adherence to standards of *conduct*, one must also have the attitudes and emotions appropriate to this conduct. Think again of the case of a family. If a father adheres to the standards of conduct appropriate to a father, then he provides for his children materially, educates them, protects them, etc. But isn't it possible for a father to do all of this and still not *love* his children, not *care* for them, or enjoy being around them, taking joy from their presence and their happiness? And wouldn't we think that these things are part of what is necessary to be a *good* father? A father who merely provides for his children but does not love them has certainly fallen far short of the ideal. Confucius recognizes this, and thus argues that more is necessary for the creation and maintenance of a harmonious community than just ritual, or contextual standards of conduct. There is also an internal element, a psychological, motivational, emotional aspect to the correct performance of ritual. It is not enough, according to Confucius, to perform ritual (thought of as adhering to one's standards of conduct), but we must perform ritual *in the spirit appropriate to ritual.* That is, we must have the attitudes that properly accompany the kind of actions that the ritual standards attached to our role in the community dictate. Thus, for the father, performance of his responsibilities in the spirit appropriate to them is performance of the activities of providing for and educating his children *with love and care*. The emotional aspects are not only important to the role of the father, but they are *even more* important than the physical aspects. Confucius teaches that the emotional ties between humans are the most important aspects of our relationships. Even if a father cannot provide fully for his children, due to poverty, for example, if he loves and cares for his children such that he tries his hardest to provide for them (and this emotional connection will generally *entail* that he does so try), we would be inclined to call him a *good* father. On the other hand, a person who provides for his children out of his more than sufficient wealth, but doesn't love or care about them, we would naturally find deficient and would be inclined to call a *bad* father.

Attitudes and emotions are central in relationships, even while standards of conduct are of crucial importance as well. It would not make sense for one who loves and cares for one's child *not* to try to provide for them. Even if unsuccessful, the attempt to provide for one's child is a key standard for the conduct of a father, and lack of such effort seems incompatible with authentic concern.

> Ziyou asked about filiality. The master said, "Today people say that filiality is to be able to nourish [one's parents]. [But] this is to be like no more than dogs and horses—they too are able to nourish [parents]. Without reverence/respect, how can one tell the difference?" *Analects* 2.7

This is where the concept of *humanity* comes into the picture. All communities, in order to become harmonious and to thrive, must be regulated by ritual— that is, each member of the community has to adhere to the standards of conduct determined by their role, in the spirit appropriate to these standards. When this happens, it creates a commitment to the community through the desire to see the community as a whole flourish—this is *humanity*. Humanity involves an "other-concern" that comes with being integrated in the right way into the community, and it is a quality necessary for a community to ultimately thrive. If the members of a community are not committed to that community *for the sake of* the community, rather than for selfish reasons, a community cannot fully thrive, even if ritual is respected by everyone within it.

> Sacrifice as if present, sacrifice to the spirits as if the spirits are present. Confucius said, "if I am not fully with the sacrifice, it is just as if there has been no sacrifice." *Analects* 3.12

Imagine the case of a person who does all the right things in a community, in the spirit appropriate to those things. She both treats her friends well and genuinely cares about them. She provides for and respects her parents and nurtures and loves her children. In other words, she is adhering to ritual in the spirit appropriate to it. But now we might consider her motivations for doing all of this. Does she have motivational states that are connected to the community and the people she cares for, or does she care for people only as a means to her own happiness? One might ask here, "What is the difference?" But we can certainly envision cases in which the difference becomes very clear. A person such as the one described above, for example, might very well begin feeling differently about and acting differently toward the members of her community if they cease giving her happiness. She might come to hate or actively work against a parent, child, or neighbor if they become difficult or for whatever reason injure her happiness or stability. We all know of people like this. They are your best friends when things are going well, but when there are problems, they disappear. It is not totally accurate to say that these people *never cared* about you, when they abandon you, as we tend to often say. They *may have* cared for you at one time. The problem was that it was a *conditional* care. "I will care for you as long as you make me happy, as long as you please me—then when you no longer do, I'll cease caring for you." This kind of person, as we considered above, is not one who will be able to attain thriving and happiness in the long run. This person is one *without humanity*, according to Confucius.[2]

> Those who are not humane cannot for long endure difficulty, and cannot for long enjoy happiness. Those who are humane are at ease with humanity, those who have knowledge profit from humanity. *Analects* 4.2

Humanity (仁) is a motivational propensity that allows one to "stick with it" when things don't go one's way. The reason for this is that the person with humanity is committed to *others*, committed to the community. The person with humanity is one who engages in moral self-cultivation not only for his or her own sake, but for the sake of others. Thus, part of what comes with humanity is a concern for and benevolence toward others. This makes one committed to the community and its wellbeing in a way the person without humanity cannot be. Humanity is crucial for building and maintaining thriving and ultimately harmonious communities that are able to weather the storms of difficult times and strained relationships. As the term 'humanity' suggests, there is something central to our nature as humans contained in this.[3] We are social animals. But we are also more than this. We can become attached to other people such that we care about them for their own sakes, and not our own. Confucius' concept of humanity thus includes *altruism*. Confucius not only believed that altruism is possible for humans, but that it represents the highest state of human development, and the only thing that can truly lead us to the thriving and happiness we desire. Again, we see something seemingly unintuitive at first, that begins to make more sense when we reflect deeper on it. Confucius taught, like a number of other thinkers we will consider, that the only way to truly find happiness, in the end, is to stop being concerned with *your own* happiness, and to cultivate a concern for the wellbeing of others and the community as a whole. Turn away from the self, and toward ritual.

## The virtues of the family and community

The thriving community, as we have seen, is for Confucius the central element of coming to have a thriving and happy life for the individual. But how do we ensure that the communities we are part of thrive? One problem is that all of us are part of a number of different communities. We are members of family communities, but we are also members of school communities, neighborhoods perhaps, sports teams, etc. And it is not always the case that there is significant (or any) overlap between these communities in the modern world. So if being part of thriving communities is necessary for my thriving as an individual, how do I ensure that the numerous communities I belong to all thrive? Do they all need to? Can I be part of one thriving community, while the others are dysfunctional, and still achieve a thriving and happy life?

The answer to his latter question, as we might expect, is *no*. Not only can one not thrive if one is a member of a non-thriving community of any kind, but the fact that one is a member of one non-thriving community will also tend to show that their *other* communities are non-thriving. In general, a person who is part of a non-thriving community won't be the kind of person who has other communities that thrive. Part of the reason for this is the learned traits, behaviors, attitudes, and emotions one picks up in a non-thriving community. Human beings, even though we attempt to compartmentalize aspects of our lives, cannot stop our attitudes and traits in one area of our life from affecting those in others. The attitudes one has in certain areas of one's life will seep into the other areas of one's life. There is lots of data to show this. People in professions in which violence and anger are prized or necessary, such as boot camp instructors, prison guards, and professional football players, have a higher incidence of domestic violence disputes than the population at large, for example. This is the reason that many traditions emphasize the cultivation of calm, benevolent, and peaceful attitudes across all situations in one's life. The anger that you direct at an enemy does not stay with that enemy—it comes home with you also, it hurts your spouse and children, your mother and father, your close friends. So, in a very real sense, when you create anger and hatred at another, regardless of what that person has done, you are not really (or only) hurting *them*, you are also hurting those you love, and ultimately hurting yourself. This is much of the force behind the oft maligned Christian notion of "turning the other cheek," a view that has parallels in a number of other religious and philosophical traditions. Two good Buddhist stories come to mind here, as a way of explaining what attitudes and mental states cultivated in one aspect of one's life can do in others.

The first story involves two monks, walking on their alms round, who encounter a rude man on the road. This man hates monks and their worldview. He hurls insults at the two monks, cursing and throwing things, saying the most horrible and crude things one could imagine. One of the monks is offended and becomes irate, and considers telling off the rude man until his sense of propriety restrains him. The other monk, however, stays calm, showing compassion for the rude man, and smiles as they pass by. Later on, the first monk asks the second about the incident. "That man said horrible things to us back there—didn't that bother you at all?"

The second monk responded, "Why should it? On the contrary, we should feel sorry for *him*. He who spits into the sky only soils himself."

The second story also involves two monks, also (as monks so often are) walking on their alms round. They encounter a woman trying to get across a long puddle of mud blocking the road. One of the monks offers to help, and carries the woman in his arms across the puddle. His fellow monk is outraged that he violated the rules for monks and had contact with a woman, but doesn't say anything about it right away because the other monk is his superior. He is torn up inside about it the whole afternoon, and finally, when the two monks return to the monastery, the junior monk can't hold it in anymore and asked his superior: "Why did you carry that woman across the puddle? This is improper!" The senior monk replied, "Are you still carrying her? I put her down long ago."

These stories, although cryptic (as good Buddhist and Daoist stories tend to be) are also instructive about the importance of attitudes, emotions, and other mental states in our thriving. Indeed, mental states are *most of what there is* to our thriving! In addition to mental states, we also gain certain patterns of behavior and dispositions from the communities we are in. When we are around certain irreverent groups of people, for example, we become irreverent. We tend to adopt the patterns of speech of the groups we are

around and are closest to. There is a good reason that a person from Boston has a New England accent and not a Georgia accent.

Living in the humane community is best. If you do not remain in humaneness, how can you thereby obtain knowledge? *Analects* 4.1

If we take this line of thought further, the most stable and developed qualities that we have as people will be developed and based in the most stable, lasting, and coherent communities we belong to, the ones most central to the self. Thus, Confucius recognizes, the *family* is an incredibly important community as it concerns development of positive qualities in the individual. It is the *most* important community, for a number of reasons: 1) it is the *first* community, in both a temporal and ethical sense. One is part of a family from birth and remains in the family throughout one's life; 2) it is the most central community to one's identity—one is closer to and more influenced by one's family than by any other community. One grows and develops as a social human being within the context of the family first and foremost, and only after this develops as a member of broader communities; 3) one gains one's basic values from the family—one's identity is constructed mainly by one's relationships in the family. One is instructed and socially contextualized based on the values provided by one's family; 4) the family serves as the mirror for all communities—that is, the rituals and relationships one develops in the family will inform all of one's relationships outside of the family. It is in the family that one first learns to make one's way through the world.

> Those who are filial and brotherly toward others yet enjoy opposing their superiors are few. To not enjoy opposing one's superiors yet enjoy bringing about disorder, such a person has never existed. The morally exemplary person attends to the root. When the root is established, the Way sprouts forth. Filiality and brotherliness, these constitute the root of humanity. *Analects* 1.2

It is important, Confucius recognizes, to have a thriving and harmonious family, because it is only within the family that important and supremely useful virtues can be developed, ones that will help us operate not only in the context of the family, but within the wider communities in the world. Familial virtues such as respect and concern for parents (filial duty, *xiao* 孝), fraternal feeling for siblings, mutual respect and cooperation, and benevolent concern are all developed most easily and deeply in the family. The idea is that if we develop such virtues as respect and concern for parents, this virtue will naturally be transformed into structurally similar virtues in our interactions with other communities, such that we will be people who tend to facilitate the building and maintenance of harmonious communities. Confucius has us consider the virtues of a person who has concern and respect for his parents, for example. One who has gained this family virtue, Confucius says, will not be the kind of person who will disrespect their superiors. Why is this? The virtue of filial duty just is the virtue of respecting and having concern for one's superiors in the context of the family. The attitudes associated with this do not simply *end* outside of the context of the family. Just like the rude and angry person, whose rudeness and anger colors his mind and comes home with him to his family, rather than staying with the person who is the intended target of anger, the person who respects and cares for his parents will find that this state of mind "infects" his other relationships. This person will tend to be one who respects and cares for those above them, because of this same "attitude seep." Just as negative mental states can infect different areas of our lives than those we intend them to, positive mental states and virtues can also influence various aspects of our lives. And the more foundational to our identity the community in which these attitudes and emotions are developed is, the more influence these attitudes and emotions will have on other aspects of our lives. Thus it is of central importance, Confucius teaches, to ensure that the familial virtues are developed. They form the root of goodness, which leads us to a thriving communal life.

But how can we ensure that all the members of a community we belong to are virtuous in the same way we are? Confucius recognized that it is not always possible to ensure that those around you are virtuous, even if you are. For this reason, Confucius taught, it is of great importance to ensure that we form communities with those who are good, those who have some semblance of virtue, and are committed to forming thriving, harmonious communities. If we form communities with those who are vicious, we run the risk of, rather than reforming these others, becoming vicious ourselves. This is just the way human nature works—we tend to become like those we are around.

> The mistakes of persons are in each case attributable to their group/community. Observe [one's] mistakes, and you will know whether they are humane. *Analects* 4.7

So does this mean we can simply "opt out" of any community when we find that the members of this community are not committed to virtue and ultimately not good? The answer to this question is complicated. We first need to recognize two distinct types of communities—*consensual* communities and *non-consensual* communities. The prime example of a consensual community might be a group of friends. One can often choose who one befriends, and it is possible to avoid befriending bad people. In fact, in a number of passages in the *Analects* Confucius suggests that we should do just that—we should not befriend those who are not as morally good as we are. On the other hand, *non-consensual* communities, such as the family, do not allow for ways out. We are stuck with our families, no matter how virtuous or vicious its members are. This does leave us at the mercy of luck or fate to some extent—we cannot control which families we are born into, and it sometimes turns out that people are born into horrible families. Are such people simply doomed to living a life without virtue and thus ultimately without thriving? Confucius says yes.

This is not wholly implausible, if we think about what is being said here. Whether we are born healthy or sickly is not up to us, but due to factors of nature outside our control. Whether we are born tall or short, intelligent or unintelligent, in one social context or the other—all of these things are dictated by features of the world over which we have no choice, no control.

However, *all* of these things are relevant insofar as they concern our thriving and ultimate wellbeing. Some people are born into war-torn areas, into poverty, or with incapacitating illnesses. We often think that it this is not fair. They did not get to choose those things. But what this should highlight for us is not the extent to which it is *wrong* that these people suffer in such ways (after all, how can be blame nature?), but the extent to which many things we require for thriving are ultimately not up to us, and are a matter of "the luck of the draw." This, of course, need not make us complacent in our attempts at moral self-cultivation. We can often improve our lot—this is one of the unique features of humans. But sometimes, we cannot. Those born into sufficiently horrible families will just be like those born into horrific poverty or war. Through no choice or fault of their own, they will be unable to live a fully thriving and happy life. This, according to thinkers like Confucius, should both elicit our sympathy and arouse our desire to help such people, and it should equally make us thankful for our own situations, which (for many of us) allow us the room to develop virtuous families, and ultimately become virtuous, thriving, and happy people.

# A life of learning

Learning without thinking leads to confusion. Thinking without learning leads to danger. *Analects* 2.15

Learn as if you will be unable to reach it, as if you are afraid of losing it. *Analects* 8.17

Learning is not something accorded very much value today in our modern society. It's seen as expedient and of only instrumental value for gaining employment or wealth at best, and useless or even corrupting at worst, as something engaged in only by nerdy people with no lives or ability to do something really important like making money or becoming famous. Sadly, it is undervalued by much of the population, even while we pay larger and larger amounts to attend university. The negative view of learning today exhibits itself not only in suspicion of those with great learning (note the "mad scientist" tropes in wide use during the late twentieth century and even into our own), but also in outright anti-intellectualism. Politicians are seen as more sympathetic and knowledgeable when they adopt an attitude of ignorance, stubbornness, and "aw, shucks" populism which shuns as distant and sinister any kind of learning, formal or informal. In a recent presidential campaign, one of the candidates was actually *criticized* for appearing too "academic" and "professorial" in his public appearances, and this was deemed by many in the public to be evidence that the candidate was "out of touch" with the country. Most often, the professional academic in our society is looked upon as a stuffy pedant, rather than someone to be respected due to their expert knowledge in a field. We shun the notion of *expertise* altogether, instead preferring what we think is a more democratic notion of collective or folk wisdom. But this is surely absurd. Have we gained the ability to fly or land on the moon or understand the causes of mental illness or cancer through folk wisdom or coming to agreement through collective consciousness? Our lack of respect for scholars and expertise is a general symptom of our lack of respect for learning, even though, ironically perhaps, we rely on learning and people who have gained it every day, in almost every action, in our high-tech world. The movies we watch, the internet we use, the cars we drive—none of these things would be possible without an enormous amount of learning gained and applied by a great number of people. Shouldn't we thus prize learning rather than shunning it? It is what helped to give us our modern world! Also quite ironically, one might think, we generally seem to have the attitude that the *more* learning one has, the less they understand about the world around them, while those who shun learning somehow have *real* or *important* knowledge. But what could a completely ignorant person say that is worth listening to?

But this, of course, is absurd. How can one know anything without learning? Humans have no magical capacity to intuit knowledge from the ether. We fool ourselves and leave ourselves open to be taken advantage of by cunning politicians, companies, and others, when we turn our backs on learning. We do not gain "folk" knowledge through refusing to learn; rather we retain ignorance about ourselves and the world around us, and when we are ignorant about these things, it will be almost impossible to get much from them. We cannot make our way through the world and live our lives in a thriving manner if we have no knowledge about these things, just as there is no way we'll be any good at basketball if we have no knowledge of the game, and will be unable to build a house if we have no knowledge of the principles of building.

Zigong asked, "how did Kong Wenzi come to be called 'wen' [cultured]?" Confucius said, "he was smart, loved learning, and was unashamed to ask those in lower positions [when he didn't know something]. This is why he came to be called 'wen' [cultured]." *Analects* 5.15

Confucius said, "Zilu, have you heard the six sayings on the six deficiencies?" Zilu replied, "I haven't heard them." Confucius said, "sit, and I'll tell you. To love humaneness and not love learning results in stupidity. To love knowledge and not love learning results in shallowness. To love honesty and not love learning results in lowness/betrayal. To love uprightness and not love learning results in deformity of the right. To love bravery and not love learning results in disorder. To love toughness without love of learning results in crazy behavior." *Analects* 17.8

I remember as a youth in high school sharing the popular view of learning. I looked down on my classes in science, language, and history, thinking (and often voicing) the common western position "I don't need this stuff for what I'm going to do. This is therefore useless and a waste of my time." At the time, I wanted to write fiction—both on the page and for the screen. What I hadn't considered at the time, however, was something that became all too clear to me later: even in such pursuits as fiction writing, how can one do well without learning? Will one's prose be any good without studying language and literature? Will one's insights and stories be of any worth without under-standing human issues and problems through history, and gaining insights into our nature and psychological makeup? Not at all. Rather, one's writing will be, as mine was, juvenile, stunted, turgid, hard to read, and trivial. Learning is, Confucius realized, necessary for *every* human pursuit. In the most central human pursuit, which we are concerned about in this work—how to live a thriving, happy life, learning plays a very important role, in a number of ways.

First, learning is necessary in the process of self-cultivation because we cannot transform our actions and attitudes if we do not have the knowledge that serves as basis for this transformation. If we don't know what the thriving life *is*, how can we learn how to move toward this kind of life? And if we *do* know what the thriving life is, but do not have the knowledge of how to attain this kind of life, how can we do anything but be miserable that we are unable to attain such a life, just like a person who knows that he could become a millionaire and who wants to become a millionaire, but sits in poverty because he has not learned the way to become a millionaire? Attaining a thriving life, Confucius understood, is not essentially different from attaining any other goal, in that it is necessary to learn in order to discover the way to attain this goal, and then apply this knowledge in practice. Thus, Confucius teaches, it is certainly true that practice is necessary—having knowledge alone is not enough (this might be something our "action-focused" society could agree with), but it is no less true that knowledge is necessary, and knowledge can only be gained through learning. A person's sincere commitment to learning is a necessary part of the path of self-cultivation. If we want to live better lives, Confucius teaches, we have to become the kind of people who prize, and are committed to, learning.

Second, learning helps us to appreciate both the world around us and our own place in that world. It contextualizes us. The understanding we gain through learning makes our lives richer, more complex, and ultimately more fulfilling. This is the quality of learning that its adherents today, including stuffy, out-of-touch professors like myself, often emphasize. Learning is intrinsically valuable and directly connected to a thriving life, not just due to its value as a means for attaining something else, as in the first use of learning I mention above. Confucius recognized this about learning, and taught that in addition to being concerned to gain learning in order to apply our knowledge to self-cultivation, we should also be concerned with learning for its own sake. There is something intrinsically valuable about having a greater under-standing of oneself and one's world. It makes our experience of life richer, and is a necessary piece of the puzzle concerning our ultimate wellbeing. Just like an ultimately thriving life requires harmonious community, it also requires a love of and engagement with learning. One cannot, Confucius recognizes, ultimately have a thriving life without a love of learning. The ancient Greek philosopher Plato had a similar view, and put things even more forcefully, claiming that the unexamined life is not worth living.

So, if we conclude with Confucius that a thriving life is, in part, a life of learning, we next have to ask the question: what is learning? Should we think of learning strictly along the lines of the kind of thing that happens in formal high school and college courses, replete with homework, quizzes and tests, and final grades? Is this what it means to learn? Of course not—learning is much broader than this. There was not, in Confucius' time, anything approximating college courses as we know them, and the kind of learning he advocated was wholly different from what we often take to be the paradigm example of learning or studying. This does not mean, of course, that learning on Confucius' view does not involve reading, writing, memorization, or engagement with a teacher at times. All of these things can be part of the learning process, but learning of course goes beyond just this. Learning to play an instrument, or to appreciate certain kinds of music and the musical structures they are built on—this is a kind of learning. Learning the principles of a sport, through engaging in it and studying the way others play it—this is also learning. Coming to appreciate the differences between different kinds of wine or coffee—this is learning. Aesthetic, moral, and scientific thought—all of these involve learning. This, interestingly enough, was the idea behind the development of the notion of the "liberal arts" as a program of learning that became popular in the western (especially American) university (based on classical Greek notions), and now, sadly, seems to be on the decline. The original idea was one Confucius would have shared—the idea that it is central to a thriving life to learn broadly, not just in the specialized fields that one will eventually work in, but more broadly in the arts, humanities, and sciences as well. Part of a thriving life, the idea went, is the ability to appreciate the plays of Shakespeare or novels of Tolstoy and the great compositions of Bach or Miles Davis, as well as appreciating and understanding the night sky and the makeup of our solar system, and the principles of mathematics. The life of learning, the idea went, is an ultimately more fulfilling life than one without learning.

> To learn and have the time to practice, is this not a delight? To have friends come visit you from distant lands, is this not joyous? To not be bothered even when people don't know you, is this not like the morally exemplary person? *Analects* 1.1

In addition, learning, Confucius taught, is not to be thought of merely as a soaking up of propositional knowledge, filling one's head with facts. Without motivation, practice, and reflection, there can be no real learning. Confucius may have been horrified by the situation in western colleges and universities today, in which students take courses to cram their heads with a number of propositions which they then show they have memorized by taking tests throughout a course. This is not real learning. Real learning, Confucius taught, necessarily involves two features.

First, it involves the motivation and investigative curiosity of the student.

> I do not instruct those who are not eager, I do not aid those who are not struggling to figure things out. If I show a student one corner of a problem, and he does not come back to me with the other three, I will refuse to teach him any longer. *Analects* 7.8

The process of learning must involve the learner. This does not mean, as is common in the terminology of higher education, that Confucius endorsed "discussion sections"—rather it means that it is essential to the process of learning that the learner *discover* things for him or herself. We learn best through discovery, rather than through explicit instruction. The good teacher, then, is one who guides the student toward solving certain problems or making certain discoveries, because it is in this way that one truly comes to understand something. How, for example, would we ever learn to ride a bike unless we got on the bike and *tried* the advice we were given by a parent?

Second, it involves the practical application of what the student learns. It is not learning, Confucius teaches, to simply memorize a proposition and leave it at that. We need to consider how this proposition connects to our experience, other knowledge, and the way we live, and *apply* it directly in our lives. Thus, for example, when we learn things about better ways to live, the best thing we can do is to go out and *try* these ways of living. It is only through practice that we will know whether what we have learned is right, and it is only through practice that we will fully integrate what we have learned into our lives in such a way that it helps us to thrive.

One who through inner effort turns away from obsession with beautiful things, is able to exert great effort in attending to their father and mother, who is able to exhaust the body in service to their ruler, and whose words in conversation with friends are honest— even if some say this person is not learned, I would definitely call them learned. *Analects* 1.7

Today, we are beginning to abandon the view that learning in general leads to thriving and happiness, in exchange for a much more "pragmatic," career-based model of learning. The idea has ascended that what is important is getting only the learning one needs to perform a particular task well, and ignoring the rest. If I am striving to become an aeronautical engineer, I should only need to learn the skills relevant to building airplanes, and nothing else. There are a few problems with this increasingly popular view, however. First, one cannot, as Confucius recognized, ultimately be an excellent engineer, accountant, or whatever else, without having robust knowledge outside of one's specific field (just as I explained above). Second, a thriving life should not be an "afterthought" in our considerations of learning. If I learn all the skills I need to be an engineer, what good are they for me if I ultimately fail to gain a thriving and happy life? After all, why choose to become an engineer, or anything else, if such a career isn't ultimately productive of a thriving life for oneself and one's loved ones? What is the point? Given our tendency to disconnect concern for human thriving from our considerations of what we're after concerning career, skills, and learning, is it any wonder that we suffer from existential strife, a sense of meaninglessness, and rootlessness as regular fixtures of our modern world? One of the most important steps we can take to counteract this suffering and move toward better lives, according to Confucius, is to arouse a love for learning and understanding in general.

> A young person at home should be filial, out and about should be brotherly, sensible and honest, broadly caring for the multitude, and close with those who are humane. Doing this, if they still have energy, then they should study texts. *Analects* 1.6

# The ideal person

What, we might ask, does the ideal, fully cultivated person look like, according to Confucius? We have seen what, in general, Confucius proposes as necessary features of the project of self-cultivation. But how do we know what the end of this process looks like?

It turns out that Confucius has lots to say about how the ideal person will act, as well as his or her attitudes, motivations, and emotions. One of the most important facts about the ideal person, Confucius teaches, is that it is only such a person who can truly be happy. Most of us coast through the world riding waves of joys and suffering, buffeted around by circumstance, our happiness dependent on things outside our control. We are often depressed, stressed out, or just generally unhappy. The morally ideal person, according to Confucius, is not buffeted by these same stresses and depressions.

An ideal person is one who has developed the virtues and communal grounding necessary for a thriving and happy life. This person's thriving or wellbeing in general is dependent upon his or her own motivations, dispositions, and communal commitments. Notice that this is not the kind of thing that is subject to the changes of nature, to the ups and downs common to external features of the world. If one is attached to wealth, health, or fame, one inevitably suffers when these things come and go, as such things tend to. The wealthy person goes broke, a healthy person gets old and becomes infirm, one's fame dwindles and vanishes. The idea here is that the person who aims at these things, without the virtues of the ideal person, cannot be happy when things go badly, because they are so attached to these external goods that their failure to obtain them throws such people into misery. The morally ideal person is not like this. There is nothing, according to Confucius, that can change the morally ideal person's virtue, his or her motivations, dispositions, and communal commitments. Whether this person is wealthy or poor, famous or unknown, healthy or sickly, they will have what they need and want, and gives them wellbeing as a human. Such persons have communal concern (which tends to create thriving communities), and they have virtuous dispositions and motivations. It is these things that make a person truly happy. And note that the ideal person's happiness is independent of the external situation. When things go badly—wealth is lost, there is war or other strife in society, people turn against us, etc.—the ideal person still thrives, still has the kind of well-being that the non-ideal person seeks in vain through things like wealth, health, and fame. Thus, only the morally ideal person can be content when things go badly.

How about the other side of this claim—that only the morally ideal person can truly enjoy when things go well? Can't, one might ask, the person who is motivated by wealth and fame be happy at the times they have wealth and fame, even if they are miserable at the times they lack these things? Think of many people you know or know of who are motivated by wealth and fame. Do they ever reach a level of wealth or fame at which they are satisfied, or do they constantly need more? We often see that for such people having great wealth and fame is the same as having very little of either, because their need for more of it is equal to the need they would have if they were without *any* wealth or fame. The attainment of these things seems to do nothing at all to satisfy their desires. We notice this kind of thing all of the time, but since we've been trained so effectively by our culture to think that gaining wealth, fame, and influence will make one happy, we find it hard to believe that people who have these things can be miserable and live much less-than-thriving lives. In fact, I've heard the sentiment echoed many times from people in our society that rich and famous people "have nothing to be upset about." People who make such statements generally dismiss stories of the troubles, strife, and stresses of the rich, famous, and powerful. These people are can't possibly suffer! The cultural training we have gained and often don't question tells us that wealth, fame, and influence are the goals of life, and that these things make one truly happy. Thus, when we see suffering people who possess all of these things, rather than taking this as evidence against the claims we have been trained to accept, we reject the authenticity of the problems these people are having. We say that they're making it all up to get attention, or that they've been "spoiled" and really aren't suffering deeply or living badly, but are unable to handle even small setbacks because their lives are such easy and fulfilling ones in general—like children who scream at the pain of a paper cut because they have not experienced more extreme pains.

This is a strange attempt to salvage a worldview in the face of overwhelming evidence to the contrary, motivated by our nearly blind faith in the proposition that wealth, fame, and influence will make one happy. It can't be that famous and wealthy people have never experienced *real* suffering (associated with poverty), because most of them didn't *begin* life wealthy and famous (social and class mobility being a common feature of the modern world). However, even if one has always lived a life of wealth and fame, why should we think that the suffering they exhibit is any less real or serious than our own or anyone else's, simply because of the fact that they have wealth and/or fame? What distinguishes between real and fake suffering? Wealth and fame? But if there is no psychological difference, then why should I take "fake" suffering to be any better, more pleasant, or easier to handle than "real" suffering? There is as much pain inherent to one as to the other. We might begin to see that our faith in this connection between wealth, fame, influence, and a thriving life is misplaced. Confucius teaches that only the morally ideal person can truly enjoy it when things go well. Such a person's thriving and happiness is not dependent on wealth, fame, or any other external feature of the world. To the morally ideal person, wealth, fame, or influence could at most be merely icing on the cake. Such a person would not need *any* of it to be truly fulfilled, but would be content with what he or she has. The morally ideal person does suffer because he or she needs more of these things, as the person who is motivated by these alone often is. Thus, ironically, only the morally ideal person, whose happiness is *not* dependent on wealth, fame, or influence, could actually ever gain enjoyment from them. The rest of us, and those of us who accept that these things are the keys to our happiness, can never truly enjoy these things.

> Zigong said, "one who is vastly charitable to the people and is able to aid the multitude—how might you describe them? Could such a person be called humane?" Confucius said, "why only go so far as to call these things humane? This is surely *sagelike*! This even makes [the ancient sage kings] Yao and Shun look inadequate! The humane person, in desiring to establish themselves they establish others, in desiring to achieve for themselves they help others achieve. To make oneself close to others and liken ourselves to them—this is can be called in the area of humaneness." *Analects* 6.30

Part of what comes with being the morally ideal person, according to Confucius, is a *natural ease* in making one's way through the world. Another, perhaps ironic, truth that Confucius recognized (along with the Daoists in the ancient Chinese tradition) is that it tends to be the case that the harder we force things and the more we bear down, the further we get from accomplishing our goals. Often, the most effective way of acting is with a natural ease, without forcing, almost as if not using any effort at all. An easy way to see this is to consider playing an instrument. If one concentrates too hard and applies too much pressure when playing the flute, one will produce a harsh, unpleasing sound. In playing a particular tune, one will miss notes, make mistakes, and generally perform badly. What will often produce the best sound is a *relaxing* of one's effort. To allow one's instincts to take over, to blow through the flute in a relaxed and natural manner, to allow one's fingers to float over the keys rather than forcing them down—this produces a crisp, beautiful sound. What is the difference? Just the natural ease with which the latter performance takes place. Confucius teaches that life is the same way. When we develop virtues, just like we can develop skill at playing the flute, we can apply those virtues to our ways of living so that we go through life with a natural ease, just like the exemplary flute performance. The morally ideal person possesses this natural ease in all that they do in part because they are free of the tension and psychic distress most of the rest of us live with, and because they are able to act without ulterior motive, without need to gain, deceive, or force. They can be this way because they are fully satisfied.

> Enacting rulership through virtue is like being the pole star—it simply keeps its place and the multitude of stars revolve around it.
> *Analects* 2.1

Confucius also teaches that the ideal person will be able to *endure* anything. Where the non-ideal person will simply give up in his or her attempt to bring about a thriving, harmonious community and society when encountering enough resistance or disappointment, the morally ideal person will push on. Because such a person is motivated by communal feeling, by the desire to realize harmony and virtue, setbacks will not deter them. They will keep striving for social harmony, even when it is difficult. They will even endure, Confucius teaches, in a situation in which they *know it is impossible* to achieve social harmony! Why would this be, we might ask, and why should we think this is a good thing, rather than a kind of insanity?

> Chang Ju and Jie Ni were plowing the fields when Confucius passed by and sent Zilu to ask where to ford the river. Chang Ju said: "who

is the master who sent you?" Zilu said, "Confucius." "The Confucius of Lu?" Chang Ju asked. Zilu responded, "yes." Chang Ju said, "He knows where the ford is." Zily then asked Jie Ni. Jie Ni responded, "who is your master?" Zilu replied, "Confucius." Jie Ni asked, "are you the disciple of Confucius of Lu?" Zilu answered, "yes." Jie Ni then said, "The world is completely flooded, and who can change this? Moreover, you follow someone who flees from other people— what if you followed someone who fled the world entirely?" He said this without turning away from raking his seeds. Zilu returned to tell Confucius. Confucius disappointedly remarked, "we cannot group together with the birds and beasts. If I do not follow the path of humans, whose can I? If the world possessed the dao, I wouldn't need to change things." *Analects* 18.6

The idea here is that the fully developed human has a fully developed *social sense* and *concern*. Part of being a morally ideal person is to have a communal concern that does not allow one to be indifferent to one's communities or neglect the well-being of one's communities. It is simply part of who the ideal person *is* to care for his or her community. If one did not have such concern, one would be less than ideal. It may help to consider the example of a loving parent. The best kind of parent, we generally think, is one who has a loving concern for his or her children. This loving concern translates into a motivation to do whatever one has to do to ensure the wellbeing of one's children. But it goes beyond this. The truly loving parent will do their utmost for his or her children *even when he or she knows* they will be unsuccessful. The loving parent who has a child dying of a terminal illness will not simply turn away and give up, ceasing to work long hours to ensure the child gets medicine because "he's going to die soon regardless." We would quite justifiably think of a parent who thought in this utilitarian manner as far from a loving parent. Indeed, most of us would rightly consider such a person a monster, or a sociopath. The loving parent is committed to his or her child such that he or she strives to ensure the child's wellbeing no matter what the situation, no matter what the inevitable outcome. This is simply part of what it is to be a loving parent. The morally ideal person, according to Confucius, has such a commitment to community in general. Such a person adheres to the standards dictated by one's role in the community, and commits him or herself to ritual action aimed at creating social harmony, *regardless* of the outcome. To do anything less would be to lack the communal concern that, in part, makes one a morally ideal, and ultimately thriving, person.

If you guide them using institutions, and order them using punish-ments, the people will avoid disorder but will be without a sense of shame. If you guide them using virtue, and order them using ritual, they will have a sense of shame, and moreover will have a standard. *Analects* 2.3

Another feature of the ideal person, that comes via his or her deep commitment to the community, is *social authority* or *moral influence*. In general, those who have the natural ease that comes with the virtue of the ideal person, and who have real commitment to a community, tend to generate respect and devotion in others. We have all seen examples of people whose wide-ranging care and concern makes him or her a beloved figure in a community—whether it is a priest whose care for his parishioners and well-performed role as guide create a mutual care and respect in his parishioners, or a sagely woman whose advice, constant concern, and supportive action toward members of her community creates a devotion and care for her in the members of the community. The moral attitudes of the ideal person will have influence throughout their community or communities. If the priest mentioned above takes a certain moral position, or adopts a certain attitude toward something, his parishioners, insofar as they are devoted to him, will tend to adopt these same positions and attitudes. This is what is meant by social authority, and moral influence. The ideal person's authority and influence will necessarily become powerful in a community, and to this extent the community will be benefitted by the presence and work of such a person. The ideal person is one who possesses the right motivations, dispositions, and communal commitments. Insofar, then, as the ideal person is a virtuous person, who for this reason also possesses communal social authority, they will also be instrumental in the *community*'s movement toward virtue. As people in the community tend to adopt the positions, attitudes, motivations, etc. of those they care for and are devoted to, they will tend to adopt those of the ideal person. Thus, the ideal person is a key element of the construction of a thriving and harmonious community. The virtue, social authority, and influence of the morally ideal person helps to mold the community into a thriving, harmonious one, in which everyone is brought closer to the moral ideal. Again, we see in Confucius' teachings, moral self-cultivation is not a solitary project. One does not develop a thriving and happy life alone. One's communities are an essential part of the picture. In the end, if we could distill the teachings of Confucius on how to live a better life down to one word, that word might be "community."

# Later Confucianism

The teachings of Confucius were perhaps the most influential in the history of Chinese thought, and gave birth to a long line of Confucian scholarship, reaching through the years even to contemporary times. Perhaps the most famous of Confucius' intellectual descendents were Mencius and Xunzi, both of who wrote during the first 100–200 years after Confucius' own life, during the Warring States Period (475–221 BCE). Unlike Confucius himself, both Mencius and Xunzi engaged with representatives of opposing philosophical schools, such as Mohism and Daoism, which rejected much of the Confucian picture of the ideal life. In addition, in later Confucianism, beginning with Mencius and Xunzi, we begin to see divisions even within Confucianism itself, surrounding important topics such as human nature, ritual, and the proper methods of self-cultivation.

## *Human nature*

It is in the *Mencius* that we first see sustained consideration of the topic of human nature (*xing* 性) as it relates to the topic of self-cultivation and creation of virtue. One common feature of almost all Confucians after the time of Confucius is their concern with virtue, generally surrounding the main concepts discussed in the *Analects*, such as ritual, humaneness, learning, filiality, and good governance. This, roughly, is what identifies them all as Confucian. Each of the later Confucian thinkers emphasize different concepts as central, however, and sometimes differ greatly on how they understand these basic Confucian concepts. In Mencius' case, he takes humaneness (*ren*, sometimes translated in the Mencius as "benevolence") and righteousness (*yi* 義, a concept we did not discuss as much above as it doesn't play as large a role in the *Analects*) as of primary importance. This focus is different from that of Xunzi, who instead takes ritual as central. We will see that much of this difference between the two can be explained by their positions on human nature.

There are two related questions we must ask in connection with human nature in Mencius and Xunzi. First—what *is* human nature? Second—what is the moral value of human nature? One has to answer the first question in order to answer the second. If we want to discover whether human nature is good or bad, we have to understand just what human nature is. That is, which attitudes and behaviors of humans are due to human nature, and which are not? It can't be the case that *everything* we do and think results from our nature, as this would entail that human nature includes contradictory things, both kindness and cruelty, intelligence and stupidity, virtue and vice.

In addition, it would be impossible to ever do anything inconsistent with our nature, and it would be of no use to analyze the concept of human nature and its moral value, as it would be useless to the task of self-cultivation. Whatever we do or are able to make ourselves do—it all comes from human nature.

Interestingly, some later Confucians in the Han dynasties, such as Yang Xiong and Wang Chong, held just such a view, that human nature is both good and bad, and thus irrelevant in consideration of self-cultivation. Neither of these thinkers can unproblematically be referred to as "Confucian," however, even while both shared a number of similarities with clearly Confucian thinkers. Perhaps the biggest divergence of their thought from that of the Confucians was their downplaying of the concept of human nature in their consideration of self-cultivation and ethics in general. Human nature was to remain a central concept in Confucian thought even down to the modern day.

## *Xunzi*

It is helpful to start by considering the *later* of the two Confucian philosophers of the Warring States period, whose position on human nature was formed in part in response to Mencius. Part of the reason for this is that Xunzi's view of human nature is likely to be closer to the view of human nature held by many in contemporary western society.

According to Xunzi, human nature is comprised of all a human's natural desires, those gained from birth, simply as a result of being human. There are a great number of desires we have that are attributable to our biological constitution. These, according to Xunzi, are the contents of human nature. So our nature contains, for example, the desire for food, survival, sex, comfort, companionship, and many other things. The question of the moral value of our nature, for Xunzi, is complex. Clearly, there is nothing *wrong* with these initial desires of our nature—in fact, they are necessary for our very survival. So it would be a mistake to call these desires morally wrong or bad. At the same time, we cannot call these desires morally right, or good, either. The desire for food alone is not something we would think of as morally positive, in the sense we would think of a right act like an act of charity or bravery, even though it is a desire necessary for our survival. Therefore, we must maintain, if all that can be said about human nature is that it contains natural human desires, then it must be morally *neutral*, that is, it is neither good nor bad.

For Xunzi, however, this is not all that we can say about nature. It is one thing to consider the basic desires alone, but we see a different picture begin to emerge when we think about how these desires will naturally develop, if left to develop on their own. We can ask the question: "If I simply allow my natural desires to play out and do nothing to diminish them, augment them, or otherwise transform them, how will they develop?" The answer to this question shows us that we *can* attach a moral value to the results of human nature's unfettered growth. *Human nature is evil* (性恶 *xing e*), says Xunzi. The reason for this is that if the morally neutral natural human desires are left to developed unchecked, they will always develop into vices. These desires have no internal cutoff point. The desire for food and material to live will naturally grow into greed—desire to have *everything*. The desire for sex will naturally grow into an unchecked sex drive and rampant promiscuity that will harm oneself and others. These desires that in themselves are neither good nor bad will, if left alone, grow unmanageable and become vices.

It is for this reason that we cannot simply rely on the cultivation of our human nature to become virtuous persons, to reach the Confucian ideal of being morally exemplary or sagelike discussed above. In particular, if we hope to become morally exemplary, we have to *constrain* our nature, to ensure that it does not grow into vice. To do this, Xunzi recommends adherence to *ritual* (*li*). Xunzi understands ritual in largely the same way it is understood in the *Analects*, but with a couple of important additions. Xunzi stresses that the most important functions of ritual is its role in limiting our desires. It is for this reason primarily (an aspect of ritual Confucius never speaks about in the *Analects*) that ritual is important for self-cultivation.

Xunzi's explanation of how ritual transforms human nature and enables us to become morally exemplary persons is a clever one. Although ritual has this single function of restraining desire, there are two important effects of this. First, it ensures social harmony if everyone follows ritual, because if desires are constrained, this will undermine the sources of conflict that lead to social disharmony. If no one is greedy and considers what they have to be enough, people will not go to war with each other to conquer territory, attain more resources, etc. Limiting our desires leads away from interpersonal conflict. Second, limiting one's desires through ritual actually ensures that our desires can be satisfied. One of the features of the person whose natural desires have grown out of check, unrestricted by ritual, is that this person's desires become overwhelming and unquenchable. Consider a greedy desire for wealth, which grows from the morally neutral desire to have enough resources. How much wealth is *enough* wealth, for such a person? One cannot possibly satisfy a desire to have an infinite amount of money. If one limits the desire for resources through ritual, however, one becomes able to satisfy one's desires. If there is a limit to the amount of wealth I allow myself to desire, then when I gain this amount, I will be satisfied, in a way the greedy person never can be.

The clever feature of this move by Xunzi is that it gives us a ready-made account of moral motivation. We often run into the problem, when considering ethical theories, that it seems hard to offer motivation for doing the right thing, being virtuous, etc. We can specify a particular type of action as right, a particular way of being as good or virtuous, but the question still stands—why should we care about doing right actions or being good or virtuous? Xunzi's theory of ritual provides a compelling answer to this question. Presumably we all want to have our desires satisfied. It just turns out that the only way to do that is to limit our desires through ritual, which also happens to be just what makes us virtuous, peaceful persons.

## *Mencius*

Mencius offers a very different picture from Xunzi concerning human nature, its initial moral value, and self-cultivation. He appraises human nature differently from Xunzi, and part of the reason for this is that he defines human nature differently. When Mencius uses "human nature," he *doesn't* mean it as the set of desires humans have naturally. Why not? As Mencius explains in a discussion with Gaozi in Book 6 of the *Mencius*, if desire for "food and sex" are human nature, then this means that human nature is the same as dog nature or horse nature, because both of these desire food and sex as well. If we are talking about human *nature*, then what we describe should be something *unique* to humans, or it doesn't distinguish them from any other animal. The basic desires common to all animals is not purely human, so how can they belong specifically to human nature? Perhaps there is, along with human nature in persons, something like animal nature that accounts for the desire for food and sex, but insofar as there is a distinct human nature, its contents too must be distinct, and set humans apart from the other animals. Dog nature includes that which is unique to dogs, horse nature that which is unique to horses, and human nature that which is unique to humans.

So what are the things unique to humans contained in human nature, according to Mencius? Initially, he explains, we have what he calls *sprouts* of virtue. Virtues like benevolence, ritual propriety, righteousness, and wisdom are, although not completely formed and coherent, elements of human nature. These "sprouts" themselves have positive moral value, and can be developed into full virtues, making us morally exemplary persons. This is the reason Mencius holds that "human nature is good" (性善).

Since human nature is good, this also entails that it will naturally develop to become even better. Notice that the kinds of desires that have the potential to become problematic or vicious are absent from Mencius' account of human nature. Instead, what we are left with are inclinations and desires that could never become bad, no matter how much they grow and are extended. Indeed, the more they grow and extend, the more virtuous a person will become. Take for example the feeling of sympathy that Mencius calls the "sprout of benevolence." This sprout could never grow large enough to become a problem. One becomes more and more sympathetic and caring— at what point could one take this to be a bad thing?

There are a couple of examples Mencius uses to illustrate what this "sprout of benevolence" is like. In one passage, Mencius discusses King Hui of Liang, who spared an ox that was taken to be sacrificed at a royal ceremony. When asked why he spared the ox, the king explained that as it marched by he saw its eyes, and noticed the fear and dread in them. After seeing this, the king could not bear to allow the ox to be killed, and had it substituted with something else in the ceremony. Mencius explained that this feeling of sympathy was the sprout of benevolence in the king, a part of his human nature. Although the king was not benevolent, the reason for this, according to Mencius, is that he had never allowed the sprout of benevolence to grow, instead always keeping it limited and checked by other desires, not arising from human nature. Given that most of the desires Xunzi spoke about are, according to Mencius, outside of human nature (perhaps part of our animal nature), one can allow these desires to get in the way of the natural growth of what is contained in our human nature, and thus obstruct the development of virtue.

But, we might ask, if a feeling of sympathy is supposed to be part of our human nature, how do we explain those people who seem to have no sympathy at all for others? There are a non-negligible number of people like this. Mencius explains that even the most hardened villains still have the sprout of benevolence, and there are certain cases that can show this. When one sees a child about to fall into a well, he says, one will feel a sense of panic and dread, followed by sympathy. Even the most wicked criminal will have such a reaction. The difference between the virtuous person and the vicious one is simply that the virtuous person has allowed this sprout of benevolence to grow unobstructed by desires that would cut it short.[4]

How, then, do these sprouts of virtue Mencius discusses grow into the full virtues that it is the goal of the Confucian to cultivate? The sprouts of virtue are extended differently depending on the virtue, but as an example, we can consider the extension of the sprout of benevolence. The sympathetic feeling that is the sprout can be extended through what Mencius calls *reflection* (思 *si*). Recall the incident with King Xuan and the ox mentioned above. How could it be the case that King Xuan is unable to bring himself to sacrifice the ox while at the same time he can allow his people to endure such great suffering through his lack of benevolent rule? It is because he fails to extend this sympathetic feeling through reflection. Using reflection, the king could imagine his people in the place of that ox. He could thus see their suffering, and this would generate the same reaction as the one he had when seeing the suffering of the ox. Reflection thus entails the ability to put oneself in the place of another, or to see what is close at hand as a proxy for what is more distant. In this way, one can generate sympathetic feelings toward more and more persons, until one eventually has the virtue of benevolence, which is understood as having sympathetic feelings toward all of humanity.[5]

Confucianism after the Han dynasty went on to become one of the most influential traditions in all of East Asian thought (perhaps the most influential in East Asia, and second only to Buddhism in Asia in general), greatly affecting the culture of almost all the countries of east and Southeast Asia. Its deep history (2500 years since the time of Confucius) is far longer than that of most other philosophical and religious traditions. Far older than Islam and Christianity, and roughly equal in longevity with Buddhism, Confucianism naturally saw many different divisions, schools, sects, and versions, many just as different from one another as they are from different traditions. This makes it hard to chart cleanly the directions of Confucianism after Confucius, Mencius, and Xunzi. There are many directions of Confucianism, some overlapping, some discontinuous, even down to our own day and the debates over both what it means to be Confucian today and who represents Confucianism. Thus, I include below in the list of further readings a number of different Confucian texts, of a variety of authors all of who take themselves to represent Confucianism in some important way.

# Further readings on Confucianism and self-cultivation

Although self-cultivation is primary among his concerns, the teachings of Confucius as recounted in the *Analects* also deal with a number of different (although not wholly unrelated) issues, including rulership, government, Zhou ritual propriety, musical knowledge, and human nature. What we've covered here is only one aspect of the more expansive vision of Confucius (although the most important part I think), and there is much more to learn about the *Analects* and the rest of the Confucian tradition, especially for someone interested in learning more about the applications of these ideas. One could spend one's entire life studying and examining the thought of Confucius, his students, and later Confucians. Of course, one of the virtues of the thought of Confucius is that it is not absolutely *necessary* to bury oneself in study, learn Chinese, read the traditional commentaries, or wade through endless scholarship in order to understand and appreciate both what Confucius taught and how we can apply it to our own lives. Even the short overview of Confucius' thought offered here can be of immeasurable value if one takes it seriously and heeds Confucius' instruction to put the teachings into practice, integrating them into one's daily life. As with all the thinkers considered in this book, the primary purpose of the thought and work of Confucius was to inspire and lead others to transform their lives, in order to become better, happier people.

Having a deeper understanding of Confucius and his teachings can help in this project. Thus, I include below a list of suggested further readings and other resources to give you a starting point for learning more about Confucius, the *Analects*, and the later Confucian tradition.

## Translations of the *Analects*

● Chichung Huang, *The Analects of Confucius*

● D. C. Lau, *Analects*

● Roger Ames and Henry Rosemont, *The Analects of Confucius: A Philosophical Interpretation*

● Edward Slingerland, *Confucius' Analects: With Selections from the Traditional Commentaries*

## Warring States Confucianism

● *Mencius*, trans. D. C. Lau

● *Xunzi*, trans. John Knoblock

## *Post Han Confucianism*

● Dong Zhongshu, *Luxuriant Dew of the Spring and Autumn*

● *Lushichunqiu*, "The Annals of Buwei Lu," trans. John Knoblock and Jeffrey Riegel.

● Jeffrey S. Bullock, *Yang Xiong: Philosophy of the Fayan.*

● *Kung tzu chia yu* "School Sayings of Confucius," trans. R. P. Kramers.

● Daniel Gardner, *Learning to be a Sage: Selections from the Conversations of Master Chu [Zhu Xi], Arranged Topically.*

● *Wang Yangming*

● Tan Sitong, *Renxue.*

## Secondary work on Confucius and the *Analects*

● Yu Dan, *Confucius from the Heart*

● P. J. Ivanhoe, *Confucian Moral Self-Cultivation*

● H. G. Creel, *Confucius and the Chinese Way/Confucius: The Man and the Myth*

● Annping Chin, *The Authentic Confucius*

● Lin Yutang, *The Wisdom of Confucius*

● Michael Nylan and Thomas Wilson, *Lives of Confucius*

## Films

● *Confucius: Words of Wisdom*, A&E "Biography" (1998)

● *Kongzi* (Confucius), Mei Hu, director (2010)

● *Confucius Speaks (Kongzi shuo)*, cartoon, Tsai Chih Chung

# A short biography of Confucius

According to the traditional accounts (compiled in the Han dynasty text *Shiji*—"Records of the Court Historian" by Sima Qian), Kong Qiu (styled Zhongni), son of the general Shu He, the man who would be known to later history as Kongzi (Master Kong—latinized "Confucius"), was born around 551 BCE in a town (present day Qufu) in the state of Lu, a vassal state in the eastern part of the ancient Zhou-controlled region (what became known as the "Warring States" not long after Confucius' life). By the time of Confucius' birth, the Zhou was already in decline and the states were semi-autonomous, vying with one another for dominance of the region, the core of which surrounded the Yellow River basin. According to legend (recounted, like many other legends, in Sima Qian's *Shiji*), Confucius was born with a misshapen head, his forehead jutting out like a small mound. This earned him the name *Qiu* (hill, mound).

Although the traditional stories do not say much about Confucius' youth, he is said to have lived in poverty, and spent his time learning the ancient rituals, music, and texts of the Zhou. He eventually married and had a family of his own, including one son who later figured in some passages of the *Analects*, but about whom little else is known. Confucius eventually became a ritual expert, specializing in reading, interpreting, and teaching the canonical Zhou texts, including the *Rites* (*Li*), *Songs* (*Shi*), and the *History* (*Shu*). Although these texts were to take different forms and were only completed as the currently known "classics" after Confucius' time, the core of these texts were available and central to the education and livelihood of scholars such as Confucius. Those most likely to have availed themselves of Confucius' services were rulers and nobles of various states. The children of these figures were expected to be educated in the ritual and classic texts that were seen as required knowledge in order to gain political legitimacy. The rituals and texts Confucius taught were at the core of Zhou cultural and political identity, and any person aspiring to rulership or an important position in government was expected to know these rituals and texts, if only to bolster their legitimacy in the eyes of a people and poltical structure still under the influence of Zhou customs, even if no longer held in check by Zhou power.

Confucius began his career in politics in Lu, gaining a reputation for his knowledge, and eventually gained position as Minister of Punishments. Although the Duke of Lu (representative of the Zhou in the old order) was nominally in control, *de facto* power in Lu resided with three families who essentially controlled the government of the state of Lu, and Confucius, in an attitude consistent with his commitment to the Zhou, desired to restore power to the Duke. Confucius engaged in a number of political intrigues in the period around 500 BCE to break the power of the three families in Lu.

In 498 BCE, due to his role in Duke Ding of Lu's unsuccessful attempt to tear down the defenses of the Meng family at Cheng, Confucius and his followers were exiled. He took his show to the road, so to speak, traveling to various states to offer his instruction in Zhou ritual and texts to the rulers and nobles of other states. Confucius did not see his offering of instruction to the rulers of other states as treasonous to or undermining of his native state of Lu, because he envisioned his project not as one of aiding states in their attempt to gain ascendant political legitimacy over their rivals, but rather as helping states see the importance of returning to Zhou rituals and conduct and ultimately regaining the social harmony (*he*) that Confucius believed was being lost with the decline of Zhou institutions and the increasing belligerence of the states. Ultimately, Confucius believed, if the rulers of states would put aside their own greed and self-centeredness and instead adhere to the rituals of the Zhou, they would develop the kind of virtuous society that would ensure social harmony both within their own states, and within the wider Zhou cultural realm. Thus, Confucius envisioned his project as a primarily ethical one. He was not betraying Lu by instructing the leaders or other states in the moral way.

Rulers in this period, as in most others, would have expected something very different for their money and support. Then as now and for most of human history, these people were primarily interested only in what could help them maintain or increase their power, whether in terms of wealth, influence, or military might. A foreign scholar with the nerve to exhort these vain figures to reflect on their faults, reject their selfishness, and cultivate virtues, would not have been received with great enthusiasm. In the best cases, Confucius was just ignored. In the worst, he was persecuted and attacked. No one likes to hear about their moral faults and what they need to do about them, least of all a vain and power-hungry petty ruler of a small and fragile state hoping to make a name for himself.

Thus, Confucius experienced failure after failure—turned or chased out of states, ignored and neglected. While in the state of Chen, Confucius and his followers went hungry, having lost their supply of food for their journey. They faced illness and starvation, but Confucius was undeterred in his determination to bring about social harmony through reestablishment of the way of virtue in his society. He used this as an occasion to teach his followers about the determination of the morally exemplary person, and the importance of persistence in the face of hardship to advance the cause of morality.

Finally, in 484 BCE, Confucius returned to Lu, his mission to influence rulers and help bring about the cultivation of virtue and social harmony in his society having ended in failure. He committed himself in his final years to teaching and editing the Zhou texts from which he had learned the way of morality and which he had tried to transmit to others, and compiling the *Chunqiu* (Spring and Autumn Annals), a history of Confucius' state of Lu from 722–481 BCE (from which the "Spring and Autumn period" takes its name). The traditional date of Confucius' death is 479 BCE.

## RELEVANT QUESTIONS

1   Does Confucius' concern for social harmony (*he*) balance with a concern for individual welfare and rights? Ought either of these have priority over the other? Why/why not?
2   Think about the social implications of the view that one's agency is dependent on integration into community? What does this say about the disenfranchised? The recluse?
3   Is filiality and family concern compatible with justice?
4   What are the "rituals"? Does our society recognize any concept of ritual? Need the Confucian rituals be accepted and followed within a narrowly Chinese context, or might they be possible for moderns and non-Chinese to adopt?
5   What implications, positive and/or negative, might the Confucian insistence on the inability to "opt out" of relationships, have for individuals or society as a whole?

6    Given Confucius' conception of learning and the ideal student, how might we train or teach people in contemporary society to become this kind of student? How might we reconfigure our institutions (schools, higher education, etc.) to foster this? Or do we already achieve it?

7    Do you think Confucius' morally ideal person will also be a *happy* person (in the conventional sense)? Is this important?

# Notes

1   All translations from Classical Chinese, in Chapters 1 and 2, are my own.

2   Such people are not necessarily *dishonest* in their concern for and commitment to a person while they are pleased by that person. Marcel Proust describes such a person brilliantly early in the fifth volume of his *In Search of Lost Time*: "The only thing was, that the virtuous enthusiasm he felt for a person who gave him pleasure, and the solemn commitments he made to her, had, in Morel's case, a debit side. As soon as the person no longer gave him pleasure, and even, for example, if the need to face up to the promises he had made her caused him any displeasure, then she at once became, in Morel's mind, the object of a violent antipathy which he justified to himself and which, after some neurasthenic disturbances, allowed him to prove to his own satisfaction, once he had re-established the euphoria of his nervous system, that, even looking at things from the point of view of strict virtue, he was now freed from all obligation."

3   The connotation is there in the Chinese term 仁 *ren* just as much as in the English translation "humanity."

4   One issue Mencius didn't consider, but we might, is that of what the existence of sociopaths says about Mencius' claim that the sprout of benevolence is part of human nature. Certainly such people will feel no sympathy for others. However, such cases don't present a problem to Mencius' account unless it is as a result of *human nature* that sociopaths are the way they are. Consider the physical aspects of humans. We hold that humans naturally have two arms—yet some people are born with only one arm. The fact that there are such people does not, however, demonstrate that having two arms is not natural after all, rather it shows that some people can be born with unnatural features. Presumably the same can apply to human nature as Mencius understands it.

5   This should not be thought of as identical to the Mohist "impartial caring" (兼愛), however. While the benevolent person cares widely, and for everyone, such a person will also recognize the greater importance of closer communities, beginning with the family, and will recognize their special responsibilities to these communities, following what we learned about the Confucians from the *Analects*.

# 2

# *Zhuangzi* and the Daoist Tradition

I am going to try to ridiculously explain something to you, and you try also to listen ridiculously. *Zhuangzi* Chapter 2

# Yangism, the *Daodejing*, Zhuang Zhou, and the retreat from society

Self-cultivation and creating an ideal life is not always a matter of struggle, development, and adherence to rigid principles. Sometimes such things can stand in the way, stunting our ethical growth, corrupting our appreciation of the world the way it *is*, and hampering our ability to move through this world with spontaneous ease. If anything approaching an ideal life is possible, mustn't it be the lived with a sense of joy and psychological freedom? Indeed, isn't the very notion of a single possible ideal kind of life antithetical to thriving? When one looks at the ideal life as something one does not have, representing a goal that has to be attained, this might turn one's life as it is into a war with oneself, a constant struggle with one's dispositions, desires, behaviors, and identity. Unless we have the dispositions, desires, etc. that the ideal person has, we must be found lacking, and to remold these intrinsic features of ourselves will involve constant struggle. And at the end of this struggle, one may simply discover that it is impossible to change human nature, and that this intangible "ideal life" can never be attained. Wouldn't it be more fulfilling, then, to simply give up on this project altogether? Instead of crushing ourselves under the need to attain some ideal state, why not just be, as Daoist text *Daodejing* suggests, "content with contentment?" Why not, that is, just learn to be happy with the way things *are*, rather than engaging in the impossible and counterproductive project of trying to mold them into what we *want* them to be? After all, isn't the person who can be happy whether it rains or is sunny ultimately better than the person who can only be happy when it is sunny and when it rains fruitlessly wastes her energy trying to make it sunny, or if this fails, sits in the house trying to pretend it's sunny outside? According to the one-of-a-kind philosopher we look at in this chapter, self-deception and fruitless attempts to change the world and oneself don't lead to the thriving life—they lead straight into greater suffering, ignorance, and disillusion.

This figure is the early Chinese "Daoist" philosopher Zhuang Zhou, better known by the honorific "Zhuangzi" (Master Zhuang), who lived not long after the time of Confucius, around 369–286 BCE, during what is commonly called the "Warring States Period". This period followed immediately after the Spring and Autumn Period, during which Confucius lived and taught, and was marked by the same decline of social order and warfare between states of Confucius' time. But by the Warring States Period, the situation had become even worse, even desperate. The battles between states were larger, more brutal, more costly in resources and lives. The stakes were higher than ever before. Even the common people, villagers and non-combatants were swept up in the chaotic whirlwind of constant and vicious war. States were destroyed, and families were annihilated. China inched closer and closer to the ultimate destruction of the states and the unification of the region under the rulership of the vicious and iron-fisted king of Qin, who would at the end of this period in 221 BC, conquer the last of the warring states and rise to power as the first emperor of the Qin dynasty—the *Qin Shi Huang Di* ("First Emperor of Qin").

For many years, people had attempted to regain social harmony and virtuous and thriving communities by using the methods of thinkers like Confucius and later philosophers influenced by him, such as Mencius. These attempts were ultimately unsuccessful. No matter how hard people strove to revive the traditional virtues in society, things quickly went the other direction. Things were getting worse, not better. And they were getting *much* worse. What, people might naturally ask, had gone wrong? Why wasn't the focus on virtue and adherence to ritual able to bring about the thriving society Confucius spoke of, returning China to the glorious "way of the former kings?" Why, instead of movement toward social harmony, was there increasingly horrific violence, centered in greed, anger, and delusion? Clearly, people began to think, Confucius must have been deeply mistaken in some of his assumptions about the effectiveness of virtue.

The first group of thinkers to offer an explanation of where they thought the Confucian approach went wrong was a semi-organized group we might call the *Yangists*, based on their agreement or adherence to the views of Yang Zhu, or Yangzi (Master Yang), who endorsed a very different kind of life than Confucius and his followers. Yang Zhu located the difficulty in the attachment of the Confucians and others to principles and ethical concepts, and to the social project in general, while neglecting personal issues. Society, ultimately, can only be an empty *idea*, because we cannot have true relationships with society as a whole, but only with those individuals close to us. When we focus on advancing the cause of society, through abstruse ethical concepts, we become cold to what is truly human—we shift our focus from real, tangible concerns, emotions, and relationships with those near us, toward something cold and abstract, a "society" and "humanity" that does not involve real people at all.

One might ask the question: how can it be that so many political, religious, and other movements that have focused on advancement of society, the "people," or some other noble idea, have ultimately helped cause the suffering of the very people they supposedly aimed to help? Yang Zhu would suggest that this just where the Confucians went wrong. We cannot focus our energies on all of society, on the "people"—as this concept is meaningless to us. This can be nothing more than a cold abstraction. One cannot have a relationship with the "people," cannot have a meal with them, share moments of joy and sadness with them, grow close to them. True relationship is only possible *where one is*, in intimate proximity with a close community, made up of people one *knows*. The "people" have no face.

It is for this reason that Yang Zhu endorsed seemingly "egoistic" claims such as "one should not damage a hair on one's head, even to save the world." Such formulations are likely purposefully provocative, intended to create controversy. Because of them, some have read Yang Zhu as advocating something like ethical egoism—the view that what is right is what advances one's personal interests. I think this is the wrong way to read these exhortations of Yang Zhu's, however. One plausible way of understanding these claims is that they represent condemnation of abstract concepts like "the people" or "the world." The hair on one's head gives us an example of something real, tangible, a concrete aspect of our lives, even if a small, nearly insignificant one. The notion of "the world" or "the people," however, does not even rise to this level. It is merely a fiction we create and use in order to feed our own egos, or, as Zhuangzi later argues, to "show off your beauty at the expense of others' ugliness" (Chapter 4).

Instead of focusing on "saving the world," Yang Zhu argues, we should focus on those things that are *authentically* close and meaningful to us. We have no real, concrete conception of "the world" we are going to save. Such a thing is merely an abstract ideal, a fanciful notion. The world has no face, has no name, we have no relationship with it. However, there *are* real people before us who do have names and faces, with whom we do have relationships and through whom we can find actual fulfillment. Our family members, our immediate communities, the people we interact with every day—*these* are the people who for us form real community, for whom we ought to work and sacrifice, toward whom we ought to aim in our attempts to become more socially integrated persons. To do anything else is to follow an abstraction that is ultimately a *lie*, a movement away from what is authentically human.

The notion of the *authentic* here is central, and it is a concept central to the thought of Zhuangzi as well as Yang Zhu. The message of the Zhuangzi might, indeed, be summed up in the exhortation "Let yourself be *authentically* human!" Most of our problems, according to Zhuangzi and Yang Zhu, arise because we construct artificial concepts and ethical notions and then try to force ourselves to act consistently with these. This inevitably rubs against our true nature as humans. To be authentic is to act consistently with *local* norms surrounding one's own community, personal interests and desires, and wellbeing. The prototypical example of the inauthentic life, then, is that of one who ignores his connection to his close community in order to hanker after some diffuse, unclear, and abstract notion of "reestablishing virtue in society" or "bringing about the thriving society"—the very things the Confucians exhorts us to do! We can see that the Yangists (and Zhuangzi) argue that the Confucians miss something central to living an ultimately fulfilling life. That is, in their concentration on *society* and *virtue* they miss the truly meaningful things in human life, the local and the small things that have nothing to do with lofty ideals like virtue, the moral *way*, justice, and the like. The ultimately thriving life consists not in the triumph of justice or "the people," but in the happy laughter of one's children, the loving caress of a spouse, the simple happiness of an evening's conversation with friends. It is the truly *personal* that is the source of our wellbeing. In this sense, Yang Zhu might be taken as concerned with the self, or ego, but this is only a concern with the self insofar as what is really valuable to the self is what is immediately available to the self. The only true source of meaning in one's life is to be found in what directly surrounds you. Yang Zhu (and Zhuangzi following him) might indeed instruct those today who are inclined to seek the way to a better life through moving forward, onward, and beyond, that "It is useless to look to another place, across the horizon, to future efforts and plans in a heroic struggle for thriving. True thriving cannot be found hundreds and thousands of miles away. True thriving is within arm's reach."

The relationship between the thought of Yang Zhu and that of the later Zhuangzi is clear enough when we notice the similarities between many of their views, and the influence of Yang on Zhuangzi's thought, but it is unclear just *how* the thought of the Yangists influenced Zhuangzi or how closely certain aspects of Zhuangist thought that go beyond what we know of Yang Zhu correspond to Yangist thought. Unfortunately, we do not have access today of very much of what we could call originally Yangist writing.

The tradition offers more clarity in the case of the purported author of the *Zhuangzi*, Zhuang Zhou. Although we can still not be certain that a single man named Zhuang Zhou is responsible for the entirety of (or even part of) the text we know today as the *Zhuangzi*, we do have a decent understanding of the man who early Chinese tradition claims was behind the authorship and the ideas of the text.

According to the Han Dynasty history *Shiji* (Records of the Grand Historian) (written c. 109–91 BCE by Sima Qian), Zhuang Zhou lived in the mid–late fourth century BCE (which would have made him a contemporary of Mencius) and hailed from a village in the state of Song. The *Shiji* claims that although he for some time held a minor local government post, he spent the majority of his life as a hermit, systematically avoiding society and government, in the mold of the Proto-Daoist hermits of *Analects* Book 18 who inspired much of his own thought.

This picture of a hermit-philosopher traveling around his region, engaging in discussions with friends like the logician Hui Shi, exhorting people to become *authentic persons* (*zhen ren* 真人), and exuberantly flouting the norms of society certainly does seem to match with what we learn about the character of Zhuang Zhou from the chapters of the *Zhuangzi* itself. Whether there ever existed a man named Zhuang Zhou and if so whether or not he was responsible for some or all of the text we currently know as the *Zhuangzi*, however, is not of central importance. The message of the *Zhuangzi* is largely coherent, if often disjointed, abstract, and difficult to grasp. It is a message intended for us, aimed at helping us radically rethink the way we live and relate to the rest of the world. The ultimate aim is to help us gain true thriving, in a way Zhuangzi claims is not possible on the narrow Confucian path. The *dao* is more expansive than empty moralizing, Zhuangzi argues, and only those who allow their minds to "wander in the beyond" can hope to realize their true potential as humans and the unsurpassable joy that comes with this realization. Let us see if we can follow Zhuangzi to better understand his strange prescriptions for living a better life.

# The perspective of the *dao*

Don't be a medium possessed by your name, don't be a stockroom for schemes. Don't take the weight of affairs on your shoulders, don't be the man-in-charge of wisdom. Become wholly identified with the limitless and roam where there is no foreboding of anything. Exhaust all that you draw from heaven and never have anything in sight; simply keep yourself tenuous. The utmost man uses the mind like a mirror; he does not escort things as they go or welcome them as they come, he responds and does not store. Therefore he is able to conquer other things without suffering a wound. *Zhuangzi* 7.6 (trans. A. C. Graham, modified)

The concept of the *dao* 道, or "way" for Zhuangzi, as for other Daoists, is central in his conception of self-cultivation in terms of living a more authentic life. The primary way to appreciate the changes inherent within the world and to come to a state of equilibrium with all things is to act consistently with the way of the cosmos itself, or *nature*. *Dao* in this sense refers to the universal process or event—the single event that all activity in the universe is a part of. One way of understanding such a process is to consider a hurricane. A hurricane is a particular weather event, a swirling wind that can span up to thousands of miles wide. Although the hurricane itself is a single continuous process—when we look at satellite photos of a hurricane we can clearly see its coherent structure, its arms and eye, the direction of the larger winds, etc.—it is also true that the process contains sub-processes, the wind and clouds of certain areas in the hurricane. There will be certain facts about how these sub-processes connect to the larger process of the hurricane, but it is clear that they cannot be taken as distinct objects related to the hurricane rather than as part of it.

So what is the distinction between a hurricane as *process* and something that is an *object*, or in philosophical terminology, a *substance*? One of the main differences between the concept of substance and that of process is the view that a process as more akin to an *event* than an *object*. A hurricane does not consist of a particular set of clouds and wind states, but rather is identified with the temporally bounded event involving wind states, clouds, etc. moving and changing in certain ways. It is the *patterns of change* that determine the event, and these patterns that are the essence of the process in question. Whereas a substance is defined by static properties (color, size, shape, etc.) associated with objects, a process is defined by patterns of change associated with events.

Thus, it is possible to *act* consistently with *dao* because *dao* is a natural process, rather than a substance or object. It is like an event, rather than an object. How could we act consistently with an object or substance? Part of the problem here would be to explain what the action of the substance consists in. Every action a substance makes or change it undergoes will necessarily be *contingent*—that is, it will be an action that the thing does not take *necessarily*, that is not necessarily part of its nature as an object. This is because a substance is not, in most cases at least, defined by its activity in the way a process is. Thus it will be difficult, if not impossible, to understand how a substance naturally acts, and to mirror the action of a substance in the sense of internalizing and resonating with the changes inherent in the substance. The situation is different if we consider processes. If we are truly familiar with a process, we understand the events constituting the process, we follow the actions and changes inherent in the process. Then, acting consistently with the process in question is a matter of acting in similar ways, following the same patterns that define the process in question. Zhuangzi exhorts us to act *like the dao*, like nature—mirroring it, and allowing our actions thus to be spontaneous and natural, *authentic* like the actions of the process of nature itself. We will have to consider in more detail below how *any* actions, then, can count as *in*authentic.

The best way to act, according to Zhuangzi, is the way that will lead ultimately to true human thriving and away from the needless suffering, worry, and general strife inherent in the way of the Confucian moralist and "civilized person" who acts based on preconceived notions of virtue, appropriateness, etc, and whose acts are aimed at construction of artificial and ultimately meaningless communities like that of "the state" or "the people." This is to mirror the activity of nature itself, of the manifest *dao*. In Zhuangzi's thought, the *dao*, nature, is vast and comprises all that there is.

Although *dao* can in some sense be considered as the process of the entirety of nature, Zhuangzi also clearly holds that the *dao* is ineffable, that nothing ultimately accurate can be said about it, because there is something essential about the *dao* that words at some level necessarily fail to capture. We can never fully capture truths about nature using language.

What it means to act consistently with the *dao* is to act in the manner that the *dao* acts, and from the *perspective* of the dao. In a sense, the best kind of action is to allow the *dao* itself to act *through* you. One of the things we notice when we look at the processes of nature (for the moment setting aside the complication of humans as part of nature) is that there is no tortuous indecision inherent in nature, no goal-directed action or action based on similar reaction to similar objects. Action in nature is spontaneous, unforced, and based on the immediate features of a situation. The wind flows downward over the tops of mountains not because it is *supposed* to or *commanded* to flow downward, such that it does so no matter what the situation, rather it flows downward based on the propensities of the current situation. There is a downward space to be filled, and the air spontaneously moves to fill it. If there were not such a space, the air would not act in this way. Nature's processes are wholly immediate and dependent on actual features of the immediate situations, not consideration of what was before and what will be after. Harmony with these processes represents, for Zhuangzi, true attunement to the *dao*, and ensures true human flourishing.

What does the *dao* have to do, then, with one's *perspective* on the world? The perspective of the *dao*, according to Zhuangzi, might be understood as the perspective that can see and appreciate *all* perspectives, but is not limited to any of the particular perspectives of aspects of the world, even its own largest perspective. Having the perspective of the *dao*, the perspective of the process of nature, is to not be limited by the narrow perspective of the specifically human, the perspective from which one sees it necessary to act based on preconceived ethical and other normative notions. Part of the problem with having a narrow, "human" perspective and acting from this perspective is that one misses various ways in which what seem like negative or painful situations from one perspective are positive or advantageous situations from another perspective. One of the keys to our thriving is to transform what would, from a limited and narrow perspective, cause suffering, to that which causes true joy and thriving through coming from the expansive and vast perspective of the *dao* itself.

How might this work? Consider an example we find in the Zhuangzi itself. Zhuangzi's wife has just died, and his friend Hui Shi finds him sitting in a grove, singing happily and beating on drums—quite a strange situation for a man who just lost his wife, assuming that he actually did care for her. Hui Shi, noticing the seeming inconsistency, asks Zhuangzi why he's expressing such joy banging on his drums. Zhuangzi gives a characteristically enigmatic response:

> When she first died, don't you think I was upset like anyone would be? But then I reflected on her beginnings. Originally she had no life. Not only that, but originally she had no form. Not only that, but originally she had no spirit. The spirit [*qi*] transformed and there was form, form transformed and there was life, and now there's been another transformation and there is death. This is like the changing of the four seasons. She lies sleeping in the great chamber, and if I were to shout and yield to tears, this would be to fail to understand and accept the way things are. So I stopped (Zhuangzi 18).

What from the narrow perspective of the human is to be dreaded and lamented, it seems, is from the perspective of the *dao* itself something to be accepted and even celebrated. The process of constant change, the "transformation of the myriad things" carries on, and we can (and should?) delight in this transformation, seeing it as a dance of colors or the changing of seasons or the fleeting enjoyment of a show on a stage. Life and death, from the perspective of the *dao*, are just part of the changes of the process of nature, just as one is inevitably oneself part of the ongoing process that is the *dao*. Why, Zhuangzi asks, does the fact of change need to depress us? Why can it not instead give us joy?

> This is the transformation of the myriad things, the node connecting [the ancient sage kings] Yao and Shun, and the culmination of the conduct of [the cultural heroes] Fuxi and Jiqu. Then how much moreso should this be for the various others! *Zhuangzi* 4.2

> Chang Ji said, "this person is footless [Wang Tai who had lost his feet through punishments], yet this Honorable Mr. Wang far surpasses the common. Now one like this, concerning the way he uses the mind, how is he alone able to be as he is? Confucius said, "death and life are large issues, but they cannot transform him. If all heaven and earth were to be smothered or drowned, this still couldn't cause him to be lost. Examining without ulterior motive, he still avoids creating 'things.' The transformation of things is fated, yet he guards his true origins." *Zhuangzi* 5.1

This might help us to understand the idea of the "narrow human perspective," what is wrong with it, and how we can (even though we are human!) free ourselves from it. Humans have a tendency to fear, suffer from, and thus resist change. We might see this as a feature of our nature—for some reason, we want things to remain as they are, and we suffer deeply when things change: when people go away or die, when our children or friends' character changes, when the world we grew up in changes to a new one as new people and new ideas transform it. What is it about humans, we can ask along with Zhuangzi, that causes us to suffer so much from change, and thus leads us to resist it so forcefully? And can we escape this, seeing instead from the *dao*'s perspective in a way that will lead to true thriving and freedom from strife? If so, how?

## "Fasting of the mind" and "listening ridiculously"

Let's attempt to answer these questions in order. Zhuangzi attributes much of the strife inherent in human life to the way we conceptualize the world, set goals, and act in accordance with these concepts and goals. If we examine closely the process of how we construct values and how we go about trying to attain goals, we will see that this process necessarily at some level undermines itself! That is, the construction of values and concepts and the attempt to achieve goals through action consistent with these values makes it impossible to ever actually realize the goals we seek or act consistently with the values we prize.

Consider the situation of the good Confucian. This person aims to bring about social harmony, thought of in terms of the adherence of society to ritual, a situation in which all social roles are performed properly, and the thriving of the individual and the society results from this proper functioning. In order to accomplish this goal, the Confucian relies on virtues, adherence to ritual action, and imitation of the sages (among other things). However, Zhuangzi says, consider what will happen when one acts in such a way consistent with Confucian values and goals.

> Yan Hui went to see Confucius, to ask his permission to travel. Confucius asked, "where are you going?" Yan Hui said, "I am about to go to Wei." Confucius asked, "why are you going there?" Yan

Hui said, "I've heard that there is a young man, the Lord of Wei, acting selfishly, carelessly directing his state, and failing to see his mistakes. Carelessly using the people, this leads to their deaths. The dead are so numerous they are laid out in the swamps, like bananas. The people have no place to turn [for help]. Master, I have heard you say that one should leave the orderly state and go to the disorderly state—that at the doctor's door there are many sick people. I want to apply what I have heard and my thoughts, in order to enact reform in the state for the multitude."

Confucius said, "Agh! This is dangerous and will only result in your execution. The manifest *dao* does not want to be scattered—if it's scattered it becomes many, and if it's many then it becomes agitated. If it's agitated then it becomes depressed, and if it's depressed then there's no salvaging it. The way the ancients arrived at it in people was first to give it life within themselves, and only after this to give it life in people. Those who give it life within themselves are not yet certain of it there, so how can they engage in the extraneous activity of trying to arrive at it in rectifying the conduct of vicious people?

"In addition, do you know what it is that washes away virtue, and what causes knowledge to flee? Virtue is washed away by gaining renown, and knowledge is pushed out by conflict. Those with renown use it to crush one another, and those with knowledge use it as an instrument for conflict. Both are horrible tools, which can't be used to bring about summative conduct. In addition, having robust virtue and solid trustworthiness does not add up to vital energy [*qi*]. Avoiding name and fame and its attendant conflicts does not add up to access to the mind. And stubbornly insisting on ritual and righteousness to restrain this vicious man through your writings and speaking—this is to use another's ugliness to show your beauty. This is called plaguing others. And to those who plague others, these others will necessarily respond by plaguing them. It's a dangerous proposition, this plaguing others!" *Zhuangzi* 4.1

In traveling to another state to reform the ruler of that state, to try to persuade him to act consistently with duty and ritual, one invites not success but only death at the hands of the ruler. Why is this? Confronting another person in a "missionary" capacity leads most often to resentment and hostility. This is because the person who is doing the "instructing" assumes that the life of their interlocutor is wrong, by the lights of *his or her own* actions and self-manufactured values. *All* values are ultimately human artifacts, made by and enforced by humans. To criticize another in light of the values one has constructed is simply to, as Zhuangzi says, "use another's ugliness to show your beauty," to reinforce one's own adherence to values deemed as good through showing that others fail to live up to these values (even if only because they reject them). There is no possibility of *converting* a ruler or anyone else to one's own values in this way, but rather what will result is alienation and hostility. To use others' ugliness to show your beauty, Zhuangzi says, is to "plague others—and if you plague others, others will plague you." The proper and likely response to missionary attempts at "restoring" virtue in people is returned hostility from those persons. The missionary who travels to a foreign kingdom that doesn't accept his or her values to "convert" the natives should not be surprised then, and should *expect* even, that the result will not be mass conversion, but either their being run out of the country, or worse, execution.

Zhuangzi suggests a kind of dishonesty on the part of the "missionary" here as well. Even though they may claim (and even believe!) that it is the conversion of the masses that is their goal, their true motivation is actually far more selfish than this. It is ultimately *human vanity* that grounds the missionary's position. They desire to use the perceived "ugliness" of others to frame and enhance their own "beauty." This is all the position really amounts to, according to Zhuangzi, and the missionary is simply engaging in some high stakes self-deception in constructing a more beneficent-sounding motivation. The ideas of *cognitive dissonance* and the construction of creative rationalizations to diffuse cognitive dissonance are relevant here. It turns out Zhuangzi had excellent psychological insight, consistent with much of what we today know about human motivation and behavior.

Consider the notion of the "goody-two-shoes." We all know people like this. Why does this kind of person's seemingly over-stringent adherence to some conventionally acceptable norm of proper action so irritate the people around them? The reason for our abrasive reaction to him or her has to do with his or her actual motivations for adhering to the norms rather than the fact of his or her adherence to the norms. The goody-two-shoes doesn't strictly adhere to the conventionally acceptable norms because he or she endorses, cares about, or sees those norms as important, but rather he or she adheres to them because he or she knows that such adherence will gain them praise by people who enforce the norms—that in the eyes of these people the goody-two-shoes will *look better* than his or her peers. They adhere to the norms out of vanity, that is, a desire to appear better than those around them, to "use the ugliness of others to showcase their beauty." We might imagine that a couple of things would follow if a person adhered to conventionally acceptable norms because he or she saw value in those norms (the prig or pedant, perhaps, rather than the goody-two-shoes): 1) he or she wouldn't be as concerned with showcasing their adherence to these norms, in publicly parading their actions; 2) he or she would likely be *less* stringent in adhering to the exact letter of the norms, because the central commitment would be to the goals they see as resulting from adherence to the norms—that is, one may adhere to the norm "do not lie to others" as a way to ensure social harmony, please God, etc. Zhuangzi suggests that most "missionaries," or those who adhere to constructed values and attempt to establish these values widely, are in actuality psychologically sophisticated "goody-two-shoes."

The motives of the goody-two-shoes are often psychologically transparent. That is, both the goody-two-shoes him or herself and everyone else knows that the actual motivation is praise, and that adherence to the conventionally acceptable norms is only a means to praise. The goody-two-shoes himself is aware that the desire for praise is his motivation, and he makes a choice to adhere to the norms as a method for gaining praise. Most "missionaries" are different from this, however. In many cases, cognitive dissonance will arise, based on the seeming inconsistency between one's commitment to certain values, which contain norms about motivation, and one's actual selfish motivation of gaining praise. Consider one common norm of many communities and societies concerning motivation: the idea that one should be motivated by other-concern rather than self-concern. Anyone who would aim at commitment to conventionally acceptable norms in order to gain praise would also thereby have to commit to *this* norm concerning motivation. Lack of commitment to this norm would undermine the central project, in that a person who did not at least *appear* to accept this norm would not gain the desired praise for adhering to the norms. So the goody-two-shoes has a dilemma: it seems their desire for praise that leads them to adhere to the conventionally acceptable norms is *inconsistent* with actual or full adherence to those norms. So one of the two has to be given up, right?

This is where the goody-two-shoes becomes transformed into the "missionary" through the reduction of cognitive dissonance that involves a key instance of self-deception. Their actual motivations being inconsistent with the values they adopt, they subsume their actual motivations, deceiving themselves into believing that they are motivated in ways consistent with the values they endorse, rather than through the desire for praise. Thus, the missionary who is filled with zeal to adhere to certain values and convert others to these values acts out of a motivation actually inconsistent with these values, while not attending to (or even aware of!) his or her actual motivation.

We see this kind of thing all the time. Consider the "holier-than-thou" type who makes a great show of his or her religious zeal, including sermonizing people he or she deems to stray from the proper standard, visibly and obviously telegraphing his or her acceptance of religious values, etc. This kind of person is often motivated not by internal motivating factors called for in the religious values he or she claims to accept, but by the desire to "use the ugliness of others to beautify" him or herslef, to gain praise, or simply out of a natural human competitive sense to prove to themselves or others that he or she is "better" than you. This is generally the source of the hostility that can arise in others toward this kind of person. We know that when he or she sermonizes the real motivation is not to convert us or help us, but simply to reinforce to those around them that he or she is, in fact, better than us. Why should this person expect anything in return other than hostility? When you slap someone in the face, shouldn't you expect to be slapped back?

The interesting feature of this case is that the "holier-than-thou" person here may not even be *aware* of his or her actual motivations, let alone endorse them. What distinguishes this kind of person from the "goody-two-shoes" is that this person has rationalized his or her behavior and reduced cognitive dissonance, deceiving *him or herself* into believing that he or she has some different motivation from that he or she actually does. Because the desire to present oneself as better than others is a motivation inconsistent with the religious values this person holds, he or she convinces him or herself that he or she is motivated by the desire to help others. So how do we know that this person does not actually have this desire to help others? Can we make sense of sublimated or subconscious desires or motivations on which people act?

It seems that we can. We can see that a desire to help others is not an *actual* motivation of such a person through what is revealed in behavior. If a person has the actual motivation to show that he or she is better than you, and not to help, they will act on opportunities in which there is a high likelihood of success in showing superiority, while he or she will not act in cases in which there is either a low likelihood or no possibility at all of achieving this goal, even though the action might help others. So, for example, we might see that the holier-than-thou person is filled with missionary zeal when there are other people around to see and admire his or her actions, but is indifferent when there are no people around. Or a strong desire for charity might arise when there are many people to witness his charitable acts, and he or she performs charitable acts in abundance in these situations, while feeling no need to be charitable when no one will know of his or her act, and avoids charity in these situations.

This kind of action and desire is consistent with not knowing one's actual motivations, insofar as it is possible to deceive oneself about one's motivations. We should not conclude that, since this person's behavior is consistent with one who desires to show that he or she is better than you, that this person realizes that this is his or her actual motivation, rather than motivations consistent with his or her purported values. It is most often the case, in fact (and *always* the case with "missionaries" according to Zhuangzi), that people operating using a narrow set of values and trying to impose these values on others are either disingenuous or (more likely) deceived concerning their actual motivations. That is, they are being *inauthentic*. Authenticity, for Zhuangzi, involves understanding our actual motivations, and leads to seeing the necessity for undermining our tendency to narrowly conceptualize the world in pursuit of the shallow and fickle pleasures that result from pleasing others or being seen as "superior", which ultimately undermine themselves and lead *away* from true human thriving rather than toward it.

Yan Hui said, "I have not yet understood. May I ask the method?" Confucius said, "You must fast! I will tell you. Having this method and acting on it, would you use it to [try to] change [others]? Those who do such are deemed improper by lustrous heaven." Yan Hui said, "My family is poor, we don't even drink wine and can eat meat only once a month. Given this, how can I possibly fast?" Confucius said, "what you have in mind is the fasting of ceremony—this is not the fasting of the mind." Yan Hui said, "may I ask—what is this fasting of the mind?" Confucius said, "Having a unified intention, you don't listen using the ears, but listen using mind. Don't listen using mind, but listen using vital essence [*qi*]. Listening stops at the ear, mind stops at the symbol/sign. As for vital essence, it is empty and waits for the addition of things. *Dao* consolidates emptiness. And emptiness is fasting of the mind." Yan Hui said, "When I had not yet begun to receive this instruction, in reality I was Yan Hui. But now that I have received it, there has not yet begun to be a Yan Hui. Can this be called emptiness?" Confucius said, "Exactly! This is what I am saying." *Zhuangzi* 4.2

The solution to the problem of inauthenticity, according to Zhuangzi, is to undergo what he calls "the fasting of the mind." In a scene in Chapter 4 of the *Zhuangzi* in which Confucius (or rather a Zhuangist parody version who expresses very un-Confucian views) is talking to his student Yan Hui (who in the *Analects* is represented as Confucius' best student, but in Zhuangzi's parody is seen as particularly slow to learn), Yan Hui explains to Confucius that he would like to travel to the state of Wei to attempt to convert the ruler to the path of virtue, engaging in the kind of missionary practice described above.

Confucius, channeling the Zhuangist here, criticizes Yan Hui's plans, and implicitly suggests that his motivations as well are lamentable, claiming that his actions will be nothing more than "using others' ugliness to establish your beauty," and equating this with "plaguing others." He reminds Yan Hui that "he who plagues others will himself be plagued," and tells him that the inevitable end of his journey will be execution rather than conversion of the ruler. Since Yan Hui's motivations, plans, and values are clearly confused, inauthentic, and ultimately dangerous, what can he do to save himself and realize true thriving?

"You must fast!" Confucius says. This is not fasting of the conventional type, refraining from eating. Rather, Yan Hui must engage in a fasting *of the mind* (*xin zhai* 心齋). This fasting of the mind is similar to that of the body, but what one refrains from here is the forming of concepts, values, and other preconceived notions and imposing them on to the world.

What does Zhuangzi mean by this? The suggestion is that when Yan Hui undergoes fasting of the mind, he will no longer see the world in terms of experiences that are valuable and those that are invaluable, acts that are the right kind and those that are the wrong kind, and even at the extreme, he will not see things as "this" or "that." When Yan Hui dreams and experiences himself as a horse or a butterfly, he will not wake up and discount that experience as "just a dream," but he will take it as the experience he had before, while he is now having the experience of being a Yan Hui. When he travels to other states, he will not see things through the colored lenses of "whether this action corresponds to the Confucian Way," but will see them purified of preconceived concepts and values, as actions of nature, of the *dao*. And seeing them thus, shorn of the way he thinks things *should* be, or how they relate to his narrow values, intentions, and goals, he will be able to respond to them much more effectively.

How might this work? Consider a case Zhuangzi mentions in Chapter 3, of a magnificent butcher who has carved oxen for years without ever changing his knife.

Cook Ding was cutting an ox for Lord Wenhui ... Lord Wenhui said, "Aha! Excellent! To have arrived at such skill!" Cook Ding put down the knife and said, "what I your servant prize is *dao*, which goes beyond skill. When I first started to butcher oxen, I saw nothing that wasn't an ox (all I saw were oxen). After three years, I could no longer see whole oxen. Now today, I encounter with the spirit, and don't use the eyes to see. Knowledge stops, and spirit acts as it desires. I rely on natural propensities, make use of the cracks and follow along the crevices with my knife—this is why I gain purchase. My skill is such that I've never passed the knife through the clumped areas, and certainly have never passed it through the large bones. A good cook yearly changes his knife, because he cuts. A mediocre cook monthly changes his knife, because he hacks. Now my knife has been in use 19 years, has carved up thousands of oxen, and the blade is still as sharp as if it had newly come off the whetstone. Although this is so, every time I arrive at a problematic point and see that it will be difficult to carve, I become anxious and proceed cautiously. My vision stops, my actions slow. I make tiny movements with the knife, and then in an instant the piece is carved, and falls like a clump of earth to the ground. Holding my knife and standing up, I look around with a satisfied attitude, clean my knife, and put it away." Lord Wenhui said, "Excellent! I have learned from Cook Ding's words how to nourish life!" *Zhuangzi* 3.2

Most butchers are unable to do this—they carve oxen for only a couple of weeks or months before their knife blades become dull and they have to change knives. But this magnificent butcher explains that not only in all his years has he never had to change his knife, but that its blade is as sharp as it was the first time he used it. Why is this? The butcher explains that when he cuts, he *does not see the ox*, but rather sees *dao* itself. He is able to see the joints and empty spaces in each individual ox, and move his knife so as to take advantage of these natural contours. While other butchers *carve* and *chop* based on how one cuts an ox, the magnificent butcher allows the ox to cut itself by following what is given in the situation, rather than rules for cutting oxen. It is important here that the magnificent butcher *does not see the ox*. It is not possible to do what he does in using the natural contours of an ox if one sees what one is cutting as an ox—because once one sees it as an ox, they project on to the object and situation before them the way they deem things are *supposed to be*, and thus they cut along "the ox's haunch" in the way one is supposed to, rather than along the natural contours. They cut thus against the grain.

There is another interesting example outside of the Zhuangzi to explain how preconceived notions and conceptualizing situations can lead to failure. When I took an art class as a high school student years ago, one of the first exercises we were given was to draw a picture of a person in a photo in front of the room. When I finished my picture, it didn't look very much like the person I was supposed to draw (and the same was the case for most of the other students). Then, we were given a second exercise, to draw the picture of the same photo, turned upside down. After finishing the picture, the photo was turned right side up. I turned over my drawing, and remarkably, I found that the result I obtained after this exercise had a much greater resemblance to the person in the photo than the first drawing. Most of the other students in the class had similar results. What, we wondered, explained this difference? The art teacher explained to us that in the first case, we added our concepts of what a person's face, arms, etc. *should* look like into the way we translated the image on to paper. In the second case, however, we were presented with an unfamiliar image that we did not conceptualize in the same way, and so drew *what we saw*, rather than what we *should* draw. We were drawing what was there, the particular lines and shades, rather than a *person*. A person is supposed to have symmetry of this type, height and weight of that type, according to our concepts. Thus, we projected these preconceptions onto the paper when we drew the person in the photo in the first case. Thus, turning the photo upside down forced us into a kind of fasting of the mind! It forced us to relinquish our preconceived notions of what the subject of the photo was *supposed to* look like, which helped us to see (and translate) what it *actually did* look like.

Zhuangzi's understanding of the conceptualizing tendencies of the human mind and how this effects our perception of the world was truly ahead of its time. The western philosophical tradition was still struggling with this in the twentieth century, when opponents of logical positivism and the "sense-data" theory of perception showed that all observation is "theory-laden," that our concepts of the world are always contained in our perception of the world. Zhuangzi, although he understood this, believed that there is a way out of this conceptualization, and this way is the fasting of the mind. We can, even if we don't currently, come to see things in the way the magnificent butcher and the skilled artist see them—non-conceptually, raw, devoid of conceptual and thus linguistic content. When we come to see things this way, Zhuangzi also suggests, we come to understand that nature itself, the *dao*, is ultimately ineffable, that is that nothing can be ultimately accurately said about it, because language is simply a manner of conceptualization, and no constructed concept can ultimately mirror the world in a way that will allow us to act *authentically* and *spontaneously* with regard to situations.

Because we rid ourselves of preconceived notions and force our concepts onto the world when we undergo fasting of the mind, one of the interesting things that follows is our loss of even our sense of identity! We no longer see the world through the lenses of particular values, goals, or other preconceived notions. But when we think about the kinds of things that fix identity, that make us different from others and individuate us as *this* person rather than *that* one, what can we appeal to other than preferences, values, goals, etc? Part of what makes me Alexus McLeod is my enjoyment of philosophy, history, astronomy, and literature, as well my acceptance of certain values and goals, such as the importance of learning. One of the things that happens, then, if I undergo the fasting of the mind is that I rid myself of all of this, and to that extent I become free of constraint in part through becoming free of my identity! Part of what I let go of through the fasting of the mind is my attachment to this *Alexus McLeod*, such that I grasp after or endorse experiences relevant to or in line with the expectations or desires of his, and instead approach my experience on its own terms, so that I can efficaciously respond to the world as it *is*, rather than as I would like it to be or color it through my preconceived notions. When I rid myself of "the self," of identity, I can become like the magnificent butcher, able to see what is before me and use the natural propensities of situations in a way I cannot when I am imprisoned in my own concepts. Trying to act with this conceptualized identity, then, is to quote Zhuangzi, to "wander around in one's cage."

One of the things we come to see when we undergo the fasting of the mind, according to Zhuangzi, is the usefulness of things deemed useless within narrower perspectives. Part of what we are constrained within when we are stuck in identity is a particular narrow perspective. I can only see and interact with the world with the values, goals, and preferences of Alexus McLeod, and this is why I perceive so much of the world as of no use, of no value. When I get outside of this narrow perspective, however, and attain to the perspective of the *dao*, my experience *blossoms*, I am able to see *everything* as potentially useful, and thus my effective power (*de* 德) becomes immeasurably vast. So how do we understand what it means to come to see "the use of the useless," and how does this translate into the attainment of a more successful and thriving life?

# The use of the useless

There is a story in the fourth chapter of the *Zhuangzi*, after the exchange between Confucius and Yan Hui concerning "fasting of the mind," about a particularly strange tree that has amazing longevity and effective power.

Nanbo Ziqi wandered through the hills of Shang, and saw a large tree there with strange features. Thousands of chariots tied together could be covered in its shade. Ziqi said, "what kind of tree is this! It's made of awkward stuff." Looking up and seeing its thin branches, he saw that they were gnarled and crooked and could not be used as pillars for structural support. Looking down and seeing its large trunk, he saw that it was uneven and separated, and could not be used to make either inner or outer coffins. Its leaves tasted rotten and would injure one's mouth. Its scent was enough to make one crazy and sick with intoxication for three whole days. Ziqi said, "This tree yields nothing of quality, and uses this to arrive at this great size. Ah! So the spirit man uses this lack of quality!" *Zhuangzi* 4.18

The useless tree in this story can teach us a number of things. First, being conventionally useless allows one to thrive in ways conventionally useful things cannot. If one has nothing that others, with their narrow and goal-directed perspectives, can use, one will be left alone, to grow, survive, and thrive. On the other hand, if one possesses the conventionally useful, that which those with narrow perspectives desire, one will be ground down and used up, chopped down like the tree with excellent wood, to be used for the projects of others. We can see examples of this when we consider those who showcase their talents in order to gain fame or realize some other goal based on identity. How many times have we seen talented administrators, politicians, or businesspeople let their sense of duty or ego lead them in attempting to be at the head of a project, company, or society, only to be "used up" by people who stand to gain from them? One narrow perspective heralds another—if you wander into a situation based on narrowly personal goals and values, you can also be sure others will respond to you with their own narrowly personal goals and values, and these will never have anything to do with *your* wellbeing. Indeed, those with narrow personal goals and values will not even *see* you when they interact with you, rather they will see a world colored with their own preconceived notions. The missionary, for example, does not see *me* when he encounters me in the desert or in a village, he sees "a heathen," or "the devil," or a "lost soul," or what have you. He sees only his own preconceived concepts and notions, which have nothing to do with *me*. The exalted politician or holy man who talks about "the people" does not see *us*—he sees a concept of his political or religious theory, which has nothing at all to do with the actual flesh and blood creatures to which he he takes himself to be referring.

Second, the way we *see* the tree will change when we undergo the fasting of the mind that both makes us conventionally useless and transforms our perception and valuation of our experience. While I might see this tree as useless when stuck within my narrow perspective, I see it as highly useful in a different way when I allow my perspective to broaden to that of the *dao* itself through the fasting of the mind. There are a number of other stories throughout the *Zhuangzi* that emphasize this aspect of the fasting of the mind and the use of the useless.

Huizi said to Zhuangzi, "The king of Wei gave me the seeds for these enormous gourds. I planted them and when they came to maturity the gourds were 5 *shi* capacity. I used it to hold copious amounts of water or soup, but it was so bulky that I couldn't lift it [to drink]. I cut it in half to use a half as a ladle, but it would not fit into my bowls. There was nothing I didn't find it too big for, so since it was so useless I finally destroyed it." Zhuangzi said, "Honorable sir, you are too dense to know how to use that which is enormous! Among the people of Song, there was a person good at making medicine for avoiding chapped hands. For generations his family had been in the business of bleaching silk. One of their customers heard about this anti-chapping balm, and offered 100 *jin* [gold] to buy the recipe for the balm. The man of Song conferred with his family and said, 'We have for generations bleached silk, and have not made much money. Now in a single morning we have the opportunity to sell this [balm] knowledge and make one hundred *jin*. Please, let's do it!' The customer bought the balm recipe, and shared it with King Wu. The state of Yue began creating difficulties, and King Wu sent the man there to conduct war against Yue. During the winter, they engaged in battle with Yue and inflicted on them an enormous defeat, smashing their installations and conquering their territory. The ability to create balm to avoid chapped hands was the same in both cases, but one conquered, and one couldn't do anything but bleach silk. It is the uses that were different. Now as for your enormous five *shi* capacity gourd, how was it you didn't consider that you could use it as a massive container to sit and float on the rivers and lakes, yet you were upset that your gourd couldn't be used as a container? It is like you have a mind full of underbrush!" *Zhuangzi* 1.6

What is "useless" from one perspective is useful from another, and to see a given thing (or experience) as useless is simply to fail to be able to adopt and appreciate the perspective from which that thing (or experience) is useful. Part of what makes it impossible for one to appreciate these different perspectives is one's being trapped within the narrow perspective corresponding to *his or her identity*, adopted concepts, values, goals, etc. Thus, the fasting of the mind will allow one to adopt the perspective of the *dao* itself, which, as vast and expansive, both contains and can see and appreciate *all* of the other narrow perspectives.

Another story from Zhuangzi—in fact, the story that opens the first chapter—explains this link between the perspective of the *dao* and the multitude of limited perspectives.

In the north, according to Zhuangzi's fable, there is a great fish called Kun. This fish transforms into an enormous bird called Peng, and flies thousands of miles at a time. Its wingspan is truly magnificent, and with one flap of its wings it can travel across entire states. This bird can see and appreciate everything below, as its vantage point is both high and broad. A cicada and a student dove in a small forest on the ground look up and see this enormous bird sailing through the sky, and they laugh at it. Where is this bird going? they wonder. He's spending his time sailing about, while we worry about getting from one branch to the next—the worries and acts that are *really* important.

In the depths of the northern waters there is a fish named Kun. Kun's size is enormous, no one knows how many thousands of *li*. It transforms and becomes a bird, whose name is Peng. Peng's wingspan is enormous, no one knows how many thousands of *li*. When it rouses itself and takes to the air, its wings are like clouds filling the sky. When the sea moves, it migrates to the depths of the southern waters. The depths of the southern waters is the well of heaven. The Book of Qixie is an account of strange tales. It says, "In Peng's migration to the depths of the southern waters, it hovers along the water for 3000 *li*, then it goes atop a wave and rides it for 90,000 *li*, and after nine months has gone by, it rests" [...]

A cicada and student dove below laugh at Peng, saying, "We make the determination to rise up and fly between the elm and sandalwood trees, and sometimes unable to complete the trip and fall to the ground and that's that! How does that thing travel 90,000 *li* to the south?" Those who go to the (nearby) grasslands carrying three meals with return with full stomachs. Those who go one hundred *li* carry grain and mortar for preparing it on their overnight stops. Those who go one thousand *li* carry with them three months worth of grain. What could these two insects possibly know? Small knowledge does not match great knowledge, few years does not match many years.

How can one know this is the case? The mushrooms that grow and die in a morning know nothing about a new moon and full moon [the length of a month]. The cicada and cricket know nothing about spring and autumn, because their lifespans are too short. In the south of the state of Chu there is a tree called Deep Spirit. For it, five hundred years is like a single spring, five hundred more like a single autumn. In furthest antiquity there was a great tree called Chun. For it, eight thousand years was like a single spring, and eight thousand more like a single autumn. And to think that today one only hears about Peng Zu as being especially long lived! The multitude of common people all want to be like this—isn't it sad? *Zhuangzi* 1.1

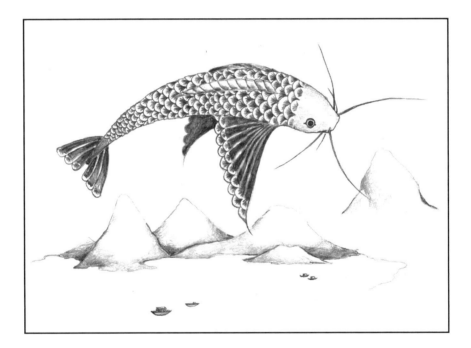

The cicada and the student dove in this story, according to Zhuangzi, are like those with narrow perspectives, who grasp on to identity, preconceived notions, values, goals, and so on. Being stuck within the narrow perspective, they cannot understand, let alone appreciate, any other, and so the person who sees and appreciates *all* other perspectives, like the vast Peng bird whose perspective is so expansive that it can access all of the others (the perspective of the *dao* itself), will be unintelligible. They laugh at the Peng bird because they think what he does is useless, has no value, because it does not conform to their narrow perspective, including their preconceived notions, values, and goals. But because they are stuck in this narrow perspective, they do not realize that the Peng bird sees their perspective as well as all others. To him, the world is not only a single tree in the forest, around which all our concerns should lie, but a far richer, more robust, and amazing place, with *innumerable* trees and forests, valleys and mountains, plains, oceans, and wonders numerous and amazing. And the Peng bird, since he is not limited by the narrow perspective of the cicada and the student dove, can not only appreciate the world in richer and ultimately more fulfilling ways than they can ever hope to, but he can also use the natural features of the world to nourish himself, to survive and grow and thrive. Part of the reason, one suspects, that the Peng bird is able to get so large is his ability to transform, adapt, and respond to situations spontaneously and without preconceived notions. He has thus found honey and nectar where the cicada and student dove have only found gnats and wind, because they will only look in the direct area of this single tiny tree.

What is deemed "useless" within a narrow perspective is deemed such because those trapped within this perspective simply can't appreciate the variety of different perspectives from within which this thing is useful. Ultimately all experience is like this. To deem a thing or experience "useless" is to fail to understand—to allow oneself to be trapped within a perspective. This is part of what Zhuangzi means by recommending "free and easy wandering." One who wanders on one's way can appreciate anything they come across during his or her wandering, while one who is *going somewhere* can only appreciate the destination, and devalues all other experiences on the journey. They are only means to attainment of the goal. But the person who has attained the perspective of the *dao* is not like this. They wander free and easy, without goals, vast and unconstrained like the Peng bird, able to survive and thrive, quick to see the value in everything. Surely such a person can surely be said to truly thrive, in a way most of us never do.

# Delighting in "the transformation of the myriad things," what we truly are, and freedom from suffering

One of the central truths about nature, perhaps *the* central truth about nature (although Zhuangzi would warn us that *any* attempt to take truth as expressible in language and using concepts is ultimately problematic), is that things are constantly in flux. Nature is not a collection of discrete, individual substances, but rather it is an ongoing process in which change, transformation, is the primary property. Zhuangzi calls this fundamental change "the transformation of the myriad things" (*wanwu zhi hua* 萬物之化). When we appreciate and are able to see from the larger perspective, which allows us to see and take advantage of the "use of the useless," another benefit that comes with this is that we gain the ability to *delight in* the transformation of things, rather than suffer as a result of this transformation, which is the normal state of those of us stuck within the narrow perspectives based on certain ways of conceptualization.

All changes in nature are part of the process of transformation that arises from the *dao* itself, even changes such as life and death. One of the features of our existence that causes us the most suffering is the inevitable fact of death. We often suffer psychic distress when those close to us die, or when we consider our own inevitable deaths. We see death as loss, as a catastrophe, as the end of all things, a fading into oblivion. For many of us, death is the very worst thing. This causes us to avoid thinking, talking about, or otherwise being open to the reality of death. The Zhuangist argues, however, that when we see nature *in itself*, when we understand the way the world really is, and attain to the perspective of the *dao*, we come to understand that death is no more a disaster or something to be lamented than is birth, no more a catastrophe than the falling of leaves in autumn, or the coming of cold and snow in winter. Birth and death are simply part of the transformation of the myriad things, part of the ongoing process emerging from the *dao*.

Two stories from the *Zhuangzi* are helpful in illustrating this point. In the first (from Chapter 18), which we considered above, we find Zhuangzi singing and banging on drums just after his wife has died. Zhuangzi's reply to Hui Shi in this story shows the benefit of understanding and taking the perspective of the *dao*—we see the world in terms of the process and the transformations, and we become able to *appreciate* the transformations and our own place in this process, rather than suffer because they happen. It is a fact about humans that we are born, grow old, and die. This is part of the process of nature, no different from the inevitable changing of the seasons. Life and death then is not something to be lamented, it is something to wonder at, to enjoy, to see as it is, the ever evolving process of the *dao*. We can draw a parallel to how we can react to the changing of the seasons. If we are attached to summer and cannot stand change, we will suffer when fall and winter come. However, if we can take the greater perspective of the *dao* and let go of our narrow attachment to summer, we can learn to enjoy what is unique about the fall and the winter, and to delight in the transformation of the seasons, recognizing the unique beauty of the fall and winter, rather than only being able to appreciate what is good about the summer. When we take a larger perspective, we become able to appreciate the value of what seems to us "useless" when stuck within the narrow perspective. One who is attached to summer sees the cold of winter as a burden and experiences it as suffering. But when we are able to broaden our perspective, we see what is good and useful about the cold. We come to understand, for example, that the cold keeps away insects, for example, or repels invaders, and makes lakes cold that we can then skate on. A world of new opportunities brought by the cold opens up when we enable ourselves to see outside our narrow perspectives. Then, we can appreciate the warm and the cold, the summer and winter, as we can see what is good in both. Likewise, we can come to see what is good in life and death, birth and decay—we can come to see ourselves as part of the process of nature. When we can come to see ourselves and our loved ones in this way, outside of the narrowly human perspective, the transformations of life and death no longer occasion sadness and suffering, but joy and (as the chapter is titled) perfect happiness.

Seeing ourselves as part of nature and subject to the transformations of nature is the central point of the next story, about the death of Zhuangzi himself. Clearly, this story cannot have been written by Zhuang Zhou himself, unless we are to accept some kind of mystical ability to author texts from the afterlife. As we considered above, however, issues of authorship are not always of central importance, especially if we are taking this text as a guide to life, rather than being concerned with the coherent thought of a historical individual. The story of Zhuangzi's death is certainly consistent with and follows the theme of what we see elsewhere in the *Zhuangzi*, and further explains the benefits of taking the perspective of the *dao*. It is fitting to end this chapter with a consideration of the end of Zhuang Zhou himself, and how we can take our awareness and perception of one's own final transformation as something that can itself be transformed, such that we delight in the natural arising and inevitable decay of all things, including ourselves.

Zhuangzi was about to die, and his followers wanted to give him a robust burial. Zhuangzi said, "I will have heaven and earth as outer and inner coffin, the sun and moon as ceremonial jade, the stars and constellations as jewels, and the myriad things as pallbearers. Aren't my burial goods already prepared? How could you add to them?" One of his followers said, "we are afraid that that crows and kites will eat you!" Zhuangzi said, "above ground, the crows and kites will eat me, beneath the ground, the crickets and ants will eat me. Taking from one to give to the other, how unfair that is!" *Zhuangzi* 32.16

The transformation of things will happen, whether we acknowledge it or not, whether we resist it or not. What is a burial other than an attempt to deny the fundamental change humans undergo on death? We have a human form, then we die and become worm food, or fertilizer for trees, part of the soil and the earth. This doesn't change if we put the person who has died into a box and then under the ground so we no longer see them, so we can imagine that they are whole and "uncorrupted," unchanged in a stasis inside the box. Denying the fundamental transformation of things will not save us from suffering—rather it will *foster* suffering! The only way we can overcome the pain we connect with death, both of those close to us and the prospect of our own deaths, is to *look directly* at it, to understand what one truly is, to let go of our narrow concepts of right and wrong, is and is not, should and should not (*shi/fei*), and once we do this, nothing can touch us. We see the world as it is, we can make our way through it with a natural ease, manifesting the height of skill in all we do, like the magnificent butcher, and we avoid the misery involved in a normal, unenlightened human life. The "authentic person" of the *Zhuangzi* floats joyfully above the hodgepodge and strife of the world, wandering free and easy like the enormous Peng bird, untouched by shallow "human" concerns. To become such a person is the height of self-cultivation, if what this process aims at is human thriving.

# Later Daoism

The "Daoist" tradition is a difficult one to characterize, especially if we are looking for a tradition influenced by and rooted in the *Zhuangzi*. There are multiple concerns of the *Zhuangzi* that take center stage in later Zhuangist-influenced work, but in many of these cases it would be difficult to justify calling these texts either "daoist" or "Zhuangist." Part of the difficulty here is that the *Zhuangzi* is one of the most unique texts in Chinese literary history, and its imitators and "descendants" are few, even if there are a number of commentaries, movements inspired by Zhuangzi, etc. Also, it is difficult to take all later "Daoist" material as standing in the same tradition as *Zhuangzi*, because it is unclear how easily the *Zhuangzi* fits into this Daoist mold, and much of the later Daoist material was more heavily influenced by texts like the *Daodejing* than by the *Zhuangzi*. Still, there are a few important texts and thinkers in the later tradition that we can clearly see as influenced by the *Zhuangzi* and attempting to build on its considerations.

# Huainanzi—"activating the genuine"

The *Huainanzi* is not a Daoist or Zhuangist text per se, but it does contain material from the *Zhuangzi*, and is clearly highly influenced by it. *Huainanzi* is a text composed in the Western Han dynasty using multiple sources, some of which were copied and some of which were changed and put into different places, in an attempt to create a synthesis of all the extant learning from the various schools and thinkers in early China. The result is a massive volume, containing bits from Confucian and Daoist texts, as well as numerous other sources, in addition to new material. The intention of the authors of the *Huainanzi* was to create a comprehensive and authoritative volume containing all current knowledge of importance to a ruler. This volume was named for the king of the state of Huainan, Liu An, a relative of the Emperor of Han. It was composed and presented to the second Emperor of Han, Emperor Wu (Liu Che), on his accession to the Han throne in 141 BCE. With the knowledge in the *Huainanzi*, and acting on its advice, Liu An implicitly suggested, Emperor Wu could ensure proper governance of the empire, and the physical and moral strength of the Han dynasty. This would have been a great concern of the young dynasty, given the spectacular failure of the first unified Chinese dynasty, the short-lived Qin, which had decisively risen to power and fizzled out within fourteen years. The Han rulers were determined to avoid this fate, and the teachings of the sages of the past were seen as key in this regard.

There are a few chapters in the *Huainanzi* that most clearly show Zhuangist influence, perhaps none of these more than the chapter "Activating the Genuine" (俶真 *chu zhen*). This chapter takes sections from the *Zhuangzi* as well as the *Daodejing*, and adds new material as well.

The chapter discusses material from the *Zhuangzi*, but understands it differently than the authors of the *Zhuangzi* did on the interpretation I give above. Specifically, where the *Zhuangzi* seems concerned with arguing against conceptualization and metaphysical speculation, the "Activating the Genuine" chapter reads the Zhuangist message as one of embracing a different kind of conceptualization. The most successful life, according to the chapter, is one in which a person can access the primordial, the aspects of reality that underlie all other phenomena, and which one might call the *dao* (Way). This is also the key to good governance. One of the interesting features of this chapter, and the *Huainanzi* in general, is that it takes the message of the *Zhuangzi* and combines it with the very Confucian concern of proper governance. We might see this as rather strange, given that the *Zhuangzi* in general seems to reject the notion of rulership or governance as something the ideal person is concerned with at all. In the *Zhuangzi*, the ideal person is one outside the confines of categories and conceptualization, and most especially outside of the meaningless clamor of politics. To Zhuangzi, the political person far from the *dao*. In the *Huainanzi*, however, the political person is seen as one who *can* attain understanding of the *dao*, and if he does this, his administration will be successful.

# Daoist "alchemy" and *Dao jiao*

Another later tradition that grew out of Daoism in general was *dao jiao*, often referred to as "religious Daoism," in distinction with the "philosophical Daoism" of Laozi and Zhuangzi. This distinction is not completely adequate, however, as much of *dao jiao* is clearly influenced by and meant to develop the teachings we find in the *Daodejing* and *Zhuangzi*. In particular, the concern with *qi* (vital energy) and its connection to *dao* is central for *dao jiao*. It was not until Buddhism came to flourish in China that *dao jiao* began to be seen as religious in nature. Daoism, like Confucianism, was given new features during this time, in order to compete with the mystical, metaphysical, and clearly religious tradition of Buddhism.

Among the major concerns of *dao jiao* was the retaining of *qi*, in terms of lengthened life and retained strength. Those who were able to "mirror the *dao*" in the Zhuangist sense, according to this tradition, protected their *qi*, just as earlier Daoists claimed. But this protection of *qi*, according to this later view, resulted in lengthened life. It does not take too much examination to see why the *dao jiao* advocates would have made such a claim. If, as earlier Daoists maintained, *qi* is ultimately responsible for our vitality and life, being the vital essence of a person, then being able to retain one's *qi* and not expend it must lead to the retaining of one's vigor and vitality, as long as one holds on to this *qi*. The complete loss of *qi* is responsible for death, and so it must be the case that as long as one can hold on to one's *qi*, one can hold on to one's life. And it follows from this that those Daoist "sages" who are particularly adept at guarding and retaining their *qi* must thereby be *immortal*. If one can hold on to one's *qi* indefinitely, doesn't this entail that one holds on to one's life indefinitely? Thus, adherents of this tradition claimed that the sages, such as Laozi and Zhuangzi, had attained immortality, and could be found in the spirit realm of the mountains still, having fully retained their *qi*. One of the results of self-cultivation at a high enough level would be attainment of immortality. Not only would one who could mirror the *dao* attain a thriving life, he or she could literally attain an *endless* life. Such an immortal life, however, would be vastly different from the normal lives the rest of us lead down here on earth. One won't find Daoist immortals walking normally among the rest of society. If one is able to attain to the level of the sages, one attains a kind of life beyond that of the normal human, a *spirit* life, in which one becomes an altogether purer and substantially different kind of entity. Such persons have cultivated themselves to the point that they have a literally inexhaustible *qi*, a substantially different type of *qi*. They become different, yet altogether greater, beings. In a sense, for the *dao jiao* the ideal person is not a *person* at all. And in this sense, it does come fairly close to the message of the *Zhuangzi*.

## Xuanxue: Guo Xiang

Another movement that was heavily influenced by the *Daodejing* and the *Zhuangzi* was the *Xuanxue* ("Mysterious Learning," also often referred to as "Neo Daoism"[1]) movement of the third–sixth centuries CE. Calling this movement "daoist" has to be qualified, however. Most of the representatives of this school were not anti-Confucian, rather they took themselves to *be* Confucians. They saw the Confucian and Daoist teachings as consistent, and took Confucius to have completely understood the *dao* discussed by the *Daodejing* and *Zhuangzi*. We might think this is kind of odd, given the clear parodies of Confucius in the *Zhuangzi*, especially that of Chapter 4, discussed above. Clearly at least some of the authors of the *Zhuangzi* collection were not fans of Confucius. The *xuanxue* thinkers, however, saw it as part of their goal to revive the authentic teachings of Confucius concerning the *dao* that they thought had been lost during the Han dynasty (206 BCE–220 CE), because of corruption of the teachings by self-serving scholars and officials.

The most prominent figure of the *xuanxue* movement as it concerns the *Zhuangzi* is the Wei-Jin period scholar Guo Xiang (252–312 CE), whose work and commentary on the *Zhuangzi* is responsible for the text as we have it today. It was Guo Xiang who divided the text into the current 33 chapters, and organized them into the categories of "inner," "outer," and "miscellaneous" chapters, which has affected how scholars read and interpret the text to this day.[2] His influence on our understanding of the text is hard to overestimate.

Guo's commentary on the *Zhuangzi* is also of interest. There are many interesting and important philosophical features of Guo's interpretation of *Zhuangzi* (which of course includes much of his own innovative views), but the most interesting for our purposes, given its uniqueness in "Daoist" thought and ethical focus, is his position concerning roles. He offers a position on the basis of the *Zhuangzi* very close to what we find in texts like the *Analects* or the *Bhagavad Gita*, which we might think are far from agreement with the *Zhuangzi*. The interesting thing about this is that it shows us alternative ways of reading such an enigmatic text as the *Zhuangzi*, as well as an attempt to harmonize the message of the *Zhuangzi* with Confucian views about community and hierarchy.

According to Guo, one's place in the social hierarchy and one's roles in community in general are fixed by one's natural abilities, which are determined by the amount of *qi* (vital spirit) one possesses. Given that one's place in society is determined by this *qi*, part of the way we can attain thriving through self-cultivation is to come to know and be satisfied with our natural place in the world. This is one way of understanding the "natural ease" discussed throughout the *Zhuangzi*. The ideal people portrayed in the Zhuangzi can be so effective in their tasks and spontaneous in their actions because they have accepted and gained ease in their natural places, determined by their allotment of *qi*.

# Further resources on Zhuangzi and self-cultivation

## Translations of the Zhuangzi and related Daoist texts

- Brook Ziporyn, *Zhuangzi: With Selections from the Traditional Commentaries*
- A. C. Graham, *Zhuangzi: The Inner Chapters—Other Daoist Works*
- David Hall and Roger Ames, trans., *Daodejing*
- D. C. Lau, trans., *Dao de jing*
- A. C. Graham, trans., *The Book of Lieh-tzu*
- John Major, Sarah Queen, Andrew Meyer, and Harold Roth, trans., *Huainanzi*

## Secondary work on Zhuangzi and Daoism

- Robert Allinson, *Chuang-tzu for Spiritual Transformation*
- Steve Coutinho, *Zhuangzi and Early Chinese Thought*
- Brook Ziporyn, *The Penumbra Unbound: The Neo-Taoist Philosophy of Guo Xiang*

## Films

- *Zhuangzi Shuo* (*Zhuangzi Speaks*)

# A short biography of Zhuangzi

Zhuang Zhou is an obscure, mysterious figure in the history of Chinese thought, just as he would have wanted (and much like his mythical Daoist predecessor "Laozi"). The only existing account of his life is given in the *Shiji*, and is likely almost completely legendary. According to the traditional account, he was born in 369 BCE, in the midst of the Warring States period, in the town of Meng (in modern-day Anhui province) in the state of Song (bordering Confucius' native state of Lu to the south).

The only other biographical information given is that Zhuang Zhou was a minor official in his state, and a story is told that suggests that he turned down an offer by the King of Chu to make him his chief minister, based on his desire to remain unsullied by the project of government and civilization. This is of course a view we see vigorously defended in the *Zhuangzi*, and this story is likely an invention to make the character of Zhuang Zhou consistent with the views represented in the text *Zhuangzi*.

It is generally accepted by scholars that Zhuang Zhou is responsible for at least some of the text today known as the *Zhuangzi*. The most popular and historically widely accepted view is that he was responsible for the chapters known collectively as the "Inner Chapters"—the first six chapters of the *Zhuangzi* text. The "Outer Chapters," comprising the rest of the text, are attributed to various disciples and others inspired by the work of Zhuang Zhou. This picture has been increasingly challenged in modern years, however. It seems likely that the inner chapters themselves are not the work of a single individual, even though it may be possible that some of the material is the work of (or at least inspired by) Zhuang Zhou. Or, it could be the case that Zhuang Zhou is a complete fiction, a sagelike character invented by the multiple authors of the *Zhuangzi*, a kind of ancient Chinese hermit King Arthur, created by the imagination of Daoist-inspired thinkers. It is impossible to know.

What is known is that the figure most responsible for the version of the *Zhuangzi* text we have today is the late third-century CE scholar Guo Xiang, who edited and compiled the text into roughly its current state, and also wrote a commentary on the text. As we know from the text of the *Zhuangzi*, whoever was its author or inspiration was clearly someone who saw the ideal life as one unencumbered by the roles, responsibilities, and concerns of "civilized" society. Whatever this person's own circumstances may have been, the commitments this person had were to the avoidance of the valuation and devaluation that come with identity, and ultimately with *shi-fei* (right–wrong) distinctions themselves.

If what we read in the inner chapters is accurate, we can know a few additional things about the life of Zhuang Zhou. He was apparently friends and intellectual sparring partners with the "school of names" philosopher Hui Shi (b. 380 BCE), and the two were associated until the Hui's death in 305 BCE. We also learn from the inner chapters that Zhuang Zhou had a wife who predeceased him—recall the famous scene mentioned in Chapter 2 above of Zhuangzi singing and banging on drums after his wife's death, having been able to overcome his grief by coming to an understanding that her death was simply another transformation of myriad things. According to tradition, Zhuang Zhou himself died in 286 BCE.

## RELEVANT QUESTIONS

1   How can it be possible to fully have the perspective of the *dao*, given that *dao* is a universal process while humans are not?

2   What is fundamentally mistaken or unsatisfactory about the perspective of the human? What does this say about Zhuangzi's view of the human? And how can this be made consistent with the possibility of the *zhen ren*?

3   Can we ever truly get rid of "identity?" How can one still act and engage in goal-directed activity of any kind (even eating or walking!) without an identity in some sense?

4   How might conceptualization make a difference in whether we see particular things as objects or as *dao*? How can we operate as normal human beings if we see everything in the mode of *dao*, rather than as discrete objects?

5   Given Zhuangzi's view on perspective and the use of the useless, how does he make sense of experiences and things that seem intrinsically of negative value to humans, like pain, suffering, and death?

6   Is there anything left the same during the "transformation of things?" If not, how can we understand change without there being some underlying thing (substance) that changes? If so, how does this square with Zhuangzi's rejection of the existence of *things* (substances)?

# Notes

**1** Neither "Neo Daoism" nor "Neo Confucianism" were called by their proponents by the names given to them in later western thought, based on their seeming influence by and place within the respective traditions. In fact, the situation might be even more complicated by the fact that the name of the school we label "Neo Confucianism" was *dao xue* ("*Dao* Learning"), which might be somewhat ironic given that we label the school referring to itself as concerning the Dao as the "Neo-Confucians" rather than the "Neo-Daoists."

**2** According to a number of scholars, including A. C. Graham and Liu Xiaogan, for example, the "inner" chapters section is the most authentic in the book, attributable to the person Zhuang Zhou (Zhuangzi), while the other sections are later additions. This view was first expressed by Guo Xiang. A number of other scholars, including Chris Fraser, argue that Guo Xiang's divisions are problematic, challenging the view that the "inner" chapters are the work of a single author, and maintain that the text is probably more syncretistic than Guo realized.

# PART TWO

# Ethics and Self-Cultivation in Ancient India

| EARLY INDIAN PHILOSOPHY—A TIMELINE | |
|---|---|
| 1700–1100 BCE | Composition of the *Rigveda* |
| tenth century BCE (traditional) | Kurukshetra war (basis of the events of the Mahabharata) |
| sixth–third centuries BCE | Earliest Upanishads composed |
| 563–483 BCE | Life of Buddha |
| 483 BCE | Traditional date of Buddha's *parinibbana* (final entrance to nirvana) [550–450 BCE] |
| 543–542 BCE | First Buddhist council, creation of the *suttas* (discourses) and *vinaya* rules (traditional) |
| fifth–second centuries BCE | Composition of *Bhagavad Gita* |
| 269–232 BCE | Reign of King Ashoka |
| 250 BCE | Third (Ashokan) Buddhist council, establishment of Buddhist missions to west and east |
| c. 100 BCE | Fourth Buddhist council (Sri Lanka), *Tipitaka* (Pali canon) first put into writing |
| first century BCE–1st century CE | Beginnings of Mahayana movement |
| 788–820 CE | Life of Shankara, key Advaita Vedanta philosopher, commentator on *Gita* |

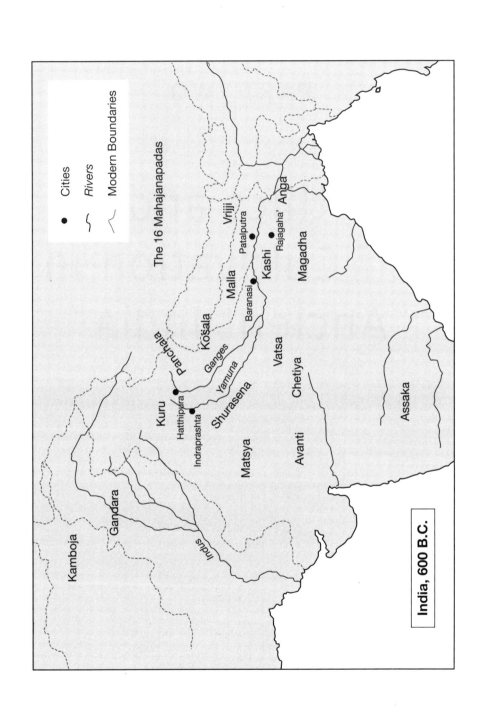

Cities

*Rivers*

Modern Boundaries

The 16 Mahajanapadas

Kamboja

Gandara

Indus

Kuru

Hatthipura

Indraprashta

Panchala

Kosala

Ganges

Yamuna

Shurasena

Matsya

Avanti

Chetiya

Vatsa

Malla

Vrijji

Pataliputra

Baranasi

Kashi

Rajagaha'

Anga

Magadha

Assaka

India, 600 B.C.

# 3

# The *Suttas, Dhammapada,* and the Early Buddhist Tradition

> He whose mind in calm self-control is free from the lust of desires,
> who has risen above good and evil, he is awake and has no fear.
> *Dhammapada* 39

# The Buddha and the early Buddhist tradition

The story of the Buddha's path to enlightenment is increasingly well known in
the west, and has all the markings of a classic of an individual's triumph over
natural adversity. It is unclear how much of the traditional story is historically
accurate, but what we do know is this: there likely lived some person corresponding to the "historical Buddha" in what is today the northern part of India
or southern part of Nepal, the leader of an influential early group, an offshoot
of the Upanishadic movements that were prevalent in the seventh and sixth
centuries BCE, similar in many ways to the earlier Jainas, who took part in the
practices of certain *Śramaṇic* (ascetic) schools, eventually branched out on
his own, and who formulated and preached the practical doctrine we deal
with in this chapter. More than this we cannot say with confidence. Virtually
*all* of the biographical claims of the traditional story are problematic, and
we can trace the origin of the traditional story to Asvaghosa's epic poem
*Buddhacarita*, which dates from the second century CE, a full 700 or so years
after the historical Buddha lived. There is a limited amount Asvaghosa could
have known about the life of the founder of his school of thought. Before this
time, the events of the life of the Buddha had not been seen as especially
important (it was his *teaching* that was important), and so biographical details
were not preserved. Beside the basic facts I noted above, Asvaghosa would
have had to rely on only his imagination (barring the possibility of a mystical
insight allowing him to access the facts about the Buddha's life). Thus, most
of the familiar traditional story is a later creation, constructed around the
time when devotion to the person of the Buddha as spiritual talisman in the
Mahayana tradition thrived.

The traditional story is interesting for its literary and ethical merits, though,
in addition to being spiritually edifying, and will thus be useful cover here.
The traditional story has multiple purposes. It is not just intended to be a
biography of the Buddha, but it also has an exhortative purpose (as most
texts in the Buddhist tradition). It is meant to motivate us and put us on the
path toward the liberation, freedom from suffering, and enlightenment, about
which the Buddha spoke. Indeed, its *primary* purpose is as a motivating
guide. As we will see below, the Buddhist view is very focused on practice.
What we ought to do is determined by what is *skillful*—that is, what helps

lead to enlightenment, the ultimate end of suffering. Insofar as the traditional biography of the Buddha can aid in this process, it is a story we should accept and cherish, according to the tradition, regardless of whether or not it accurately depicts the actual life of the historical Buddha. Indeed, whether or not it did so may not even have been an afterthought of the author of the *Buddhacarita* and its earliest readers. They were less concerned with the historical incident in the life of the Buddha than with the spiritual message he taught and (to them) embodied.

According to the story, a prince of the Gotama clan named Siddhartha (Siddhattha in Pali) was born in the kingdom of Magadha to the ruler of the state and his wife. At his birth a wise man, perhaps akin to the traveling mendicants one still sees in the Indian countryside today (referred to as *sadhus*), gave his parents the spiritual prediction that this newborn child would become either a world-conquering ruler or a great renunciate sage. Siddhartha's father, as himself a king, did all in his power to ensure that the wise man's first option was realized. He raised Siddhartha to become a king in his own mold, even going beyond himself in strength, influence, and ability. Siddhartha lived in the lap of luxury, was instructed in all the royal arts, and was insulated from the world outside the palace, all to ensure that he would become a king rather than a wandering holy man. Siddhartha had everything a man of the world could have wished for: riches, pleasures, education, and leisure. But even with all of this, Siddhartha was unsatisfied. There was something empty about all of it. Even when a desire was fulfilled, he noticed that there was an enduring emptiness that would not be filled no matter how much enjoyment, work, or anything else was used to fill it. Siddhartha wondered: could this really be all there is to life? Hankering after one desire only to feel the same emptiness and lack of satisfaction when that desire was fulfilled, then moving on to the next one, continuing this chain of inevitable suffering? Siddhartha was beginning to realize what is the major motivation of those who contemplate self-cultivation and the way to a better life, as we have done throughout this book: that a normal, unreflective way of living life, where pleasures and freedom from harm are the main goals, is deeply unsatisfactory, and that in order to live a truly thriving life, we must transform ourselves through contemplation and self-cultivation.

But how, Siddhartha wondered, could we make our lives better? What would help us to truly thrive? Siddhartha, although he felt this dissatisfaction with life and harbored these difficulties, continued to perform his duties and live on in the palace in his life of luxury, eventually marrying and having a child as well. The question of how to avoid the inherent unsatisfactoriness (*dukkha*) of life subsided into the background of his life for a few years as he prepared himself for his future role as king. Siddhartha's experience one day on a parade through his city, however, returned this question to the forefront of his mind. It transformed his thought on the matter, showed him the core of the problem, and suggested the beginning of a response.

As Siddhartha rode an elephant through the city on a parade, he saw the townspeople he had been mostly sheltered from his entire life, and noticed how they lived. There were three things in particular he saw that shook him to the core, and showed him the root of the inherent dissatisfaction he felt with life. First, he saw a sick person on the side of the road, suffering deeply from his illness. Next, he saw an old man, struggling to walk, weary and pained by the ravages of age. Finally, he saw a dead body in an alleyway off the side of the road. Siddhartha had an epiphany. *This* is the root of the dissatisfaction. Everything we do—all human life, no matter how noble, pleasurable, righteous—it all ends in illness, old age, and death. It all ends in *suffering*.

Siddhartha now understood that it was the seeming inevitability of suffering that caused the dissatisfaction that seemed inherent in any life. Suffering cannot be avoided by accruing wealth, losing oneself in pleasures, or becoming famous. The suffering inherent in illness, old age, and death awaits us all. And there are many types of suffering beyond these. The root of the problem, Siddhartha realized, is this suffering. But what can we do about it? Are we simply doomed to a life of suffering?

Siddhartha tried to go back to his normal life after this experience, but simply could not move away from the question of suffering. He neglected his duties, became lethargic, and fell into a deep depression. Coming to an understanding of the human condition had rattled him to the bone. Can we really do nothing to avoid the suffering inherent in life? If not, what is the point of even living? Life began to lose its meaning for Siddhartha, and his suffering increased.

Then, one day, Siddhartha had another experience that again helped him progress in his thinking and on his path. He saw a wandering mendicant monk begging for food, wearing ochre robes symbolizing the retreat from the worldly lives of most people. Such wanderers, Siddhartha had learned, studied, meditated, and searched for the truth about human life and the world, distant from everyday life in the city, wandering in the wilderness. Perhaps, Siddhartha thought, this is the way to find the answer to the problem of suffering. If there is an answer to be found—if it *is* possible to escape the human condition, it must be in the wilderness in contemplation and not in the worldly life that it is to be found. Involvement with pleasures and duties cannot be conducive to learning the answer and overcoming suffering.

So one night Siddhartha left his wife and child and all of his possessions behind and fled into the dark night, going deep into the wilderness to seek the answer to the problem of suffering. He exchanged his lavish princely attire for a simple ochre cloth covering. He sought a teacher among the forest monks, who could guide him to the answers he sought. The first teacher he found was an ascetic who wore no clothes at all, neglected his health and body, and focused all of his attention on meditation and contemplation. Siddhartha followed this path for some time, determined to find the answers he sought. He became an extreme ascetic, wearing no clothes and eating only one pea every day. He spent all of his time in meditation, but became so weak from malnourishment that he could not even stand. He decided that this could not be the correct path to find the answers he sought. The asceticism was so strict that it sabotaged his search! How can one find the path to end suffering if one cannot even think or properly function due to starvation? So he began to eat again slowly, regained his strength, and once again fled into the wilderness. His next teacher was the opposite of the last. He taught that to escape suffering one should indulge in sensory delights and avoid refraining from anything. It did not take Siddhartha long to realize that this was not the right path. How was this different from the way he had lived for many years in the palace, albeit with more power and wealth? Siddhartha decided to leave once again, and this time he went out on his own, to be his own teacher.

Siddhartha wandered alone for some time, practicing, contemplating, and meditating, looking for the answer to the problem of suffering. But nothing was forthcoming, and his frustration grew. Was there simply no answer after all? Then, one day, he had enough. He vowed to either find the answer or wither away and die. He decided to stay underneath the peepal tree he had taken shelter under the day before and not to move from there until he solved the problem of suffering once and for all. He would either discover the answer beneath this tree or he would starve and die, ending the entire fruitless and meaningless journey.

After days of contemplation and meditation, almost miraculously, Siddhartha discovered the key to ending suffering, and became "enlightened." He finally understood that there was a path to end suffering, and that this path consisted in a number of steps of self-cultivation. This revelation came through gaining an understanding of what causes suffering, and the ways we can undermine the creation of suffering. Siddhartha's own suffering slowly disappeared, and underneath the peepal tree his face brightened, revealing the enigmatic smile we know today on the figure famous across the world, represented in millions of statues, paintings, and arts of all kinds. Siddhartha had become an *enlightened one*. He had become a *buddha*.

What was it that the newly enlightened Buddha learned underneath that tree? What was the answer to the problem of suffering, and how did he think self-cultivation entered into the picture? The thought of the Buddha, perhaps more than any others we have examined in this book so far, was focused almost solely on self-cultivation. The key to living a better life is to achieve at a life completely without suffering, which, according to the Buddha's teaching, is possible. There are many features of the path to ending suffering he discovered, and in order to be effective, he argued, self-cultivation must be carried out following these principles that lead away from suffering and ultimately to its extinction.

## Suffering and the eightfold path

Now, monks, this is the noble truth of suffering: birth is suffering, aging is suffering, death is suffering; sorrow, lamentation, pain, distress, and despair are suffering; association with the unbeloved is suffering, separation from the loved is suffering, not getting what is wanted is suffering. In short, the five clinging-aggregates are suffering.

And this, monks, is the noble truth of the origination of suffering: the craving that makes for further becoming—accompanied by passion and delight, relishing now here and now there—i.e., craving for sensual pleasure, craving for becoming, craving for non-becoming.

And this, monks, is the noble truth of the cessation of suffering: the remainderless fading and cessation, renunciation, relinquishment, release, and letting go of that very craving.

And this, monks, is the noble truth of the way of practice leading to the cessation of suffering: precisely this Noble Eightfold Path—right view, right intention, right speech, right action, right livelihood, right effort, right mindfulness, right concentration. *Dhammacakkappavattana Sutta*, (trans. Thanissaro Bhikkhu, modified)

In the first of the Buddha's teachings (according to tradition), given to a group of ascetics the Buddha knew during his time with his first teacher, he outlines the core features of the truths surrounding suffering and the method he discovered to end suffering through self-cultivation. This teaching is contained in early Pali text *Dhammacakkappavattana Sutta* ("Discourse on Setting in Motion the Wheel of the Teaching"), part of a collection of early *suttas* ("discourses") representing the earliest known written material on Buddhism, which set out key tenets of the system.

The Buddha's discovery beneath the peepal tree was based on four basic truths concerning suffering, which have come to be known as the "Four Noble Truths." The first noble truth is that there *is* suffering, connected with every aspect of human life. Birth, aging, and death cause suffering, as do the inevitable loss of things we possess, including loved ones. This loss, which comes about through *change*, cannot be avoided. One central truth about the world is that things are constantly changing. The very existence of change entails decay. An entity cannot remain in being if all of its aspects are constantly changing. The particles that comprise a human being, for example, in their constant change, will not, of necessity, always form a working body, as they will eventually move elsewhere, forming new things. The Buddha emphasizes this fact of change in a principle I have often found one of the most profound and the most simple of the entire Buddhist system, and fittingly the last words of the Buddha to his monks as he lay dying of old age many years after his enlightenment: "*all conditioned things are of a nature to decay.*"

Another way of saying this is that *anything that is born inevitably dies*. A conditioned thing is something that comes into being from some cause, something that is brought into being based on a change in the world. Tables, then, are conditioned, being created by human labor, as are all animals including ourselves, being created in the process of reproduction. Indeed, *all* phenomena and things that we see, have, and experience in the world are things that are conditioned, that have come into existence based on causes. Even the universe itself, according to modern science, is thus conditioned. If something caused the big bang, then the universe itself is inevitably headed for decay and death at some point. The only things that are not subject to decay are those things that are unconditioned, that have not been brought into existence by a cause. If there were eternal, uncaused entities, these would not be subject to decay.

> Consider this body! A painted puppet with jointed limbs, sometimes suffering and covered with ulcers, full of imaginings, never permanent, for ever changing. This body is decaying! A nest of diseases, a heap of corruption, bound to destruction, to dissolution. All life ends in death. *Dhammapada* 147–8, (trans., Mascaro)

But why think that this is true? Why does something inevitably decay if there is a condition or cause for its existence? Couldn't there be something that is caused but is not subject to decay once it exists, lasting forever? The answer to this depends on the underlying notion of change at the heart of causation and decay. Anything that has come into existence through a cause is constructed of parts that have undergone *change*. Things that change *constantly* change, or they would not have changed in such a way that led to the creation of the conditioned entity. If these things constantly change, however, then eventually they will further change in such a way that entails the extinction of the conditioned entity they compose and the creation of new entities. The tree that dies and falls to the ground decays and provides nutrients to the soil and food for bacteria, for example. But why not think, one might respond, that certain entities can change and then reach a point at which change ceases, and thus the formed, conditioned entity is not subject to decay? What reasons do we have for thinking that this cannot happen? It seems the only available reply for the Buddha here would be to claim that this would be to accept an arbitrary limit on change. What would it be about certain compounds that would *stop* the constant change we observe in all features of the world? That is, given that everything appears to us in motion and constant change, we require an explanation of what could *stop* this change, rather than what can create it. The burden of proof is on the one who claims that there are some conditioned things that do *not* change and thus are not subject to decay (conceding here that if parts are constantly changing then the wholes they comprise will inevitably decay), and this is a burden the opponent of the Buddha's view cannot bear, as our experience shows us only constant change of conditioned things rather than stability.

The second noble truth builds on the notion that all conditioned things are subject to decay. According to it, the *origin* of suffering is attachment to conditioned things. In particular, *craving* in connection to things that inevitably decay is the source of suffering, and understanding how craving generates suffering is a key of discovering the way to ultimately undermine suffering. The creation of suffering by craving is explained by the Buddha in the somewhat complicated system of *dependent origination*, which, although not mentioned directly in the *Dhammacakkappavatana Sutta*, is a key feature of the second noble truth, discussed in other *suttas*.

And what is dependent origination? From ignorance as a requisite condition come fabrications. From fabrications as a requisite condition comes consciousness. From consciousness as a requisite condition comes name-and-form. From name-and-form as a requisite condition come the six sense media. From the six sense media as a requisite condition comes contact. From contact as a requisite condition comes feeling. From feeling as a requisite condition comes craving. From craving as a requisite condition comes clinging/sustenance. From clinging/sustenance as a requisite condition comes becoming. From becoming as a requisite condition comes birth. From birth as a requisite condition, then aging and death, sorrow, lamentation, pain, distress, and despair come into play. Such is the origination of this entire mass of stress and suffering. *Paticca-samuppada-vibhanga Sutta* (trans. Thanissaro Bhikku, modified)

The chain of dependent origination explains the causal connection between a number of mental states that ultimately lead to the creation of suffering. Each link on the chain creates the next, and the process culminates in suffering. According to the Buddhist formulation, ignorance causes mental fabrications, which cause consciousness, which causes name-and-form, which cause the six sense perceptions, which cause contact, which causes feeling, which causes craving, which causes clinking, which causes becoming, which causes birth, from which follows old age, illness, death, and the *entirety* of suffering. While it would take an entire chapter in itself to explain each link of the chain of dependent origination, what is important for our purposes here is to understand *ignorance*, *craving*, and *suffering*. The second noble truth points to craving and our attachment to things as the primary source of suffering, and we see from dependent origination that such craving ultimately has its source in ignorance. This suggests the beginning of an answer to the question of how to undermine the creation of suffering.

The third noble truth is basically the statement that it is possible to end suffering. Having understood that all things in life are involved with suffering insofar as they are conditioned or caused, and that this suffering comes about through the causal chain of dependent origination, one can come to see that it is possible to end this suffering.

This leads to the fourth and final noble truth, which lays out the path to the end of suffering. This truth contains the central message of the Buddha insofar as it concerns self-cultivation, and can be taken as the core of the Buddha's practical teaching. In order to end suffering, we have to look to the first two noble truths. Since it is craving and attachment to conditioned things that ultimately causes suffering, we must get rid of this craving and attachment, and seek the *unconditioned*, if such a thing exists. The only truly stable joy will come about from involvement with (note, not *attachment* to, in the sense of craving) something unconditioned. As we saw in considering the second noble truth, the source of craving is ignorance. Thus, to undermine our craving and attachment to conditioned things, we must free ourselves from ignorance, which entails that we must understand and experience the truth about things. These truths are concisely summed up by the Buddha in what have come to be referred to as the "Three Dhamma ('law', 'teaching') Seals": *all things are impermanent, all things are unsatisfactory, all things are without self.*

For now, we'll shelve discussion of the third of the *dhamma* seals, which will be the subject of "The enlightened person and *nirvana*" (pp. 117–19). The first two of the *dhamma* seals we have seen in the earlier discussion of the noble truths. All things are impermanent. This, of course, means that all *conditioned* things are impermanent. The key here is the word *thing* (*dhamma*—a distinct use of the term "*dhamma*" as "teaching" or "law" above). Anything that can be called a *thing* is necessarily conditioned. All material objects, mental formations, anything tangible or a process of thought—all of these are conditioned. And this is just what we mean by *thing*. Something that can be grasped, that can be the object of thought, and that can be possessed. I can have a Lamborghini, and I can also have an emotion of disgust or a thought of an abstract entity. There is, however, something that is *unconditioned*, but it is not a "thing," in the sense that it is not something that can be possessed, that can be the object of my thought, that is not created and destroyed. This something (for lack of a better term) is *nirvāṇa* (Pali *nibbāna*). It *is* the unconditioned—and there is nothing else in the world that is unconditioned. In fact, *nirvana* is not something in the world at all. In that it is unconditioned, it is transcendent, completely distinct from and not affected by things in the world. Indeed, it cannot even be said to "exist" in the same sense that things in the world exist. As unconditioned, it has no beginning and no end, it is not compound, not in space or time, not within the world of phenomena. *Nirvana* is notoriously difficult to define (necessarily so, as it lies outside all categories of conditioned things), and the Buddha almost always talks about it in terms of what it is *not*: it is not conditioned, not impermanent, and one who achieves it does not suffer.

Go beyond the stream, Brahmin, go with all your soul: leave desires behind. When you have crossed the stream of delusion, you will reach the land of *nirvana* ... He who has cut all fetters and whose mind trembles not, who in infinite freedom is free from all bonds—him I call a Brahmin ... Who is free from anger, faithful to his vows, virtuous, free from lusts, self-trained, whose mortal body is his last—him I call a Brahmin. Who clings not to sensuous pleasures, even as water clings not to the leaf of the lotus, or a grain of mustard seed to the point of a needle—him I call a Brahmin. He who even in this life knows the end of sorrow ... him I call a Brahmin. *Dhammapada* 383–402 (trans. Mascaro)

This gives us a key to understanding the first and second *dhamma* seals. All *things* are impermanent. Anything we experience or possess in life is necessarily, as conditioned, subject to decay. And from this the second *dhamma* seal follows: all things are unsatisfactory. No thing can fulfill our wish to be truly happy, completely without suffering. Every conditioned thing not only allows us to suffer, but causes us (if we are attached to it) to suffer.

The key to breaking the chain of dependent origination and thus freeing ourselves from suffering is to engage in self-cultivation by following what the Buddha calls the *eightfold path*, which is the core of the fourth noble truth, the way to end suffering. This path consists of eight steps to overcoming craving and thereby undermining suffering: 1) right view; 2) right intention; 3) right speech; 4) right action; 5) right livelihood; 6) right effort; 7) right mindfulness; and 8) right concentration. One easy way to categorize these aspects of the path is to divide them into the classes of *wisdom* (1 and 2), *moral conduct* (3, 4, and 5), and *mental cultivation* (6, 7, and 8). The Buddha teaches that self-cultivation requires a holistic approach. Not *only* is understanding necessary, but also positive moral action and aspects of concentration. We have seen in previous chapters different accounts of how understanding or wisdom and morality are necessary to self-cultivation, but the Buddha's message is unique in what we've seen so far in suggesting that cultivation of our abilities of concentration and attention are necessary for self-cultivation. We will see in the next section below how this works.

Those who think the unreal is, and think the real is not, they shall never reach the truth, lost in the path of wrong thought. But those who know the real is, and know the unreal is not, they shall indeed reach the truth, safe on the path of right thought. Even as rain breaks through an ill-thatched house, passions will break through an ill-guarded mind. But even as rain breaks not through a well-thatched house, passions break not through a well-guarded mind. *Dhammapada* 11–14 (trans. Mascaro)

The wisdom aspects of the path have to do with understanding the truth about suffering and what causes it. Having right view is to see and understand all aspects of the four noble truths, and right intention is to have the goal of ending suffering as result of this understanding of fundamental truths about human life.

The moral conduct components of the eightfold path are meant to control one's *karma*, an essential feature of reducing and ultimately ending suffering, which is discussed further in "The role of compassion and moral conduct" (pp. 109–12). The moral aspects of the Buddha's teaching are often neglected or downplayed in western coverage of Buddhism, in favor of more esoteric aspects of Buddhism surrounding mental cultivation, although interestingly in Asian cultures the moral aspects are primary in the thought and practice of most Buddhists, and mental cultivation is often seen as primarily a monastic pursuit.

The most well-known component of the eightfold path in the west is that of mental cultivation. Perhaps this is because this feature of Buddhism is not often central in many of the ethical systems of self-cultivation we in the west are familiar with, and so most clearly defines Buddhism as something other, unique, or exotic. Interestingly, though, while many western systems of self-cultivation do not put emphasis on mental cultivation in the Buddhist sense, many Indian (and some Chinese) systems have such components, and Buddhism not particularly unique in this aspect of its system. This could be part of the reason mental cultivation is not seen as so important in Asian Buddhism as it is in the west (with the exception of meditation-heavy schools like Zen). Arguably, of course, the early Buddhists (and the Buddha himself) may not have taken mental cultivation (including meditation) as central to the Buddhist path in the way many contemporary westerners seem to. For the Buddha, mental cultivation was *one aspect* of the path, not the entirety of the path. The contemporary western tendency, on the other hand, is to read all other aspects of the path as facilitating mental cultivation, which is seen as directly causative of the end of suffering. While this is an interesting derivative of Buddhist thought, it doesn't represent the ideas of early Buddhist thought. Part of the reason for this focus on meditation in Buddhism may come from the influence of the Zen Buddhist tradition on the west.

The early Buddhist system, based on the teachings of the Buddha, represents a system of holistic self-cultivation involving a number of different aspects of human life. As we have already seen, Siddhartha Gautama had some very interesting and insightful things to say about human nature and the way to becoming a better person and living a better life, even if one does not accept his entire picture about the human condition and the possibility escape from this condition through *nirvana*.

Be quick in doing what's admirable. Restrain your mind from what's evil. When you're slow in making merit, evil delights the mind. If a person does evil, he shouldn't do it again and again, shouldn't develop a penchant for it. To accumulate evil brings pain. If a person makes merit, he should do it again and again, should develop a penchant for it. To accumulate merit brings ease. Even the evil meet with good fortune as long as their evil has yet to mature. But when it's matured, that's when they meet with evil. Even the good meet with bad fortune as long as their good has yet to mature. But when it's matured, that's when they meet with good fortune. *Dhammapada* 116–20 Thanissaro trans.

# Controlling the mind

Since there are many misunderstandings surrounding meditation and the idea of mental cultivation in Buddhism, we start our consideration with this aspect of the eightfold path, which is comprised of *right effort*, *right mindfulness*, and *right concentration*.

The first misunderstanding I wish to address is that mental cultivation is *opposed* to discursive thinking. One often hears that meditation, in the Buddhist tradition, is meant to undermine or somehow otherwise subvert rationality, reflection, or active thinking, which are seen as negative because it traps one in attachment and suffering. There are even some Buddhist schools today that endorse this reading of the early Buddhist teachings (perhaps, but not necessarily, Zen among them). This is simply not true, however. Meditation/ concentration and discursive thought are not mutually exclusive in the early Buddhist view. Indeed, they could not be such, as the Buddha claims both are necessary in order to fully end suffering, to gain enlightenment. How can one possibly have right view and right mindfulness at the same time if having mindfulness and concentration is incompatible with the discursive thought required for having right view? If meditation were opposed to thought, the Buddhist path would be contradictory, bordering on incoherent. In addition, the early descriptions of the Buddha's enlightenment and teachings given in the Pali *suttas* and other early texts do not, in the way common today, malign discursive thought. On the contrary, they detail such thought as itself a crucial element of the Buddha's enlightenment. A rich and robust philosophical tradition built up both in India and later in China around Buddhism, which would certainly not have been possible if Buddhism rejected rational, discursive thought.

In the *Ariyapariyesana Sutta*, one of the earliest Pali accounts of the Buddha's enlightenment experience, he is described as in thought, contemplating the truths of the path underneath the famous peepal tree as part of his final push to enlightenment.

> How delightful is this countryside ... I sat down right there, thinking "this is just right for exertion." Then, monks, being subject myself to birth, seeing the drawbacks of birth, seeking the unborn, unexcelled rest from the yoke, unbinding, I reached the unborn ... Knowledge and vision arose in me: "unprovoked is my release. This is the last birth. There is now no further becoming." Then the thought occurred to me, "this *dhamma* that I have attained is deep, hard to see, hard to realize, peaceful, refined, beyond the scope of conjecture, subtle, to-be-experienced by the wise." *Ariyapariyesana Sutta* (trans. Thanissaro)

There is nothing there about *going beyond thought*, there is thought and concentration together, which (with the formerly prepared moral behavior) bring about enlightenment. Indeed, in the later Sanskrit *Buddhacarita* (mentioned in the first section above), from which the bulk of the traditional story of the Buddha's enlightenment comes, the Buddha's enlightenment experience *itself* is described as a series of thoughts and considerations concerning truths about the existence, formation, and removal of suffering—that is, clearly discursive thought about the four noble truths. One can only discover and formulate truths by thinking—propositions, one might say, do not simply appear in one's head through imageless and thought-less meditation. To hold that the Buddha discovered the four noble truths through meditation would be as odd as to say that Einstein developed special and general relativity through imageless meditation—he simply focused on his breath, then one day the theory was just *there*. Surely the Buddha, with his deep insight into human nature and the mind, understood that the human mind does not work that way.

Thus, contrary to some contemporary readings of Buddhism, the early Buddhist view is not that thought is the *enemy*, or that meditation is inconsistent with or somehow undermines thought or objective truth (another target of contemporary interpretations). Anti-intellectuals and skeptics will not find an ally in the Buddha, no matter how hard they may try to appropriate his thought for their purposes. In the system proposed by the Buddha, one must know the objective truth about the world and human life in order to free oneself from suffering, and knowing this truth requires thinking hard about one's own life and mind. It turns out that the Buddha was likely closer to the philosopher than to the mystic after all.

In what, then, does mental cultivation consist? In particular, what is meant by *right mindfulness* and *right concentration*? These, according to the Buddha, are two ways of *controlling the mind*. Gaining control over the mind is essential in the path to ending suffering. It is the mind, according to the Buddha, that is the main source of suffering, not the outside world, and so to answer the problem of suffering, we have to address how the mind creates suffering, rather than focus on external conditions, which will change nothing.

The centrality of the mind and one's mental state in suffering or happiness is a key feature of a number of systems of Indian philosophy and religion, and one we will see again (albeit in a different guise) in the next chapter. The idea is that what causes us to suffer is *not* our external condition, but rather our mental state. There is some plausibility to this claim. We can imagine two people, one of whom is rich beyond the dreams of most and the other who has very little. The rich person, however, may be horribly depressed and thus suffer greatly, while the impoverished person might have a positive outlook on the world and thus have a comparatively much greater amount of joy in her life. There have been psychological studies, for example, linking the temperament of a person (optimistic or pessimistic) and that person's reported happiness. Even more obviously, people can have chemical imbalances in the brain that result in severe depression, whether they are rich or poor. While such states are certainly not caused by or even linked to wealth, this does show us that suffering is most directly connected to the mind, and a cause of suffering will be whatever creates the conditions in the mind that bring forth suffering.

But perhaps the materialist can take another swing. Sure, it's true that depression can afflict the rich as well as the poor, but does this show that wealth and other external conditions have *nothing* to do with suffering and joy? The non-depressed rich person will, in general, be happier and have less suffering than the non-depressed poor person, one might claim, and if this is so, it is likely due to the external situation. The mind, this person could claim, is the *direct* source of suffering, but external features of the world *affect* the mind, and so poverty can cause the mind to be in the conditions for suffering. If the external world could not affect the mind in this way, then it would be impossible for things like drugs to have any effect on our behavior or experience. Drinking alcohol would not make one tipsy, drinking coffee would not make our thoughts race and our rate of speech increase. The fact that external features of the world *do* affect our minds shows us that we should not dismiss the connection between suffering and one's external, physical situation. Situations can, indirectly, cause suffering. In the parlance of modern science, we can say that features of the world have effects on the brain, and the brain is explanatorily linked (in some way, this is a mystery cognitive scientists and philosophers still struggle to solve) to the mind. Thus features of the world have effects on the mind.

The Buddhist might respond to this in a number of ways. First, he or she can appeal to the observed irregularities concerning the mental effects of features of the external world. For example, some people make lots of money and are relatively happy, while others can make a similar amount of money and suffer more. If this is so (and one doesn't have to look far to see that it is), then it can't be the wealth that is the determining factor in the happiness of wealthy (or poor) people. Indeed, there have been psychological studies to back this up. The reported levels of happiness of people with massive wealth on the whole *does not* differ from those of people with an average amount of money. It seems to make no difference to one's happiness whether one has billions of dollars or thousands. Interestingly, though, under a certain lower limit, happiness levels seem to drop dramatically. That is, above a particular income level, there was no difference in happiness, but below this income level, there was markedly less happiness. Surely *this* shows that there is a connection between external features of the world and suffering.

Perhaps the Buddhist view could accept some correlation between external features of the world and suffering, while still holding that one's mental state is the key determinant of suffering and that this mental state is independent of one's external situation. Think about what the above mentioned study actually commits one to. It does *not* show that, below a certain income level, a person will *necessarily* suffer. It simply shows that suffering tends to increase below this income level. But the Buddhist view can accommodate this level of connection between external situations and suffering. It will, they can claim, be more difficult for people to free themselves from suffering within certain conditions, because of this general connection between external conditions and the mind. But as long as there is no connection between the two such that some external condition *necessarily* causes some mental effect, the Buddhist view can make sense of the cleft between external situation and one's state of suffering. While the person in an extremely impoverished life may have to work harder to bring about the mental states that lead to the extinction of suffering, it can be done even in this context.

It is the Buddha's understanding of the connection between external features of the world and states of the mind that leads him to recommend that those on the path abstain from taking intoxicants, such as alcohol or other drugs. These things produce effects in the mind that are not conducive to the destruction of suffering, and thus help to keep one trapped in the chain of dependent origination. This is part of the reason for keeping free from intoxicants being included in the moral component of *right action*.

Furthermore, abandoning the use of intoxicants, the disciple of the noble ones abstains from taking intoxicants. In doing so, he gives freedom from danger, freedom from animosity, freedom from oppression to limitless numbers of beings. In giving freedom from danger, freedom from animosity, freedom from oppression to limitless numbers of beings, he gains a share in limitless freedom from danger, freedom from animosity, and freedom from oppression. This is the fifth gift, the fifth great gift—original, long-standing, traditional, ancient, unadulterated, unadulterated from the beginning—that is not open to suspicion, will never be open to suspicion, and is unfaulted by knowledgeable contemplatives and brahmins. *Abhisanda Sutta* (trans. Thanissaro)

Controlling the mind is essential in the Buddha's teaching as it is only through control of the mind that we can avoid craving and the attachment to conditioned things that is the source of suffering. We find it natural and easy to crave things and become attached, and to resist this we must have a firm control over our minds, such that we do not allow these cravings to get started. Such control requires an understanding of dependent origination. If we know how craving arises, we know the specific ways in which we must control the mind in order to avoid the creation of the antecedents of suffering.

Some may be wondering at this point: okay, while we can see that controlling the mind might be necessary to avoid craving and attachment, why should we accept the Buddha's view about dependent origination in the first place? Why think that it is craving and attachment that cause suffering, and not something else, even if we concede that it is not ultimately external features that directly cause it? After all, a life free of craving and attachment would not only be a life without suffering, it would also be a life without joy. Can we ever truly be happy or live a thriving life without love, devotion, or various desires, like the desire to be successful in a career, to see our children be happy, to enjoy the pleasures life has to offer? If the Buddha is suggesting that we should rid ourselves of craving and attachment, it sounds like he is suggesting that we should live the kind of bland, dry, ascetic, and world-denying life he himself rejected in the wilderness during his search for enlightenment.

Part of the Buddha's response to this would be to draw a distinction between pleasure and joy. It is not the case that one has to give up all good things in life in order to live without suffering—one just has to give up the unhealthy craving and attachment we tend to make a part of our connection with these good things. There is nothing inherently bad about enjoying a meal, or sexual pleasure, or having wealth—it is just that we easily become attached to these things through craving in such a way as to create suffering. This is why, for example, the Buddha prohibits his monks from engaging in sexual activity altogether. It is very difficult for someone to control themselves with regard to certain things. Because one on the path is attempting to control their mind to undermine attachment and craving, it is best to abstain from those things that exert the most influence over our minds and that are thus most difficult to avoid negative craving and attachment to—things like drugs, sex, and wealth.

> The hunger of passions is the greatest disease. Disharmony is the greatest sorrow. When you know this well, then you know that *nirvana* is the greatest joy. Health is the greatest possession. Contentment is the greatest treasure. Confidence is the greatest friend. *Nirvana* is the greatest joy. When a person knows the solitude of silence, and feels the joy of quietness, then he is free from fear and blemish and he feels the joy of the *dhamma*. *Dhammapada*, 203–5 (trans. Mascaro, modified)

The difference between pleasure and true joy, according to the Buddha, is that true joy is to be able to enjoy the good things in life without the craving and attachment that causes suffering. An enlightened person is not a prig who takes joy in nothing and for that reason has nothing that bothers him. Rather, he is one who is able to enjoy the taste of good food, to delight in the pleasures of the world, while understanding that they are conditioned, and thus fleeting, and without craving them and creating attachment. He is happy with them when they come, and happy with them when they go. In Zhuangzian terms, we might think that such a person is lives a life almost like the Daoist sage who delights in the transformation of things. The similarities between the Buddhist and Daoist views on this and a number of other points was a large part of the reason for the use of Daoist terminology to explain Buddhist concepts by early translators who tried to render the Pali and Sanksrit Buddhist texts into Chinese when the Buddha's teaching first moved into China in the first few centuries CE.

So how, according to the Buddha, are we able to control the mind in order to avoid craving and attachment? Right mindfulness and right concentration at first glance may appear to be the same thing, but we begin to see the important differences between them when we look beneath the surface.

What is commonly called *meditation* in the early Buddhist tradition (and in contemporary Theravada Buddhism) is based on a combination of mindfulness and concentration. Although scholars do not know what these two processes originally signified for the earliest Buddhists and the Buddha himself, looking to the Theravada tradition as it exists today may help us gain some idea. The Theravada tradition prides itself on remaining as close as possible to the oldest, historically contextual understanding of the Buddhist path. The name for the tradition translates from the Pali as "Way of the Elders." The tradition takes as canonical only the Pali texts, which are the oldest scriptures of the Buddhist tradition. The Theravada tradition is the closest school existing today to the oldest teaching associated with the Buddha (although there is no way of saying whether it is the most *accurate*—the Mahayana schools claim that *they* have the most complete teachings intended by the Buddha). The Theravada school today is most flourishing in south-east Asia, including Sri Lanka, Thailand, Burma, Cambodia, and some parts of Vietnam (having been mostly displaced, like other schools of Buddhism, in its homeland of north India, Pakistan, and Nepal). While much of the system of the Theravada school today is likely very different from the original system of the Buddha, the Theravada position on mindfulness and concentration might be as close as we can approach to the historical views of the Buddha. Despite human attempts to hold things static in time, teachings, concepts, and views inevitably change. As Buddha himself recognized, this is simply part of the human condition, and part of the way of the world. If all conditioned things inevitably change and decay, this necessarily applies to the Buddha's teaching, if not the *goal* of the teaching and the path itself, which is the unconditioned *nirvana*.

> The enlightened, constantly absorbed in *jhana* (the levels of meditative concentration), persevering, firm in their effort: they touch *nirvana*, the unexcelled rest from the yoke. Those with initiative, mindful, clean in action, acting with due consideration, heedful, restrained, living the *dhamma*: their glory grows … Heedful among the heedless, wakeful among those asleep, just as a fast horse advances, leaving the weak behind: so the wise. *Dhammapada* 23–4, 29 (trans. Thanissaro)

Taking the Theravada tradition as a guide, *mindfulness* is the awareness of a person of her thoughts, activities, and full mental life. One who has mindfulness has awareness of the processes of her mind. In the person with fully developed mindfulness, nothing happens within the mind without her total awareness of it. There are no hidden activities. This is much different than the state of the normal person. When we reflect on our mental lives, we can see that there are many times that things happen in our minds without our notice. We can become infatuated with something without knowing how we became infatuated, without seeing the process by which this attachment was created. We can become irritated by something that changes our mood, without realizing what we are irritated by or even that we are irritated at all. Sometimes we don't realize what is going on in our own minds until others point out our behavior and we are forced to introspect, then we realize something is going on. We humans can be remarkably unaware of what is going on in our own minds.

If we are unaware of the processes going on in our minds, then we cannot hope to stop the process of forming attachment through craving. We have to *see* the process in order to cut it short. When we develop mindfulness, according to the Buddha, we develop the ability to notice what is going on in our minds. We are able to be attentive to the changes and causal chains, to the decisions and emotions, and most importantly to the process of dependent origination. Once we can employ mindfulness to perceive the process, we can then begin to control our mental activity to undermine the process. This control is the second aspect of mindfulness. Mindfulness makes us aware, but it also effectively constrains the construction of craving and attachment. Thus, mindfulness has both perceptive and active purposes.

*Concentration* on the other hand is what directs mindfulness and allows it to investigate the mind. It allows us to fix our attention on the activities of the mind, which we can then apply mindfulness to. Concentration and mindfulness therefore must work together in order to be effective in giving us control of the mind. This is indicative of all elements of the eightfold path, however. All of them must work together in order for one to achieve liberation from suffering. The concentration that leads to the proper focus and functioning of mindfulness can be developed (according to the Theravada view) through *meditation*. This is where the well-known aspect of Buddhism comes into play. We can see that meditation is one aspect of the path the Buddha devised to end suffering, and not the entirety of the path, as contemporary westerners are sometimes inclined to understand Buddhism. This does not mean, however, that meditation is not important in the Buddha's teaching. Rather, it has a specific function, and should not be mistaken for the core of the teaching.

Through meditation (of various kinds), one becomes able to observe the processes of one's mind, including the chain of dependent origination, and, through following the other elements of the eightfold path, one can employ mindfulness as a way to undermine the origination of craving and attachment. Mindfulness and concentration are essential parts of the process, and the direct means by which we control our minds. But if we do not have wisdom and proper moral conduct, we will be unable to control the origination of craving and attachment. We may gain a great deal of control over our minds, but we will not be able to control what counts—we will not be able to refrain from creating suffering. Mental cultivation, according to the Buddha, is not enough. We can sit in the lotus position on a mat, meditating with fragrant incense burning and the harmonious sounds of birds in the forest for the whole day—for a whole *life*, even, and without the other elements of the path, we will make no progress toward ending suffering. Likely we'll even make things worse. It is crucial to see the place of moral conduct and wisdom in the Buddhist path.

## The role of compassion and moral conduct

There is the case where a monk might say, "Although compassion has been developed, pursued, handed the reins and taken as a basis, given a grounding, steadied, consolidated, and well-undertaken by me as my awareness-release, still viciousness keeps overpowering my mind." He should be told, "Don't say that. You shouldn't speak in that way. Don't misrepresent the Blessed One, for it's not right to misrepresent the Blessed One, and the Blessed One wouldn't say that. It's impossible, there is no way that—when compassion has been developed, pursued, handed the reins and taken as a basis, given a grounding, steadied, consolidated, and well-undertaken as an awareness-release—viciousness would still keep overpowering the mind. That possibility doesn't exist, for this is the escape from viciousness: compassion as an awareness-release." *Nissaraniya Sutta* (trans. Thanissaro)

Probably the second most well-known feature of Buddhism in the west, after meditation, is the notion of *compassion* as central to the path. Compassion, however, like meditation, is a more contextual and specific feature of the Buddha's teaching than is often understood. It is included in the division of the eightfold path dealing with *moral conduct* (including right speech, right conduct, right livelihood). But we might notice that this division does not include anything such as "right compassion." Compassion is in one sense a general virtue that might be seen as part of right conduct, and in another sense a mental state underlying and necessary for right speech, conduct, and livelihood. Compassion, however, is not the only virtue or mental state that plays such a role—there are a number of moral and intellectual virtues a person has to cultivate in order to attain the steps of the path. In this section, we will examine a few of those virtues, connected with the moral conduct division of the path. Although there are intellectual virtues that are as necessary as the ones discussed here, I will save discussion of these to the next section, and will focus mainly on the behavioral outcomes of these virtues (the *knowledge* gained from the virtues of intellectual honesty and wisdom, for example) rather than the virtues themselves.

Right speech and right livelihood are fairly particular. One can aid the creation of suffering, according to the Buddha, through one's speech and livelihood. If one engages in harsh, false, or hateful speech, this can lend itself to the creation of suffering. How does this work? The primary concern here is not that one's hateful speech harms another and makes that person suffer, although that is also true. Shouting curses at a loved one might make them depressed or angry and contribute to their suffering. More importantly, however, if I speak harshly, falsely, or hatefully, I contribute to *my own* suffering. This might seem counterintuitive at first. Isn't the recipient of my negative speech the one who we would expect is the victim of such speech? When I should angrily at another, it is the person I'm shouting at who is made nervous, angry, or sad—I certainly don't make *myself* so.

If we more deeply consider the results of such speech on our disposi- tions, behavior, and mental state, however, we can see that the one who suffers most from such negative speech is the person who initiates it. Harsh speech of the kind the Buddha says we should refrain from is caused by negative mental states, such as hatred, anger, delusion, lust, or greed. These mental states are exactly the ones connected with suffering that we are trying to rid ourselves of when we follow the Buddha's teachings (Buddhists often speak of these states together as "greed, anger, and delusion"). Any negative speech is connected to greed, anger, and delusion in two important ways. First, these negative mental states are present if negative speech is present, and so if one engages in negative speech, this shows that one is to some extent still mired in greed, anger, and delusion. More importantly for purposes of self-cultivation and the path, however, negative speech *reinforces* the greed, anger, and delusion that bring it about. Consider a person who has negative mental states of greed, anger, and delusion. This person may be constantly angry at everyone around him because he has not been as successful in his life in terms of worldly gain as he wanted to, and due to his craving and attachment to such a conception of himself and his success, he lashes out at the world. Speech born of the greed, anger, and delusion of this person, the Buddha claims, will help continue the pattern of suffering he is engaged in, while positive speech will help to undermine it. If he verbally abuses those around him, this will reinforce the negative mental states he has. His hatred will be further fed by his hateful words. If he refrains from such speech, however, he will avoid this trap, thus making it easier for him to ultimately remove these negative mental states that cause him to suffer.

Speak only the speech that neither torments self nor does harm to others. That speech is truly well spoken. Speak only endearing speech, speech that is welcomed. Speech when it brings no evil to others is pleasant. *Subhasita Sutta* (trans. Thanissaro)

The fool who does evil to a person who is good, to a person who is pure and free from blemish, the evil returns to him like dust thrown against the wind. *Dhammapada* 125 (trans. Mascaro, modified)

Right livelihood works in a similar way. When we have certain kinds of career or job, this can aid the creation of suffering in us. If one is a butcher, for example (a stock example of wrong livelihood in Buddhist texts), one kills living beings and causes suffering for a living. This kind of job surely creates greater suffering for the person who performs it. To understand how this is, however, we have to go beyond the explanation given above concerning speech, and understand the Buddhist notion of *karma* (Pali *kamma*). According to the Buddha's teaching, the concept of *karma* (literally, "action") is central to the story of dependent origination. Every action has some positive or negative result insofar as it concerns suffering. When we perform acts that create suffering, such as killing, harming others, or acting from greed, anger, and delusion in general, we accrue negative karma, which means basically that we cause ourselves suffering, through the link of dependent origination. An act that creates suffering, by definition, is an act of greed, anger, and delusion linked to craving and attachment. This craving and attachment is reinforced in the person who performs the act and thus leads to the continuation and deepening of this person's own suffering, and this act also has the potential to contribute to the suffering of others. Any act, thus, that proceeds from greed, anger, and delusion, or causes this in others, is a karmically negative act that will necessarily produce suffering. It follows from this, of course, that having a job or career that requires one to perform karmically negative acts will be an obstacle to overcoming suffering. Thus, one should reject jobs and careers linked with karmically negative acts.

Let us return to the virtues grounding right conduct mentioned at the beginning of this section. We have seen now how avoiding karmically negative actions is conducive to undermining one's suffering. But what about the flipside of this? Are there any actions, mental states, or virtues that positively *aid* in the elimination of suffering? The virtue of compassion is one such mental state/virtue, along with other virtues such as honesty, perseverance, and wisdom. It is true, however, that the Buddhist view holds a special place for compassion, seeing it as the most noble and positive of the virtues, the most instrumental, perhaps, in subverting suffering through undermining craving and attachment. We will see in the next section below that compassion is the natural response when we understand the truth about the world and the self—that all things are impermanent and that there is no autonomous, individual "self."

Compassion works almost like the reverse of greed, anger, and delusion. When we act compassionately toward another, we do things that aim at relieving the suffering of others, at undermining the craving and attachment of others. This attitude, of course, thinking back to the causal chain of dependent origination, tends also to undermine our own craving and attachment. Just as negative acts and attitudes create suffering in two ways, compassion destroys suffering in two ways—it conduces to the end of craving and attachment in others, and in ourselves. Think about what follows from greed, anger, and delusion. If one is greedy, one grasps in ways that fortify craving and attachment. Compassion, however, undermines this craving. Out of compassion for others, one is willing to let go of the things one has, willing to give for others. This kind of attitude naturally undermines the craving that leads to suffering—the need to have, to possess. The same works for anger and delusion. Compassion undermines the features of these mental states that create craving and attachment and hold us stuck in suffering. Compassion, then, is one of the roots of right conduct. The Buddha enjoins compassion for all living things as a necessary feature of the path to end suffering.

# The role of wisdom and the insubstantiality of the "self"

When you see with discernment, *"All fabrications are inconstant"*—you grow disenchanted with stress. This is the path to purity.

When you see with discernment, *"All fabrications are stressful"*—you grow disenchanted with stress. This is the path to purity. When you see with discernment, *"All phenomena are not-self"*—you grow disenchanted with stress. This is the path to purity. *Dhammapada* 277–9 (trans. Thanissaro)

All of what we've explored so far ties to the "doctrinal" aspects of Buddhism, and the knowledge that the Buddha claims one must have before one can come to attain the mental states required of the path and control the mind in such a way as to end suffering. The *wisdom* division of the path (including right view and right intention) is often neglected in contemporary western interpretations of Buddhism. It is sometimes claimed (even by proponents of the Buddhist view) that Buddhism is a non-doctrinal religion, without a creed or belief system that guides and grounds it. It is, these interpreters claim, simply a *method*. It cannot even properly be called a religion (because of the lack of doctrine or creed), but must be called philosophy, or rather a method for living. If we look closely at early Buddhism, we can see that this interpretation is, even if in earnest, somewhat flawed. The Buddha's teaching *does* involve a doctrine and (one might call it) a creed, without which the Buddhist practice would never get off the ground. Not only are there doctrinal elements of Buddhism, but these elements are at the very core of the Buddhist system of self-cultivation. Without them, all the other elements of the path would be useless, according to the Buddha. What makes it possible to end suffering at all is an understanding of the truth about human life and the world. Without this understanding, there can be no freedom from suffering. *Knowledge* is necessary, according to the Buddha. And knowledge requires belief (even if belief does not require knowledge). No one can *know* a thing she doesn't believe.

But what is it that we have to know in order to end suffering? This brings us back to the concept mentioned earlier in this chapter of the *three dhamma seals*. The knowledge that we must gain is that of the truth about the world and human life, as it relates to suffering. Primarily, this truth is contained in the Four Noble Truths. Without knowing these truths, we cannot hope to end suffering. As part of understanding the four noble truths, of course (particularly the second), we come to also know and understand the three dhamma seals: 1) all things are impermanent; 2) all things are unsatisfactory; 3) all things are without self. We've considered in an earlier section what the first two of these entail, and how they translate to ending suffering. If we understand the impermanence and intrinsic unsatisfactoriness of things, we will naturally be less inclined to crave and form negative attachments to these things. But what about the "self"? What does it mean to say that all things are without self?

The Buddha's view of the self has to be understood in light of the conception of the self as it existed in the philosophical thought of his contemporaries. This view of the self that the Buddha opposed is not unique to ancient India, of course—it is a view roughly shared by a great number of figures in the western tradition, including such central figures as Plato, Aquinas, Descartes, and most Christian philosophers.

The Upanisadic movement (today called Vedanta) was roughly contemporary with the life of the Buddha, originating somewhat earlier, and continuing through his time and beyond. This would have been the major influential strain of philosophy during Buddha's time, and some of the early Buddhist concepts are formulated in response to the views of the Vedic/Upanishadic thinkers. We will discuss both the Vedas and (especially) the Upanishads in greater detail the next chapter, on the *Bhagavad Gita*, but here it is necessary to give a short account of the dominant view found in this tradition on the "self."

According to the Upanishadic thinkers, the self (*Ātman*) is something like a spirit or soul that animates the human, and with which a person is identified. A person is not a body; rather a person is a *self* that occupies or animates a body. One interesting difference between the Upanishadic view and that of some western thinkers is that this self is not identified with the *mind* any more than it is with the body. The self is not the mind or the body. Rather, the self has a conscious awareness and life that grounds the mind and body and can possess a mind and body. The self is, in some sense, pure consciousness, devoid of any other individuating characteristics. There are some important reasons for their acceptance of this view, and it also leads to some very interesting commitments.

Philosophers in ancient India, as much as those throughout the western tradition, worried about the problem of identity through time, particularly in the case of persons. What makes me, you, or anyone else the *same* person now as the person we were three years ago? What will make us the same person 20 years from now that we are today? In order for two things, *a* and *b*, to be identical, they have to share the same defining features in what makes them what they are. For example, we can say that tennis ball *T* at time 1 is identical with tennis ball V at time 2 because the two balls are the quantitively the same physical stuff—ball V is made of quantitatively identical material to ball T. Since there needs to be something quantitatively the same for multiple entities to be identical (the person called "the Dalai Lama" at 9:44 on July 17, 2011 and the person called "the Dalai Lama" at 9:44 am on July 17, 1989), we need to locate these features. But there is a problem. When we search for quantitatively identical features of ourselves at different times, we seem to find nothing quantitatively the same between two distant enough entities. For example, what qualitatively similar features can I find that belong to both myself today and to myself as a one year old? Certainly no physical states. All the atoms and cells comprising my body today are completely distinct from those that comprised my body as a one year old. In addition, we don't take body to generally be a criterion of identity, as one can lose one's arms and legs but we still call him the same person.

What if we move to psychological features of the person? It looks like a similar difficulty obtains here. Today, I am completely psychologically different from the way I was as a one year old (don't be fooled by the "I" talk here—the fact that I am referring to an identity in each case as "I" and "me" does not itself show that there is some self underlying the two entities, because we've not yet learned if I am justified in so claiming identity). There are almost no thoughts, attitudes, and mental dispositions I have today that I had as a one year old (perhaps aside from basic things like the desire to eat and sleep, which can't count as identifying features of a self, because then we would have to conclude that every human and animal who has such a desire is identical!). So it looks like there is nothing that I can point to that is qualitatively the same between the two entities, that makes the one-year-old me same as the me who exists today. (The name won't do it, as I can call two distinct things 'Alexus McLeod,' because naming is a function of the speaker not the object).

So if there is a self, it cannot be identified with any of the specific physical or mental features of the individual person. But then what could a self be? Does it exist at all? The Upanishadic thinkers held that there is such a self, and that it is *pure consciousness* or spirit (*atman*). This is something that does belong to the one-year-old me and the me of today. The two share the same consciousness, the same pure awareness and spirit. It is important to see, however, that this consciousness is pure, and without individuating features. So the particular thoughts, attitudes, dispositions, etc. that I have are not my self. My self (*atman*) is pure consciousness alone, which underlies all of the contingent features of me as a person. Those things all change, are born and die, while the self as pure consciousness endures.

This view has a couple of interesting results. First, if the self does not have features and is pure consciousness, it does not *change*. It does not gain and lose features, and is thus not subject to the growth and decay of conditioned things. The self is unconditioned. As such, it is not born, and it does not die. The self is eternal. According to the Upanishadic view (derived from earlier Vedic views), although the body and mind die, the self continues, and takes new bodies and minds. The self is reincarnated over and over, as it endures through time. A second result of the self view is that it ultimately entails that there are no discrete, autonomous individuals. If the self is pure consciousness ultimately without identifying features, what is the difference between *my* self and *your* self? The Upanishadic view, at the end of the day, will admit that there is no difference between the two, and that the self of each person is ultimately identical to *Brahman*, the universal spirit. We will discuss this further in the next chapter, on the *Bhagavad Gita*.

The Buddha takes a different view concerning the self. Why, we might ask, think that anything like the self exists at all, given the various reasons we have for thinking that there are no quantitatively identical features shared by persons at different times? Rather than giving us reason to think there is some featureless self of pure consciousness, perhaps we have better reason to think *there is no self at all*! And more importantly, think about the results this understanding of the self would likely have concerning the construction of suffering through dependent origination. If it turns out that there is no self, then I have no good reason to grasp after, crave, or attach to conditioned things, because there is no sense in which I can ever "own" or attain these things. Not only because the things themselves are impermanent, but because there is no I to possess them! The person who craves some thing today wants to gain possession of this thing, but the entity in the future who gains possession is not identical to "me," because there is no self. It is just the same whether someone I refer to as "myself" has this thing or someone I don't so refer to has this thing. When we understand, according to the Buddha, that the concept of the self is a fiction, our craving and attachment disappears. We see that there is no point to it, and that it is impossible to ever attain what this craving and attachment seeks.

Clearly, much more needs to be said about this unintuitive view that there are no selves, and the Buddhist philosophical tradition spends many hundreds of years constructing arguments and justifications of this view which cannot be covered in this short chapter, but for our purposes here, it suffices to show that the results of such a belief in the non-existence of the self will conduce to the dissipation of craving and attachment, which is just what the Buddha's teaching aims at. Of course, the Buddha cannot use this expediency claim as a justification for the *truth* of the teaching that there is no self, but he can show that the undermining of the causes of suffering is a positive *result* of understanding this fundamental truth about the world. If all things are without self, then there is no reason to crave and grasp.

There is the case where an uninstructed, run-of-the-mill person—who has no regard for noble ones, is not well-versed or disciplined in their

Dhamma; who has no regard for men of integrity, is not well-versed or disciplined in their Dhamma—assumes form [the body] to be the self, or the self as possessing form, or form as in the self, or the self as in form. He is seized with the idea that "I am form" or "Form is mine." As he is seized with these ideas, his form changes and alters, and he falls into sorrow, lamentation, pain, distress, and despair over its change and alteration [same for the other four aggregates] ... And how is one afflicted in body but unafflicted in mind? There is the case where a well-instructed disciple of the noble ones—who has regard for noble ones, is well-versed & disciplined in their Dhamma; who has regard for men of integrity, is well-versed and disciplined in their Dhamma—does not assume form to be the self, or the self as possessing form, or form as in the self, or the self as in form. He is not seized with the idea that "I am form" or "Form is mine." As he is not seized with these ideas, his form changes and alters, but he does not fall into sorrow, lamentation, pain, distress, or despair over its change & alteration." *Nakulapita Sutta* (trans. Thanissaro)

# The enlightened person and *nirvana*

Now that we have considered the truths about suffering and the Buddha's prescription for how to end suffering, through following the eightfold path, we can consider the *enlightened* person. What is such a person like, who has attained to the pinnacle of self-cultivation, completely eliminating suffering? The Buddha calls such a person an *arahant*. As opposed to a *Buddha*, an *arahant* is one who has attained enlightenment through instruction, while a *buddha* attains enlightenment on his or her own, as did Siddhartha Gautama. There is no difference between the level of enlightenment of the two, however. They both have attained *nirvana*, they both have gone fully beyond suffering.

One obvious feature of the fully enlightened person is that such a person will be completely without suffering. We might wonder what it means to say that a person has eliminated all suffering. Does this mean, for example, that the Buddha never felt pain or exhaustion after his enlightenment, and lived in a perpetual state of happiness and joy? No—the enlightened person, according to the Buddha, still has pains and pleasures, still aches, gets hungry and tired, and feels pleasure when eating something tasty. What the enlightened person *does not* have, however, is craving and attachment to these states, and thus does not have suffering. We must remember that it is not pleasure and pain that cause joy and suffering, but rather our mental states concerning attachment. We can be in pain without suffering, because suffering is a matter of the attachment and identification with what we feel. There is a fundamental difference, according to the Buddha, between the person who is in pain and thinks of this pain as belonging to themselves, desiring to get rid of it, and the enlightened person who experiences this pain as simply pain, not belonging to him or her, and thus not grasping after the state of pleasure, or non-pain. The enlightened person can hurt without suffering, and can have pleasures without suffering. In a way, then, we can say that the enlightened person is the only kind of person who can truly experience the world as it is, without suffering, without projecting his or her own mental formations on to things. They are the only ones who can truly *enjoy* what is good, and *endure* what is bad. There are elements of the Buddha's ideal person that should remind us of the ideal persons of the Confucian and the Daoist both.

Another interesting feature of the enlightened person, according to the Buddha, is that such a person will not be reborn again. Early Buddhism adopted a similar view of reincarnation to that in the Vedic/Vedantic tradition, holding that what keeps a person being reborn is craving and attachment, which creates the karmic result of continual birth. Recall the chain of dependent origination, discussed earlier in this chapter. Craving and attachment lead to suffering *via* becoming and birth. Thus, craving and attachment are not only conditions for suffering, but more immediately are conditions for becoming and birth, which are themselves conditions for suffering. As long as we crave and are attached, then, we create the process of birth and becoming, which inevitably leads to old age, illness, and death. When we *become*, we are committed to *decay*, and becoming only comes about when there is prior craving and attachment. Thus, in an interesting divergence from the Vedic/Vedantic view of reincarnation, *we* are responsible for our continual rebirths, which entail continual re-deaths. The enlightened person, however, as one who has completely erased craving and attachment, also undermines becoming and birth. Such a person brings the process of dependent origination to a halt, and thus is not further reborn. This person is thus fully free from suffering, as rebirth entails suffering.

There is an interesting problem that arises here, however. If we understand the goal of Buddhism as destruction of the chain of dependent origination and the end of rebirths, doesn't this simply amount to self-annihilation? Is the Buddha prescribing something like suicide as the answer to human suffering? Is he basically saying that if you no longer exist, you can't suffer? Not quite. What saves Buddhism from being nihilistic is the notion that *nirvana* is not annihilation; rather it is something *transcendent*, outside of the world of conditions and causes. Nirvana is the only thing that is unconditioned, not subject to birth and decay, and thus not involved with suffering. But because *nirvana* is outside the categories of the world, we cannot fully understand it using these categories. The enlightened person who attains nirvana is thus not reborn, but it is also not the case that such a person is annihilated or destroyed, never to return. The Buddha denies the application of these categories to *nirvana*. On the question of existence after death for the enlightened person, the Buddha says things like "it is not the case that the enlightened person exists after death, and it is not the case that the enlightened person does not exist after death." It is simply, given the transcendence of *nirvana*, an inapplicable question. It is like seeking a yes-or-no answer to the question "Have you quit smoking yet?" put to a person who has never smoked. Neither possible answer is applicable. So it is not the case that the Buddhist view is nihilistic. The enlightened person is not reborn, but rebirth is involved with suffering. Whatever the enlightened person has, which is *nirvana* and cannot be fully conceptualized using language, is far better than rebirth in the conditioned world. This gives the enlightened person an ease and joy others are unable to find. The enlightened person, like the Zhuangist sage, we might imagine, can truly wander free and easy, delighting in the transformation of things, and ultimately aiming to help others find their way out of the prison of suffering.

# Later Buddhism

Buddhism is one of the two oldest of the traditions considered in this book (along with Confucianism), but it is by far the most diverse and varied of all of them. Part of the reason for this is the geographical and cultural extent of Buddhism. It gained influence in by far the largest geographical area of any of the four traditions we are studying (Confucianism coming a distant second). Even in the ancient world, its extent was truly vast, but today it is expanding its influence even further, well into Europe, the United States, and Australia. This cultural variety may be one of the reasons that there are so many very different kinds of Buddhism. The number of schools, sects, and traditions within Buddhism are so varied that any two of them can sometimes look like completely different religions or philosophical systems. Schools under the Buddhist rubric vary from the spartan simplicity of the Thai Forest tradition of Theravada to the lavish deity-filled cosmology of the Tibetan Tantric tradition. The variations in Buddhist schools are dizzyingly vast.

To offer some help through this wide array of traditions, I give a short account of a few major, influential schools and the ways they develop and adapt the basic message of the Buddha discussed in this chapter. While Buddhism produced an enormous number of philosophical schools, especially in early Indian Mahayana, the philosophical debates tended to be around metaphysics and epistemology more than ethical self-cultivation, although they had some to say about this as well. This was probably because the participants in the debates saw the ethical teachings of Buddhism as clear and not in need of philosophical clarification. Thus, although I do focus in this section on one explicitly philosophical school (Madhyamaka), the other groups I focus on are various denominations of Buddhism. Each of these are much broader and more complex than I could possibly express here, but since we are interested primarily in ethics, specifically the ethics of self-cultivation, I focus on these elements of the traditions and schools.

# Early Mahayana

The Mahayana school introduced the first and biggest transformation in the history of Buddhism. A major shift happened with the early Mahayana movement, and new *sutras* began to appear claiming authority alongside of (or sometimes in *replacement* of) the early *suttas* discussed above. The proponents of these texts argued that these texts were presenting the full and complete teaching of the Buddha, which he did not give at first because he understood that people were not ready for it, and so instead taught the positions of the early *suttas* recounted above. Instead, the teachings were kept secret until the right time, and now the Mahayana was revealed, which was meant to supersede the earlier teachings.

The term '*mahāyāna*' itself explains much of the core of the school. The Sanskrit term (by this time Sanskrit, rather than Pali, was being used among Buddhist groups) translates to "great vehicle." The Mahayanists meant by this that their teaching represented the greater vehicle for carrying people "across the shore" from suffering to *nirvana*. The word "great" here had a few senses. First, it signaled a value claim that Mahayana was *better* or more efficient than previous schools, which they called *hīnayāna* ("lesser vehicle").[1] Second, the "greatness" refers also to the *size* of the vehicle. Mahayanists saw their school as the school of the people—that which could take *everyone* to the other shore, to the end of suffering, and not only monastic types who could follow the kind of discipline prescribed by the Theravadins and abandon their worldly place and join the *sangha* (community) of monks. The Mahayana school taught that *anyone* could gain enlightenment. One need not be a monk, or live like a monk, to attain *nirvana*. The "lesser vehicle," on the other hand, taught a program that only a few with the time and ability to become monks could follow. For everyone else, there was just suffering, and the round of rebirths.

A third way the Mahayanists understood their school as "great" concerns a distinction between two conceptions of the ideal person, lying at the heart of the dispute between Mahayana and the other schools. According to the Theravada school, the goal of Buddhist practice is to gain enlightenment, to become what is called an *arahant*, one who has completely eradicated suffering, and will no longer be reborn once died, just like the Buddha himself. The Mahayana school argued that this ideal was lacking. If part of the path is to become compassionate toward all beings and truly care about relieving their suffering as well, then why would a truly enlightened person accept arahantship and commit to *nirvana* for him or herself, never coming back in future lives to help others climb out of suffering? Such a decision looks far from compassionate, it looks selfish. Thus, the Mahayana school argued, the truly ideal person is one who through following the Buddhist path gets to the level at which they *could* enter into arahantship and completely end the cycle of rebirths and suffering, but who holds back out of a desire to be reborn and help others out of suffering. Such a person commits to future rebirths, to continued suffering, in order to help others, out of compassion. It is this person who is truly ideal, according to the Mahayana school. Such a person, called a *bodhisattva*, takes a vow not to enter into enlightenment themselves until all beings have become enlightened. The Mahayana school calls this the "Bodhisattva vow."

It is primarily the *bodhisattva* ideal that distinguishes the positions of the early Buddhist schools and Mahayana on the aim of self-cultivation, but there are also a number of philosophical distinctions concerning metaphysics and epistemology that are fleshed out primarily in the philosophical schools associated with the Mahayana movement. We will look at only one of these, the *madhyamaka* (Middle Way) school of the philosopher monk Nāgārjuna.

## Madhyamaka

Madhyamaka philosophy probably captures most clearly the essence of the Mahayana movement, and is fairly continuous and consistent with important positions of early Buddhism as found in the *suttas*. Before Nagarjuna's time, there had been an explosion in schools and philosophical positions on the basic categories and concepts of Buddhism, and metaphysical theorization and speculation ran wild. It seemed as if the main purpose of the numerous philosophers discussing these issues was to construct an adequate metaphysical explanation of basic Buddhist truths such as the working of karma, the nonexistence of the "self," the insubstantiality of all things, and the creation of suffering. These philosophers used conceptual analysis and argumentation to try to uncover correct explanations of these claims. The differences surrounding the early Buddhist position that there is ultimately no self can provide us with an example of the philosophical attempts and divisions among the schools. According to some philosophers, there are basic substances called *skandhas* (aggregates), such as mental formation, body, and intention—these things exist, but selves do not. When we use the term "self" we refer to certain *collections* of *skandhas*, but only the *skandhas* are ultimately real, and the "self" is simply a useful convention to refer to such sets of *skandhas*.[2] Other philosophers disagreed with this, and held that the theory of *skandhas* violated the Buddhist view that all things lack substance. Instead, they argued, what exists is mind alone, and although it *appears* to us that substances such as bodies exist, this is merely illusory. Following one of the main tenets of the Mahayana school, these philosophers said, clarifying or going beyond the early Buddhist position, that all things are ultimately *empty*. This claim of emptiness was understood differently by the philosopher Nagarjuna, the major representative of the Madhyamaka school.

According to Nagarjuna, the Mahayana claim about emptiness can be understood in the same way as the earlier schools understood the claim about insubstantiality. That is, we can see the Buddhist teaching as one denying the essence or efficacy of metaphysics altogether. To say that the self is ultimately empty and that there is "no self" is to say that it is *neither* the case that some metaphysical entity exists *nor* the case that no metaphysical entity exists. Both options are denied. This follows very closely with things the Buddha says in the early *suttas* concerning metaphysical topics such as the self. When asked questions such as "Does the self continue after death?", the Buddha often answers that it neither continues nor does not continue. Nagarjuna gives an analysis of emptiness that takes it to entail something very similar. It suggests that ultimately there are no answers to these metaphysical questions that people spend so much time and effort debating over. We begin to understand the Buddhist path and see the way toward ending suffering when we come to realize that such questions are illusory, and ultimately empty. When we understand this, we are naturally directed back toward the what is important, namely the Buddhist path to attainment of *nirvana*. Cultivation of conduct, wisdom, and concentration. The third of these aspects of the Buddhist path was the focus of a major sub-school of the Mahayana tradition that began in China, after the movement of Buddhism into East Asia, and ultimately flourished most strongly in Japan. It is probably the school that has most influenced the western understanding of Buddhism, for better and worse. This school was known in China as *Chan*, but is better known in the west by its Japanese name, *Zen*.

## Chan/Zen

The Zen school was born of a combination of two philosophical systems we have examined in this book—Buddhism and Daoism. Much of the enigmatic and jocular while serious character of Zen reminds one of the *Zhuangzi*, and much of the Zen antagonism toward conceptualizing the path comes from Daoism, also in particular the *Zhuangzi*. We might imagine Zen as what Zhuangzi would have taught were he a Buddhist. The Chinese word *chan* derives from the Sanskrit *dhyana*, which translates as "concentration" or "meditation." We see right away, then, that the Zen school takes meditation as a central focus, which was unique among the Buddhist schools. As we saw above, early Buddhist schools saw meditation as *one* aspect of the Buddhist path, but by no means the *central* aspect. It is only one part of the eightfold path. For the Zen school, however, meditation took center stage. It is through mental cultivation, according to Zen teaching, that the other aspects of the path are realized. Ultimate victory—the attainment of *nirvana* and the end of suffering—comes only indirectly through the other aspects of the path, but comes directly through meditation. Thus, the Zen school understood the other aspects of the path in a secondary sense. It is important to have wisdom and exemplify right action because these are necessary in order to put one's mind in the proper place for meditation. One can only be truly equanimous and one-pointed in concentration if one has cultivated wisdom and proper action. It is like lighting a match—a match can only be lit in certain conditions, where the air is dry enough, and there is little enough wind, but ultimately only striking the match directly leads to its lighting.

Considerations of this kind led to a controversy within the Zen tradition concerning the attainment of enlightenment. Some Zen sects insisted that enlightenment, like the lighting of a match, happens instantaneously, once all the proper conditions have been put into place. This entails an "all or nothing" view—one is unenlightened while one builds the foundation, then one finally attains full enlightenment, in an instant. Other sects argued that enlightenment is gradual, that as one progresses on the path, one comes closer and closer to enlightenment, attaining more of the features attributable to that state, until finally one has them all, and one is enlightened. The "sudden enlightenment" sects, such as the *Rinzai* (Chinese *Linji*, named after the Chinese monk who founded the school), became the dominant ones in later Chinese and Japanese Zen history, and it is these which have also had the most global influence. The Rinzai sect is truly Zhuangzi-like, with people demonstrating enlightenment through strange, irreverent, and spontaneous actions, and heavy reliance on the *koan*—short questions that a student is given to answer that cannot be answered through rational analysis, but that instead force the student to transcend and put aside the normal categories of thought in order to break into enlightenment. Given that the Zen mind, the mind of enlightenment, is wholly different from the normal mind of suffering, stuck within its categories and modes of thinking, we have to abandon the normal mind to become enlightened.

The anti-rationalist strain of Rinzai Zen shares this feature in common with another school of Buddhism that became popular in both China and Japan, referred to as the "Pure Land" school.

## Pure Land

Part of what was revolutionary about the Mahayana movement was that it was concerned with opening up the Buddhist path to those outside the monastic *sangha*, such that anyone, even "householders" in the midst of the world's activity, could attain enlightenment. The Pure Land school took this cause even further. Not only can some people not become monks due to worldly responsibilities, lack of ability, or health, but it is also the case that most people, spending the vast majority of their time just attaining the means to survive, cannot spend much time in meditation. Are these people doomed to continue on life after life in the round of rebirths and suffering, just because they are poor or unintellectual?

The Pure Land school argued that there is another way. Devotion to the next Buddha, Amitabha, can guarantee one rebirth in his "pure land", in which he awaits his birth as the next Buddha. From this realm, it is much easier to attain full enlightenment, as there is both the time, the motivation, and the atmosphere to ensure success on the Buddhist path. Amitabha's pure land is basically a kind of Buddhist paradise, from which everyone achieves enlightenment. There is no regression there, only improvement.

According to most versions of Pure Land, the main way to ensure rebirth in Amitabha's realm is though devotion, represented by chanting of *mantras* (short verses) concerning Amitabha and his pure land, to ensure the proper mental state. A popular practice based on this is to (if able), chant Amitabha mantras when one approaches death, in order to help ensure rebirth in the pure land. Although the Pure Land variant of Buddhism is still very popular today, perhaps the most widely practiced form in contemporary Asian societies, in the west a very different form of Buddhism is far better known, which most of us know as "Tibetan Buddhism," but is more properly referred to as a collection of schools of *Vajrayana* or *Tantrayana*. Most of the existing Tibetan schools come from this tradition, including the Gelug-pa school, well known as the tradition of the Dalai Lama.

## Tantrayana

The Tibetan Buddhist schools were formed in the tradition of *Vajrayana*, which is another school of Buddhism very different from the early Buddhist schools. The Vajrayana, or "thunder vehicle" school took itself to be a third major division of Buddhism, along side the early schools like Theravada and the younger Mahayana. It surrounded the use of Tantric rituals in place of the meditative aspects of other traditions such as Zen. Through such rituals, the Vajrayana school argued, one could cultivate the same mental states as one could through meditation, even more efficiently. Again, we see here a tradition aimed at encouraging lay Buddhists and offering a program they would have seen themselves as able to engage in, involving ritual and devotion rather than asceticism, meditation, and other monastic practices. We will see in the next chapter an example of a system based on just such considerations in India, in the attempt to synthesize Vedic religion, Upanishadic thought, and Buddhism, as well as make liberation from the round of rebirths attainable for everyone—not only renunciates and ascetics, but even those who must stay within the confines of the "worldly" life.

# Further resources on Buddhism and self-cultivation

The resources on the Buddhist tradition in general are truly vast, as with most major world religions. Even limiting this to the Theravada tradition and early Buddhism alone does not make the literature any more manageable. Like Confucianism (and to a lesser extent Daoism), Buddhism and early Buddhism have captured the imaginations of people across the world for thousands of years, and have inspired seas of literature, art, philosophy, and other human enterprises. The list of resources here is mainly meant to give you an example of a few good readings and other materials primarily on the Theravada and early Buddhist tradition, and also concerning the later traditions discussed above as an entry point to better understanding the self-cultivation teachings of the Buddha and his early followers.

## Translations of the Pali texts

- B. Nanamoli and B. Bodhi, trans. *The Middle Length Discourses of the Buddha*

- M. Walshe, trans. *The Long Discourses of the Buddha*

- B. Bodhi, trans. *The Connected Discourses of the Buddha*

- J. Mascaro, trans. *Dhammapada*

- F. Max Müller and T. W. Rhys-Davids, *The Questions of King Milinda*

- Online resource of translations of much of the Pali canon at *Access to Insight*; www.accesstoinsight.org

## Later Buddhist texts

- B. Watson, trans., *Lotus Sutra*
- D. T. Suzuki, trans., *Lankavatara Sutra*
- Red Pine, trans., *Bodhidharma*

## Secondary works on early Buddhism and Theravada

- W. Rahula, *What the Buddha Taught*
- S. Collins, *Selfless Persons: Imagery and Thought in Theravada Buddhism*
- D. Kalupahana, *Buddhist Philosophy: A Historical Analysis*
- Sumedho, *The Way It Is*

## Films

- *The Buddha*, PBS

# A short biography of Siddhartha Gautama, the Buddha

The man known to history as the Buddha was born around 563 BCE in the Shakya capital city of Kapilavasthu (in modern-day Nepal), son of the king Suddhodana. His identity as a member of the Shakya clan was the basis for one of his post-Enlightenment monikers "Shakyamuni" (sage of the Shakyas). The prince took his family name Gautama (Pali Gotama), and according to tradition he was given the name "Siddhartha" (Pali Siddhattha), which translates roughly to "the accomplished one." It is unclear whether the historical Buddha was a prince at all (though most scholars accept that a person corresponding to the figure of the Buddha in fact existed), but I will here follow the traditional story of the Buddha's life, with the caveat that little of this is historically verifiable. It is likely that the Buddha was an actual historical person, and it is clear that he founded a philosophical and religious movement that would go on to become highly influential throughout India and even into East and Southeast Asia, but other than this we cannot know much with confidence, as with the other figures discussed in this book.

According to the traditional story, Prince Siddhartha grew up in the sheltered Shakya court, pampered and closed off from the outside world by a paranoid father who took to heart a prophecy made at the birth of his son. The priest told Suddhodana that his son would become either a great world-conquering king or a great renunciate monk. Fearful lest his son become a monk and foil his plans for succession, Suddhodana tried to ensure that his son be exposed only to the palace and its delights, and experience none of the suffering of life outside the walls. But Suddhodana's wish was not to be realized. It appeared to be Prince Siddhartha's destiny to become a monk and to discover the truth about life, suffering, and liberation from suffering.

Siddhartha was eventually married to a woman named Yasodhara, and with her had a son, Rahula. However, all was not well. The story continues that at age 29 (534 BCE, if we accept the above date of his birth), Siddhartha became dissatisfied with his constrained and meaningless life within the palace, and took a journey outside the walls to see and meet with the people of his father's realm. During the ride in his chariot on this journey into the land, Siddhartha made a discovery that shook him to the core. He saw an old person struggling to walk, his body weakened by age. Either on this trip or future trips outside the palace (depending on which version of the story we consult), Siddhartha next saw a diseased person, sick on the side of the road, and finally a corpse aside the road. He came to realize that these three modes of suffering are inherent in all of life. No matter how powerful, rich, or famous we are, all of us are destined for old age, sickness, and death.

Prince Siddhartha became obsessed with this problem—the seeming inevitability of suffering. Was there no way out of it? A possible way out seemed to be offered him when he witnessed, on one of his trips, a wandering renunciate. Perhaps, he thought, this was way to discover the answer to the problem of suffering, its origin, and whether it can be ended. Siddhartha made up his mind to leave the palace and his family behind, and escaped out into the night with no possessions to become a wandering monk, looking for the answers to the problem of suffering.

During his journey as a monk, Siddhartha studied under two different teachers, each of whom offered a different path and a different answer to the problem of suffering. His first teacher, Kalama, emphasized yogic meditation practices, and the renunciation of worldly things. Siddhartha learned all he could from this teacher, but felt that there was still more that he could not gain from him, so he left and joined with another teacher. Eventually, he found that this new teacher did not have all of the answers either, and again went out on his own. Finally, Siddhartha joined with a group of ascetics practicing extreme austerity—rejecting the things of the world so thoroughly that they wore no clothes and would eat nothing more than a single bean per day. The idea was that suffering could be overcome by a complete rejection of the world. It did not take long for Siddhartha to arrive at the edge of starvation. Recognizing that this could not be the right path, Siddhartha again went off on his own. He realized that if he were to find the answer, he would have to do it on his own.

According to the traditional story, it was after many days of meditation under the famous peepal tree, at 35 years old (528 BCE), that Siddhartha discovered the principles of the Four Noble Truths outlined in Chapter 3, finally solving the problem of suffering, and becoming enlightened. Siddhartha was now the Buddha (also in the Pali texts called "Tathagata," "one who has passed beyond [the cycle of dependent origination]"). According to tradition, the Buddha's enlightenment took place at the site of modern day Bodh Gaya, in the northern Indian state of Bihar. Soon after his enlightenment, the Buddha began his teaching ministry, traveling throughout what is today northern India and Nepal, offering the Four Noble Truths as the solution to the problem of suffering. Around the Buddha grew a community of monks who followed his teachings and his ways, a group that came to be called the *sangha* ("community").

The Buddha traveled, taught, and took on students, eventually even his son Rahula and his wife Yasodhara, who both in time gained enlightenment, becoming *arahants*. The Buddha's teaching ministry lasted for 45 years, until his death and final entrance to *nirvana* (*parinirvana*) at 80 years old (483 BCE).

## RELEVANT QUESTIONS

1   How might ethical reflection or philosophical reflection in general be relevant to the matter of liberating oneself from the cycle of suffering—birth, death, and rebirth?

2   Why think that attachment to conditioned things must cause suffering in the way described by the theory of dependent origination? Couldn't one have a more *modest* attachment to things, enjoying them but recognizing and accepting their impermanence? Does the Buddhist position on ending suffering entail that we *should not* enjoy impermanent things (that is, everything that is not *nirvana*)?

3   According to early Buddhism, both mental and moral cultivation are necessary factors of the path, but how might controlling one's mind and mindfulness in general help in the *production* of moral action?

4   Is there a connection between compassion and acting? That is, might there be certain kinds of action incompatible with compassion, or is there a more radical disconnection between act and mental state?

5   If there is ultimately no self, how do we explain the apparently unified character or our experience? (That is, perception with five senses, of a subject, with memory, etc.)

6   If *nirvana* cannot be positively defined, then how can we avoid the conclusion that it is ultimately nihilistic? That is, if *nirvana* is nothing in the world, and is also nothing *outside* the world, nothing that becomes (because all things that arise inevitably decay), then how can we avoid the conclusion that it is in fact *nothing at all*?

7   Would a Buddhist renunciate be able to function in a Confucian society? What might Confucius think of such a person?

# Notes

1   This term applied to the older schools, including the *Theravada*, but was only used by Mahayanists, as the other schools certainly would not have considered themselves "lesser". In some older western literature one sometimes sees scholars refer to "Hinayana" schools, but this is a convention clearly influenced by Mahayana tradition, and has been for the most part stopped, as it is offensive toward Theravada.

2   Notice that we are not committed to the independent existence of the self by referring to it as the "set" or "collection" of the *skandhas*, as the existence of this set is wholly conventional. There are no facts about the set (we might say the set does not exist) prior to our conventional construction of it. It works in the same way that one might pick out random objects on the ground, class them together, and coin a term to refer to this set of things. No separate entity from the random objects exists, and the person has not brought anything into existence by classing these objects together—what has happened is just that the person has created a new way of classifying things.

# 4

# The Message of the *Bhagavad Gita*

*One should remember*
*man's spirit as the guide*
*the primordial poet,*
*smaller than an atom,*
*granter of all things,*
*in form inconceivable,*
*the color of the sun*
*beyond darkness.*

*BHAGAVAD GITA* 8.9 (TRANS. MILLER)

## The background—Vedas, Vedanta, and the *Mahabharata*

As mentioned in Chapter 3, most of the philosophical and religious tradition of ancient India grew out of or was otherwise related to the enormously influential system of the Vedas. The Vedas had such an overwhelming influence on Indian thought and culture that they seeped into the very background assumptions of thinkers in India. We might liken it to the effect of the Enlightenment on contemporary western thought. The views and positions that arose out of the Enlightenment are very often the unquestioned assumptions of western society, taken as universal and "self-evident" truths. Think of concepts like those of "freedom," "rights." "autonomy," "democracy," and "rationality." In western societies it is almost universally assumed that these are necessary goods or values, and the dominant view of the best human life revolves around these concepts. We often accept this without argument, however, simply taking it as obvious and self-evidently true that, for example, all people have basic "human rights," ought to be free, represented in a democracy, should operate with reason as primary, etc. However, it is not obvious that these statements are true, and it is only relatively recently in human history that anyone thought things like autonomy or democracy were either universal or even minimally acceptable. So it can't be right to hold that such things are either self-evident or universally accepted (even if it seems so because of their acceptance within our society). Even if such views are ultimately true, they are not obviously true or self-evidently true, and it is important to see the role that our cultural background plays in our acceptance of these views.

We can thus say that the values of the Enlightenment stand in need of justification and argument just as much as those of the Vedas or any other cultural system. That these basic cultural values are often *not* argued for but rather assumed, however, cannot be taken as the basis for a dismissal of a particular view or system, otherwise we would be forced to dismiss most ethical and other systems ever devised by human beings, including all of "our own." Instead, we should try to understand *why* one would adopt certain background beliefs, examine what kinds of systems grow from these various backgrounds, and ask ourselves whether we *ought* to accept the relevant backgrounds.[1]

The multiplicity of backgrounds, however, should not necessarily show us that there is no truth or that there is no single true method, claims, or set of values. Even if we necessarily have a problem *demonstrating* the truth, this does not entail that *there is no truth*. The skeptic can only show us that our claims to knowledge are problematic—he or she cannot go further and claim that we cannot have knowledge, lest he or she commit the same mistake he or she charges us with. In addition, it does not follow logically from the multiplicity of background values and outlooks that there is no single correct set of values and outlook, anymore than it follows that, in a math class, if five students give five different answers to the question "what is 2+2" that there is no correct answer. One of the five students may have given the correct answer, or they may have *all* got it wrong. But there is surely a correct answer: 4.

In the time of the Buddha and the *Bhagavad Gita*, the positions expressed in Vedic tradition were strong background assumptions, quite as much, or even more so, than the values of the Enlightenment in contemporary American/western society.

The Vedic tradition was based on the concepts, rituals, and values discussed in the *Vedas*, a collection of religious texts written from around 1500 BCE through 500 BCE. The main focus of the Vedas is religious ritual and symbolism. We see in the Vedas creation stories along with elaborate explanations of the forces of nature through religious and metaphysical system building. We are introduced to a pantheon of gods, who represent and control different aspects of the world—to some extent like what we see in the religion of ancient Greece. Thus, the first feature of Vedic thought we can point to that has definite influence on subsequent Indian thought is the *polytheistic* worldview. Some contemporary Hindus, of course, and also some of the past, would argue that the tradition that grew out of the Vedas (today generally called "Hinduism") is more accurately described as *henotheistic* (where the multiple gods taken to represent aspects of one single supreme God) rather than polytheistic (where multiple gods are seen as autonomous and distinct). Although there is a henotheistic strain in later Hinduism, especially after the introduction of Islam and the west, ancient Vedic religion itself does appear to be genuinely polytheistic, and it is this polytheism that had an influence on Indian society in the time of the *Bhagavad Gita*.

The polytheism of the Vedic tradition is a key to understanding the central character of the *Bhagavad Gita*, Krishna, as *avatar* (or incarnation) of the god Vishnu, and on a deeper level, as a representation of the spirit of the entire universe. Although the Vedic tradition itself is polytheistic, in later Indian thought, including in the *Gita*, we see a move toward *pantheism* (the view that God is comprised of all that exists, including human beings, or that there is a *part* of all things that is identifiable with God).

Another major feature of the Vedic tradition is the notion of *rebirth* of souls, and reward for moral action through rebirths. The traditional belief is that each of us has a soul (*atman*) that transmigrates from life to life. One can be reborn as a human, or as another kind of animal, depending on the moral quality of one's life. One's present life is the result of the moral quality of previous lives. The concept of *karma* grows out of this consideration of rebirth and moral reward or punishment.

There are two misconceptions surrounding Vedic culture and the *Gita* that it would be helpful to dispel here. First is the notion that the Vedas and the *Bhagavad Gita* represent an organized religion called "Hinduism." Before the introduction of Islam in the subcontinent, there was no such term "Hindu." This term was an invention of the conquerors, meant to distinguish those who practiced generally Vedic-based religions from the Islamic conquerors. The term derives from the name of one of the major river systems of the subcontinent, the *Indus* ("*Sindhu*" in most South Asian languages, including Sanskrit), from which the word 'India' is also derived.[2] There was no organized single religion called Hinduism in those days; rather, there were a number of distinct and interrelated religious and philosophical systems influenced by and to a large extent contained within the Vedic tradition. There did not exist then anything like a "church" of Hinduism, and such a thing does not exist now either. Despite the claims of some Hindu nationalists, systematizers, and syncretists, who attempt to isolate and elaborate a concrete "Hindu religion," the religious and philosophical thought of the Vedic tradition is highly decentralized, diverse, and distinct. Unlike western religions such as Christianity and Islam, there is no creed, belief system, ritual or practice that all Hindus will accept or engage in and that defines them as Hindu. In a sense, this confusion arises because of the historical fact that the Islamic conquerers used a catch-all term to refer to native forms of religion distinct from Islam, which works very well as a negative boundary condition (that which is *not* Islam), but cannot capture at all a coherent religious and philosophical system or outlook (what native Indian religion *is*). It is more helpful to think of "Hinduism" and Vedic thought in general as similar to categories like "Indian religion," "Chinese philosophy," etc., in that it refers to a widely diverse tradition consisting of multiple systems, views, tendencies, and practices, most of which are in dialogue with each other and influence each other in various ways.

The second misconception surrounds the position of the *Bhagavad Gita* as religious text. One will often hear it said today that the *Gita* represents the "essential teaching" of Hinduism, or that it is the "bible" of the Hindu religion. We ought to be skeptical of this right away, once we understand what has been explained above about "Hinduism." But there is an additional problem with this view. The *Gita*, although it certainly is a wonderful text, and in my opinion one of the greatest works on self-cultivation and spirituality ever written, did not hold a particularly special place in Indian religious and philosophical thought until relatively recently, many thousands of years after it was written, sometime during the period between 400 BCE and 200 CE. In particular, the *Gita* gained popularity among westerners and the English (perhaps as it shares some similarities with western philosophical and religious concepts) after it was translated into English and praised by progressive thinkers across the western world. This western appreciation of the text boosted it into a position of primacy in the Hindu tradition. Gandhi took it as the essential core of Hindu teaching (also reading it in a very allegorical sense, perhaps even beyond what was intended by the authors), and many Hindus themselves began to present it as *the* central text of the tradition, reordering its historical significance. This is not to say that before the western interest in the *Gita* that it had little or no importance—rather, that it tended to be treated as one text among a number of important religious texts, including other parts of the *Mahabharata*, the *Upanishads*, *Puranas*, and other texts.

The *Gita* is not a self-standing text, but a single chapter of a larger religious epic called the *Mahabharata* ("Great Bharata [War]"). The work is truly an epic, spanning over twenty volumes in its (still-unfinished) English translation.[3] It tells the story of two clans, the Pandavas and Kauravas, and a massive war for supremacy between the two. The Pandavas are rightful holders of the throne of Bharata (a name still used to designate all of India

today, but during this time referred to a smaller domain in current north west India), but through duplicitous means the Kauravas have come to control the realm. The *Mahabharata* tells the story of this usurpation, the war between the clans, and the eventual restoration of the throne to the Pandavas. While this sounds like it could be the plot to a Hollywood (or Bollywood, as the case may be!) picture, this action-packed plot is merely the external motivating vehicle for what is essentially a religious and moral tale, focusing on Vedic ritual and religion, concepts of duty, action and rebirth, religious devotion, and of course moral self-cultivation. The *Mahabharata* can be considered a moral and religious epic, in which the conventional events are meant to symbolically (and sometimes explicitly, as in the *Gita*) express moral, religious, and philosophical views. Sometimes the *Mahabharata* is compared with the Bible, but I think a more accurate comparison is to the Elizabethan English epic poem *The Faerie Queene* by the poet Edmund Spenser, which both tells a national founding epic (for England, as the *Mahabharata* does for India), and uses its plot in symbolic ways with the primary purpose of expressing religious and philosophical positions through a surface story involving swords, knights, and maidens (in its case, derived from Arthurian legend).

The events of the *Gita* take place at the beginning of the war between the Pandavas and Kauravas, as the two armies face each other on the battlefield of Kurukshetra. The *Gita* is written as a dialogue between two central characters, Arjuna, the mightiest warrior of the Pandava clan, and Krishna, his friend and chariot driver, who also happens to be an incarnation of the god Vishnu, who is, in the Hindu pantheon, the preserver and protector of the universe. We can guess that his role in the *Mahabharata*, then, is to help the Pandavas take back their rightful place as rulers of Bharata. But it is in the crisis Arjuna has on the battlefield and, more importantly, in Krishna's response to it, that we hear the timeless message of the *Gita*, which speaks of self-cultivation and the ultimate purpose of humanity and the entire universe.

# The crisis of choice

There Arjuna could see, within the midst of both parties, his fathers, grandfathers, teachers, maternal uncles, brothers, sons, grandsons, friends, and also his fathers-in-law and well wishers. When the son of Kunti, Arjuna, saw all these different grades of friends and relatives, he became overwhelmed with compassion and spoke thus—Arjuna said: "my dear Krishna, seeing my friends and relatives present before me in such a fighting spirit, I feel the limbs of my body quivering and my mouth drying up. My whole body is trembling, my hair is standing on end, my bow is slipping from my hand, and my skin is burning … I do not see how any good can come from killing my own kinsmen in this battle, nor can I, my dear Krishna, desire any subsequent victory, kingdom, or happiness. Krishna, of what avail to us are a kingdom, happiness, or even life itself when all those for whom we may desire them are now arrayed on this battlefield?" *Bhagavad Gita* 1.26–1.32 (trans. Prabhupada)

On the surface, the teaching of Krishna given in the *Bhagavad Gita* is in response to an existential crisis of Arjuna's. Arjuna, as *kshatriya* and member of the Pandava clan, who are rightful heirs to the throne of Bharata, has a moral and religious duty to fight against the usurping Kauravas to regain control of the land. This duty is of highest importance—it is Arjuna's *dharma* ("sacred duty"). There is a hitch, however. The Kauravas are related to the Pandavas, and many of Arjuna's relatives, friends, and past mentors and teachers are on the side of the Kauravas. In addition to the obvious fact that killing these people will cause great emotional pain to Arjuna, it also seems that there is a conflicting moral duty here. Doesn't Arjuna have a moral responsibility to help and protect his relatives and friends? Thus, we have an emotionally charged conflict of responsibilities that Arjuna cannot dissolve, and cannot find a way around. What is he to do? Unable to decide, he becomes inert and depressed, dropping his weapons and failing to advance.

> Better for me if the sons of Dhrirarashtra, weapons in hand, were to kill me unarmed and unresisting on the battlefield ... Arjuna, having thus spoken on the battlefield, cast aside his bow and arrows and sat down on the chariot, his mind overwhelmed with grief. *Bhagavad Gita* 1.45–1.46 (trans. Prabhupada)

This is the situation that immediately leads to the teaching of Krishna, the answer given in the *Gita* to not only dissolve this difficulty, but to show us the way to cultivate the self and perfect ourselves in a way most of us never dreamed possible.

There is, of course, more to this story than we see on the surface. Not only does Arjuna's crisis of choice represent more broadly conflicts of moral responsibility, but on a deeper level it represents the constant conflicts that all of us deal with on a daily basis concerning the direction of our lives, our actions, motivations, and responses to the world. It concerns, that is, the essential duality and opposition of the human will and the natural order of the world. The assumption here is that such things as moral/religious responsibilities are built into the world and are not a matter of our decisions. What I have a moral responsibility to do is determined concretely by features of my biology, environment, and role, and is fixed independently of my choices or attitudes. Arjuna is a *kshatriya* warrior, but he is also a family member, relative, and friend. We also recognize, however, that there is an element of the self that chooses, that assents, that accepts or resists, and that does not seem (at least) to be determined by the forces of nature. The Gita (as we will see below) accepts such a distinction between elements of human life, and speaks of them in terms of the undetermined *spirit* (*atman*) and the rest of the person, which is physically and mentally determined.

According to the *Gita*, the main source of strife in human life, of suffering and psychic distress, is disharmony between this spirit, the free and sensitive will, the order of nature, the physically and mentally determined elements of humans, and the rest of the world. It is this conflict, according to the *Gita*, that is at the heart of all existential suffering.

We can try to understand this in a more practical and contemporary way through a consideration of our own modern lives. Straightforwardly, we are often distressed by choices. We are confronted every moment by a plethora of choices, more than our ancestors hundreds of years ago could have imagined. We have in large part become a society based on *choice*. Things that would have been determined for us in the past, like which bread and toothpaste to buy (whichever one the store has), our profession (we would have done what our parents did or told us to do), school, activities, religion, friends, and even in many cases spouse, are today largely left up to us. In many ways, we have become overwhelmed with choice. This is likely in part a function of being part of a consumer society in which products, institutions, and other things must compete for our attention in order to survive. There have become so many choices to make, from where to live (something else that in years past would have been determined), what car to drive and clothes to wear, all the way to what identity group to be a part of. Am I a jock or a nerd? A liberal or conservative? Mac or PC? Coke or Pepsi? The choices we have been asked to make in every area of our lives are truly overwhelming, and all these choices, even seemingly the most trivial (what kind of phone we buy, for example) have been tied to our identities. The human sense of connection to identity and construction of identity is immensely strong, and companies market their products by trying to tie our choice of them to our sense of and construction of identity. Although in some ways this enormous amount of choice can be a good thing, it can also lead to a sense of helplessness, panic, or complete withdrawal and apathy, which is what Arjuna experiences at the opening of the *Gita*. He is overwhelmed, he cannot choose, and simply shuts down.

In western cultures, we may have a particular problem with this, because we seem to hold choice as one of the highest values of human life. We can sometimes even deem horrible situations acceptable, as long as those in them have chosen to be in them. Many in our culture would be inclined to say that there is no exploitation or moral problem wherever a person of her own free will *chooses* to be exploited. Likewise, people can sometimes discount the suffering or oppression of other people in situations they chose to be in, as if a person's choice removes all moral responsibility of all other parties concerning the results of that choice. The drug dealer defends himself by pointing out that the addict chose to buy his product, just as the sweatshop owner tries to justify himself by claiming that the employees chose to work there. Many seem to take choice to trump all other moral considerations.

This, according to the thought of the *Gita*, lays too much emphasis on choice. If we do have moral responsibilities, how does what we or others choose change those responsibilities? If dealing drugs is wrong because it harms others, does it cease to be wrong simply because the buyers have chosen to be harmed? Presumably if it is wrong to harm others in itself (and the wrongness of harming others is not based on the wrongness of violating choice, which is a separate issue) then it is wrong to harm them whether they choose to be harmed or not.

Another pressing issue involving choice is that of the seeming meaninglessness of choice, and its suggestion of an even deeper meaningless of life itself. Arjuna's difficulty thus can be seen in terms of the classic *existential crisis*. We see the things of life as giving no lasting joy. The dissatisfaction underlying all things and the realization of our eventual death and decay often brings on such a crisis. Prompted by the situation at hand, Arjuna has come to see that all things are ultimately unfulfilling—a similar realization to the one of the Buddha as a young man discussed in the previous chapter.

> We don't know which weight is worse to bear—our conquering them or their conquering us. We will not want to live if we kill the sons of Dhritarashtra assembled before us. The flaw of pity blights my very being; conflicting sacred duties confound my reason. I ask you to tell me decisively—which is better? I am your pupil. Teach me what I seek! I see nothing that could drive away the grief what withers my senses; even if I won kingdoms of unrivaled wealth on earth and sovereignty over gods. *Bhagavad Gita* 2.6–2.8 (trans. Miller)

This dissatisfaction with the world Arjuna expresses does not entail that he thinks nothing is satisfactory, or that nothing is enjoyable. Rather, it signifies that even those enjoyments we encounter during life leave us ultimately unsatisfied. We have a sense that we have not gained something lasting or truly meaningful.

## Sacred duty and the fruits of action

It is in Krishna's response to Arjuna and his difficulty that we encounter the core of the teaching of the *Gita*. The first part of his teaching involves the concept of *dharma* (sacred duty) and offers an explanation and a motivation for adhering to sacred duty. Krishna's opening words to Arjuna might be unexpected and somewhat jarring, especially given that Krishna is represented in the *Gita* as an incarnation of the god Vishnu and ultimately as a representation of *Brahman* itself, the single infinite spirit of the universe.

Why this cowardice in times of crisis, Arjuna? The coward is ignoble, shameful, foreign to the ways of heaven. Don't yield to impotence! It is unnatural in you! Banish this petty weakness from your heart. Rise to the fight, Arjuna! *Bhagavad Gita* 2.2–2.3 (trans. Miller)

His response to Arjuna is simple: *why are you upset about this fight?* The first part of Krishna's teaching focuses on three points, all of which aim at undermining Arjuna's existential strife and agony over the prospect of fighting and killing relatives and friends in the Kaurava camp.

## The indestructibility of the self (*atman*)

Nothing of nonbeing comes to be, nor does being cease to exist; the boundary between these two is seen by men who see reality. Indestructible is the presence that pervades all this; no one can destroy this unchanging reality. Our bodies are known to end, but the embodied self is enduring, indestructible, and immeasurable; therefore, Arjuna, fight the battle! He who thinks this self is a killer and he who thinks it killed, both fail to understand; it does not kill, nor is it killed. It is not born, it does not die; having been, it will never not be; unborn, enduring, constant, and primordial, it is not killed when the body is killed. Arjuna, when a man knows the self to be indestructible, enduring, unborn, unchanging, how does he kill or cause anyone to kill? *Bhagavad Gita* 2.16–2.21 (trans. Miller)

Krishna explains to Arjuna that they and all their enemies on the battlefield have always existed, and will always exist. So what point is there of grieving for them, of being upset that his duty calls him to fight and kill them to restore rightful rule to the kingdom?

Some backtracking here is necessary, to consider the doctrines contained in another ancient Indian group of texts, the *Upanishads*. The *Upanishads*, describe the equality between what is called the *atman*, or "self," and *brahman*, or "ultimate reality." The *atman*, according to this tradition, is the substantial part of the mind within each person, similar to the western conception of the soul. The *atman* is the unique spiritual essence of each person, but it is stripped of all the pieces of character of each individual person. It doesn't contain one's humor, intelligence, or depression. Thus, the *atman* is spirit or soul, but without particular characteristics. It is that which makes one an individual thinking thing. It may help to think of *atman* as that which distinguishes a human from a pencil. The pencil is made of matter, but does not think, does not have what one might call an *animating spirit*. One way to think of *atman* is as this animating spirit within a person. The concept of the soul is somewhat similar, though as far as I know the soul is said to possess the properties a person has with respect to their character. A soul can be intelligent, sad, quick-tempered, etc. *Atman* does not have these characteristics. Such properties are certainly considered part of the mind in Hindu philosophy, or *citra*, but the *citra* is not the same as the *atman*. In the western tradition of philosophy, soul and mind can sometimes mean the same thing. In fact, Descartes seems to have used these terms inter-changeably, as did later philosophers during the Enlightenment period, as well as some before it.

There is another spiritual component of the universe, according to the *Upanisadic* thinkers—*brahman*, the "ultimate reality", or "infinite spirit."[13] One way of understanding *Brahman* is as akin to the *atman* of the entire universe. Each of us has an *atman* that distinguishes us from things without experience or spirit, and likewise, the Hindu philosophers said, the universe itself, or the totality of everything there is, has its own *atman*. This is *brahman*. Now this is where things get interesting. According to the Advaitic understanding of the *Upanishads*, the *atman* within each person is *identical* to *brahman*, or the infinite spirit. This can be construed as a pantheistic notion, but it goes beyond even this.

Given this identification of one's individual soul with the soul of the entire universe, the Advaitic thinkers posited that the way to achieve realization of the infinite spirit (that is, true recognition of and unity with the infinite spirit) was to achieve realization of one's own spirit, that is, illumination of one's own mind. The infinite spirit, *brahman*, is eternal, according to the *Upanishads*. It is not born and it does not die. In fact, *brahman* can be thought of as similar to the concept of God in much of Hindu thought (especially contemporary Hindu thought). It is for this reason that you will hear much contemporary Hindu talk of "God-realization." If, then, *atman* is ultimately the same as *brahman*, then *atman* too is immortal, is not born, and does not die. Indeed, this is just what the ancient thinkers said about the *atman*. This is often tied in with the Hindu notion of rebirth. If one's *atman* does not die, even though one's body (and mind!) appears to, then the *atman* must continue to exist after one's death. Thus the most central part of a person, one's soul or spirit, survives death. Since new things are born as old things die and the entire universe is thus in flux, those *atmans* that are yet not embodied will become so, and thus the *atman* I leave behind on death is embodied in a new person, and I am reborn. There's not a whole lot of argument here (remember, the point here wasn't argument and counter-argument, but an illustration of the commitments of held beliefs). Krishna explains this to Arjuna as his first response to Arjuna's difficulty in killing relatives. Although you might kill their bodies, he says, you cannot really kill them, because the *atman* lives on.

There is no reason for Arjuna to despair, because he is unable to really kill these relatives and friends he must fight. The vital part of them, the *atman*, will live on regardless. But we may find this reasoning less than compelling. Even if the *atman* lives on, isn't it still morally problematic to kill a *person*? After all, we don't take the fact that one cannot destroy the atoms that constitute one's body with a gun to offer sanction for murder. All of the unique features of an individual belong to something other than the bare *atman* or spirit. When Arjuna kills one of the Kauravas, he is indeed ending that which is unique and individuating. He is killing the *person*, if not the *true inner self*. Why isn't this still problematic? The author(s) of the *Gita* may have recognized this problem, and thus offer two additional arguments to dissolve Arjuna's dilemma.

## Adherence to *dharma* (sacred duty)

Also, you should reflect on your caste duties. You should not get agitated. In fact, for a warrior there is nothing more noble than a just war. The opportunity arises by pure chance, and the doors to heaven open. Arjuna, those warriors are happy who get the opportunity to fight such a war! But if you will not participate in this just war, a war of sacred duty, you will have abandoned your caste duty and your honor as well, and you will have won only evil for yourself. The whole world will talk of your permanent dishonor, and for someone of your stature dishonor is worse than death. *Bhagavad Gita* 2.31–2.34 (trans. Thompson, modified)

The second response Krishna gives to Arjuna is that it is his sacred duty to engage in the coming fight. Arjuna is a member of the *kshatriya* class, the class of warriors and rulers. As such, it is his sacred duty, his *dharma*, to protect the people, as well as to protect the integrity of the kingdom. Remember the story of the *Mahabharata*, and the usurpation of the throne by the faction Arjuna is fighting against. It is Arjuna's side that is in the right, and so if Arjuna backs down from this fight, it will be an infraction of his sacred duty, which is to always fight for right and for the protection of the people.

There is obviously appeal to vanity in Krishna's response here, but the adherence to *dharma* is the main point being made. Those who do not adhere to *dharma* "gain evil," shame, slander, and suffering in general. The suggestion seems to be that through adherence to *dharma*, one can lessen one's suffering, whereas infractions of *dharma* lead to increased suffering. Since Arjuna's dejection is caused by the suffering brought about by the thought of killing his relatives, Krishna recommends adherence to *dharma* as a way of banishing this suffering, through doing what it is Arjuna should do.

There is a passage from the other great epic of Indian culture, the *Ramayana*, which describes what adherence to *dharma* means for the classes in general:

> Even though Ayodhya had thousands of brahmins, people did not neglect the performance of household sacrifices and rituals. Brahmins were committed to the performance of public rituals and were allowed to accept gifts. They were learned and had conquered their senses because of their exalted characters. There were no unbelievers, nor were there any ignorant or unrighteous people in Ayodhya. There were no libertines either. There was no sadness or poverty. Men and women were beautiful and wealthy and they were all devoted to their king.
>
> A guest was honored as a god in the homes of all four castes. People took refuge in the truth and lived well into old age. The ksatriyas placed the brahmins first and the vaisyas followed the ksatriyas. And the sudras, according to their duty, served the other three castes. *Valmiki Ramayana* 18 (trans. Sattar)

For *brahmins*, learning the sacred literature and performing rituals is the sacred duty, *dharma*. For *vaishyas*, it is to do the laboring allotted to them and to buy and sell goods. For *sudras*, it is serving the other three castes. The ideal person is one who adheres to his or her own *dharma*, rather than attempting to perform the duties of another. There is no reward for "upward mobility," as the ultimate value comes in performing one's own sacred duty, even if one may be better at performing another's.

> It is better to perform one's own duty poorly than to perform another's well. By performing action that conforms to one's own nature, one does not accumulate guilt. Arjuna, one should not give up the work that one is born to do, even if it is harmful. For harm accompanies all our involvements, just as smoke accompanies fire. *Bhagavad Gita* 18.47–18.48 (trans. Thompson, modified)

The *sudra* who serves his masters perfectly following *dharma* is thus better than the *brahmin* who neglects his duties. Part of this is meant to support the caste structure. A *sudra*, for example, should not think that it is better to be a *brahmin* or a *kshatriya* than it is to be a *sudra*. A *sudra* would not be following *dharma* if he or she were to try to follow the duty of some other caste, pulling themselves upward. This, the Gita says, is the wrong way to think about things. We have a sense in the contemporary west that one's worth is largely based on one's class. It is "upward mobility" when one goes from poor to rich, low caste to high caste, suggesting that the person who does so has somehow bettered themselves. The *Gita* presents us with an alternative picture of self improvement. According to the Gita, to improve oneself and one's position is to more perfectly adhere to one's own *dharma*. One does not gain anything by changing caste, but by performing well the duty of their own caste.

## Inaction within action

Krishna's third response to Arjuna focuses on what will become a major theme for the rest of the *Gita*, and what is truly new and unique to this teaching. In performing his duty, Krishna instructs, Arjuna should relinquish *attachment to the fruits* of his actions.

> Be intent on action, not on the fruits of action, avoid attraction to the fruits and attachment to inaction! Perform actions, firm in discipline, relinquishing attachment; be impartial to failure and success—this

equanimity is called discipline. Arjuna, action is far inferior to the discipline of understanding; so seek refuge in understanding—pitiful are men drawn by the fruits of action. Disciplined by understanding, one abandons both good and evil deeds; so arm yourself for discipline—discipline is skill in actions. *Bhagavad Gita* 2.47–2.50 (trans. Thompson)

What does Krishna mean by this? Most things that humans do, we might observe, are done as means to certain consequences prized by the person. We go to work every day in order to make money, because money is necessary to gain the basic means of survival, and we also think money can be instrumental to our happiness. We do things with and for our friends because being with them will make us happy, or alternatively for the instrumental effect it has on our friends. Our actions are commonly *goal oriented*, in that they are performed to attain the most obvious and direct results of such action.

Krishna suggests something very different for performance of one's sacred duty. Even though our sacred duties have certain instrumental outcomes (Arjuna's duty to fight the Kauravas has as its aim, for example, the restoration of Pandava rule) in order to achieve realization of the *atman*, the highest goal of self-cultivation according to the thought of the *Gita*, one must relinquish attachment to the results of one's actions. One cannot, that is, engage in one's duties in order to attain some valuable result from these dutiful actions insofar as it concerns the world. If Arjuna performs his duty as a *kshatriya* and fights, but does so in order to enjoy the comforts of the kingdom, or even to rightfully restore the kingdom and thus attain justice, he is not acting in a way that will lead him to realization. Krishna explains that he must act out of duty alone, without concern for the results. This kind of action removes one from the worldly concerns that tend to keep one stuck in the karmic cycle of pleasure and pain, joy and suffering.

If we reflect on why it is we suffer, as well as why it is we feel pleasures (often *neurotic* and unstable pleasures—those who have lived long enough will recognize that sometimes the pleasures we feel are torturous, inherently stressful pleasures, pleasures without calm joy, manic pleasures that bring with them more suffering in the long run), we find that there are the results of certain actions. We strive to avoid or engage in certain types of action in order to attain the fruits of these actions or avoid pains connected with alternative actions. Our motivations surround the consequences of action, and our reasons for performing certain actions tend to lie only in this. Krishna's suggestion here, however, is that this is exactly why we suffer.

When we act without concern for the results of our action, we avoid the kind of natural stress that tends to come along with such concern with action and its success or failure. Why do we generally face the kinds of existential strife Arjuna feels on the battlefield concerning our actions? It is never usually because we are unsure of what our responsibilities are in a given circumstance (though there are separate questions about this). Arjuna knows exactly what he is *supposed* to do in the circumstances he is in. He knows his *dharma*. As a *kshatriya*, his primary responsibility is to protect and preserve the kingdom, and as such it clearly calls for him to fight.

Krishna suggests that we should act in a different way. We can, he says, act without attachment to the fruits of our actions. How do we do this? When we realize, he says, that this limited, illusory "*I*" actually does nothing, the various desires we attach to this illusory "I" vanish, and we no longer worry about the results of given actions insofar as they concern this illusory self. The *real* self, however, is above all results of actions in the world. As Krishna has already explained, the real self cannot be killed, and is not born, cannot be cut, injured, cannot suffer. The true self is the eternal subject, pure experience.

But what is the significance of this in terms of action, and specifically action consistent with one's *dharma*, or sacred duty? Krishna explains that the person who realizes the true nature of the self will necessarily act, because they understand the necessity of action for all beings. Such a person will see that performance of one's sacred duty without concern for the fruits of action is the way to liberation from the suffering inherent in delusion of the world. One who acts in the proper way performs action *as a sacrifice*, in devotion to Krishna, or, more properly, the universal spirit (*Brahman*) he represents.

But why, we might wonder, is the performance of *dharma* necessary here? If we realize that the conventional self is ultimately not real, and that we find true joy in action without attachment to the fruits of action, made in sacrifice through devotion to Krishna, why shouldn't *any* action done in such a manner suffice, rather than just those actions specified as our duties (because of conventional features such as birth, communal roles, etc.)? These are all features of the *jiva*, the ultimately unreal conventional "I," so how can these features carry any normative weight? That is, how can the duties I gain through these conventional features be relevant to how I, the *atman*, should act?

There are a few different ways a proponent of the thought of the *Gita* might answer this question. First, one might respond that the *atman* in itself does *not* act. It is pure consciousness alone, and separate from action. Only the *jiva* acts. So the norms that constrain and guide our action then are linked to features of the *jiva* rather than the *atman*. The reasons to act consistently with our *dharma*, then, have to be independent from our reasons to act without concern for the fruits of action. The idea is that if we act *otherwise* than the ways our *dharma* specifies, we are necessarily acting from attachment to the fruits of action. We have a roadmap that tells us what to do, and the only reason for straying from this would be because we choose to do some other action. But what reason could we have for choosing some other kind of action? Could we choose this completely randomly, or irrationally? We only make choices given certain reasons, and if we realize the truth about the self then we would have no reason to desire actions not cohering with our *dharma*.

There is another response available as well, suggested by something Krishna says in Chapter 3:

> In the three worlds, there is nothing I must do, nothing unattained to be attained, yet I engage in action. What if I did not engage relentlessly in action? Men retrace my path at every turn, Arjuna. These worlds would collapse if I did not perform action; I would create disorder in society, living beings would be destroyed. *Bhagavad Gita* 3.22–3.24 (trans. Miller)

Proper action, Krishna says, is necessary in order to keep the world in motion. If people do not follow their *dharma*, the society and the world in general will be thrown into disorder. Even Krishna himself must act, to sustain the existence of the world as a whole. Since this is the case, one must perform one's *dharma* as part of the activity of sustaining the order of the world. Neglecting one's *dharma* and acting in a different way will lead to disorder and chaos, and will make it more difficult for one to free oneself from attachment to the fruits of action.

One key objection may occur to some readers at this point. Does this account of duty suggest an objectionable tyranny of some classes over others? If one is in the position of a servant, the *Gita* seems to suggest that one should not try to better one's position, but instead be content with performing one's duties as servant, even if one has the talent to be a better leader, priest, or warrior than those in society who actually perform these roles. This kind of stifling social system, one might think, represents the worst kind of oppression of its members, especially those unfortunate enough to be born in the lowest classes.

One possible way to respond to this objection is to allow for some amount of mobility. In some class-based systems such as that advocated in the *Gita*, there is a conception of justified class mobility, and class based on natural quality. In the system recommended by Plato in his *Republic*, for example, he suggests the construction of a caste system very much like that of ancient Indian society, with rulers, warriors/guardians, merchants, and servants. Membership in a class, however, is not to be determined by the mere fact of birth from parents of a certain class. Rather, class membership, on Plato's account, is to be determined by the natural features demonstrated by individuals. The child of servant parents, for example, might demonstrate early ability in complex thought, and thus manifest the qualities of a ruler. This child could be moved to the class of rulers.

The *Gita* itself in some places seems to suggest this kind of enlightened view of caste movement, when it attributes features of caste duty to the nature of persons. Brahmins (priests), for example, are said to naturally have "serenity, self-control, austerity, purity, patience, honesty, as well as knowledge and discrimination, and religious faith ..." (*Gita* 18.42). It is hard to plausibly argue that such features of nature can be transmitted through genetics, such that the child of a Brahmin, for example, will necessarily have children with the qualities of a Brahmin. It does not take much experience of the world to recognize that children sometimes have very different qualities than their parents. The child of an unintellectual athlete can have a child who turns out to be an unathletic scholar, and vice versa. Thus, if class membership is fixed by natural qualities, we should expect lots of movement back and forth.

Other passages in the *Gita*, however, seem resistant to the possibility of class mobility. One must stay in the class one is born into, *even if* one is better at the duties of those in other classes. This seems to be just what 18.47 is claiming—even if one is better at the duties of a *kshatriya*, if one is born into the class of servants, one should perform the duties of a servant. We might imagine that there is a basic inconsistency here in the position of the *Gita* on class structure and duty. While it can be very enlightened and plausible in some areas on the idea of natural features and differences, in other areas it seems to be harsh and oppressive, lending ideological support to a fundamentally unjust social system. Such a fundamental contradiction must be left to stand, like many other things in the *Gita* and elsewhere. We might take this to represent two different strains in ancient Indian culture, both evidenced in this syncretistic and pluralistic text. One of the remarkable things about the *Gita* in general is its attempt to and ability to synthesize the many different religious and philosophical viewpoints and schools of thought in its day, bringing them into a more or less consistent system meant to transcend them all. This must be seen as part of the purpose of Krishna's full revelation of himself in Chapter 11, which will be discussed in Section 5 below.

# Discipline—knowledge, action, and devotion

According to the *Gita*, the highest kind of action, done without concern for the fruits of action—the inaction within action considered above, is the highest kind of discipline (*yoga*). This Sanskrit word *yoga* carries conjures a particular image for many westerners that it would for the authors of the *Gita*. When many in the west think of "yoga" they imagine people in a gym stretching and contorting themselves into flexible poses on exercise mats. The term *yoga* is used for this activity because in general every type of profession, activity, or pursuit was taken to be tied with some *yoga*, which is a more general action term, and certain groups who popularized in the west the kinds of physical exercises some sadhus and renunciants engaged in adopted the term for their mode of meditative exercise. The term *yoga* in Indian thought has a wide range of uses, then, but is always employed to talk about some form of activity—similar to the term "discipline" in English. We can speak of *disciplines* in the university: some people engage in the discipline of physics, while I engage in the discipline of philosophy, etc. In the *Gita*, *yoga* has a more specific technical use. Although it does still stand for "discipline" in the above sense, it more importantly signifies action that constrains the will of the individual, both taming and liberating him or her from concerns connected with action. It is a happy coincidence for translators of the *Gita* that this use of *yoga* is also echoed by a similar use of the English "discipline." One sense of "discipline" is ordering—a regimen of action, guidance, or other means to control important aspects of our psychology and behavior. To act in a disciplined manner is to act in a careful and mindful way, maintaining control over one's actions and mental states. Indeed, the word *yoga* derives from *yuj*, which means "to yoke or tie up." Through discipline, one ties up one's mind, controlling and subduing it, in order to gain liberation.

How is this supposed to work? One might question this move right away. If we are aiming to gain liberation, how does putting *more* control on our minds through acting in the specified *dharmic* manner without attachment to the fruits of our action help? Doesn't it seem like common sense that this would tend to move us *away* from liberation? Any liberation that consists in our constrained action, not only such that we have no choice over our own actions, but also that we cannot even take enjoyment in the results of our actions, must ultimately be considered a path to self-oppression rather than self-liberation.

But we can think more deeply about this. Is it really so that more choice, more freedom to act outside constraints, more options, liberates us from existential strife, from pain and grief? We need not rely only on a consideration of Arjuna's dilemma to see that such a view is problematic. Think of examples that come up all the time in our contemporary society. Often times, the more choice we have, the more miserable we become. All of us *think* we prize choice, until we get it. When there is only one school possible for us to attend, we go right forward and attend. When the only profession we can possibly succeed in is clear and lying before us, we go this direction, without worry. What other choice do we have? But what happens when we have choice? What if we get into Harvard *and* Oxford? What if we could be an astronomer, pro boxer, or firefighter? Choice is hard, and brings with it responsibility, stress, and doubts that we simply don't have when there is one clear option for us. Choice is inherently *stressful*.

There is another problem with choice, closer to Arjuna's own problem at the beginning of the *Gita*. There is an *ethical* problem with choice. When we have a clear duty, and this duty both specifies what action we should take as well as gives us an identity, we can perform our duty as an expression of what we are, *because* this is what we are and it flows from our nature, rather than performing our duties with the aim of attaining certain consequences. We see that the world often problematizes our attempts to gain certain results from our actions. If it is my duty to ensure the safety of the state, then I fail in my duty if my attempts to ensure the safety of the state fail. Thus, if the results of action are part of my duty, I will necessarily be in a kind of psychic distress concerning my duties. The situation in the world could make it such that not only do I fail in my duties, but I *necessarily* fail in my duties. The possibility of devastating earthquakes that I cannot control or do anything about, for example, makes it the case that I cannot perform my duty.

And there is another part of this general problem. If my duties include the consequences of my actions, then there is the possibility that my duties could conflict with other duties. This is Arjuna's dilemma in the beginning of the *Gita*. His duty to fight to regain the kingdom conflicts with his care for and his responsibility not to harm his friends and relatives who are members of the Pandavas. Because he is concerned at first with the *results* of action (the death of friends and relatives in the Pandavas vs. the regaining of the kingdom), he is brought to a point of existential crisis. Either decision leads to negative results (either he fights and regains the kingdom but kills relatives and friends, or he saves relatives and friends but does not fight and thereby loses the kingdom). *Neither* option is right, if what makes an action right is the moral value of its consequences.

This is a problem one can raise with all kinds of consequentialist theories of right action. A *consequentialist* theory is one that takes the rightness of an act to be based on some quality of the consequences of the act. It often happens, however, that the consequences of all actions available to us at a given point are bad ones. And even worse, in cases like this one, all of the actions available have *equally bad* consequences. A consequentialist would have grounds for action even if every action produced bad consequences as long as one option produced *less bad* consequences than the others. But one of the special features of Arjuna's case (and many that occur in real life) is that there seems to be no ground for deciding which consequences are worse. Is it worse to kill one's friends and relatives or to through inaction allow one's state to fall? These are both among the worst things we can think of. Any attempt to order these consequences in terms of better or worse would ultimately have to be arbitrary.

We are often, more often than many ethical theorists would like or care to admit, in situations in which we are faced with *no right choice*, and a number of options that are as bad as one another. In such situations, we seemingly have no moral grounds from which to choose. But then how can we act? Krishna suggests that action performed in *sacrifice* answers this problem. We can, through discipline, perform our actions as sacrifice, in devotion to the divine.

If we reconsider the concept of *dharma*, or sacred duty, discussed above, we see that each of us has only one real choice in any given situation. Although there may be a conflict between actions all of which are wrong in some external sense, there will always be a single option that coheres with our own sacred duty. In Arjuna's own case, the situation is likewise. While each of his options might be wrong in a consequentialist sense, only one option coheres with his *dharma*—taking up the fight to defend the kingdom. But how can Arjuna *discipline* himself through this act?

When we adhere to our *dharma* in the right way, Krishna argues, we escape the implicit psychic distress associated with action, and liberate ourselves from the suffering inherent in attachment to action and its results. Thus, we should engage in our *dharma* in a detached manner, committed to its performance only because it is our sacred duty, and not for desire for the results of the action. But why should we do this? And how can this possibly help?

Krishna explains to Arjuna that, regardless of what he chooses, action will happen. The people Arjuna is avoiding fighting will be killed, and there is nothing Arjuna can do to stop this. The physical causal mechanism of the universe has been set in motion, and no one can stop it. Thus Arjuna can either resist, based on attachment to the fruits of action, and suffer, or commit to performing action consistent with *dharma* as sacrifice and thus liberate himself from such concerns. The idea of physical determinism is relevant here. What Krishna says brings him very close to a contemporary view about the state of the universe—that all events are completely determined by prior states of the universe. The physical state of things at this instant is the causal result of the state of things at all previous moments of the system. The physical system of the universe, that is, is closed under causation. Notice that this leaves no room for things like agent causation based on free will. If our will is free, it cannot be caused to act in the way it does, because to be caused is not to have had the ability to be otherwise—causation involves necessity. Krishna thus seems to be suggesting something like physical determinism.

If, then, physical determinism is true and one ultimately has no choice about which actions will happen and which will not, how can it be relevant to talk about choosing actions in any sense? Isn't Arjuna's crisis, his depression, his inability to fight, and all of this determined? Krishna answers *no*. Although *acts* are determined, our *mental state* is not determined. This is the true choice one has—how our minds react given certain actions. We can act in such a way as to be attached to the fruits of our actions, or we can act in a way such that our minds are focused on devotion and sacrifice to the divine, to Krishna.

Arjuna, the lord resides in the heart of all creatures, making them reel magically, as if a machine moved them ... Relinquishing all sacred duties to me, make me your only refuge; do not grieve, for I shall free you from all evils. *Bhagavad Gita* 18.61, 18.66 (trans. Miller)

This is a radical claim, and one at the heart of the *Gita*. What is it that truly makes us suffer, the *Gita* asks. Is it a bad physical situation? Do we suffer because of pain, not enough food, the death of loved ones, the failure of our actions? It cannot be these things in themselves that cause us to suffer, because rocks do not suffer when they are punched, things without reflective minds like flies do not suffer when genetically related flies die. What is it about these acts that causes us to suffer? It is, of course, how they affect the *mind*. What suffers is the mind. But the mind, we see, is not constrained by physical determinism in the way described above. The mind is the only part of the person that is, or at least *can be* truly free. Whether one is in pain or a loved one dies—these things are physically determined, and one can do nothing about them. They are necessary, and caused. But the state of one's mind given these actions—this is not determined. I can, through attachment to the world, grieve and suffer on the death of a loved one, or I can, understanding that, as Krishna explains in Chapter 2, what is truly important and central to this loved one, the *atman* or self, cannot be destroyed and continues on, remain in equanimity, my mind restrained from attachment. And in addition to freedom from suffering, we gain another positive quality through abandoning attachment to the fruits of action—*skill* in action.

This claim is not so startling when we consider our own experience. Often, we become anxious and suffer because of anticipation of the results of certain future acts. I have seen it to be the case in job interviews, for example, that candidates can sometimes be so nervous about doing badly that this ends up *causing* them to do badly. Why is this? Krishna might explain it by saying that these people are attached to the fruits of action. They have such a strong desire to get the job (result of the interview) and a fear of not getting the job that their minds are in turmoil because of this attachment. And of course, anyone with such a rattled mind will not be able to perform as well as someone with a calm and clear mind who can focus and bring a calm, one-pointed energy to bear on the task at hand. The person who is too attached to the outcome of the interview will never be able to do this. Her attachment is too great, and she will be a nervous wreck worrying about the possibility of failure. The person who abandons the fruits of action, however, and goes through the interview out of a sense that it is his duty, will perform much more effectively. This person is not worried about whether or not he gets the job; rather, he is focused on performing his duty as well as he can. If he fails, it is of no consequence—what matters is how well he did his duty given his abilities. The only way they can fail in this is to not exert the proper energy or have the right motivations. It is completely *internally* dependent. Whether or not I succeed in doing my duty is totally up to me. When one is attached to the fruits of actions, however, whether or not one succeeds is *externally* dependent. No matter how hard a person tries, he or she still may fail to get the job, still may fail to defend the kingdom. But, as Krishna points out, what ultimately determines suffering or joy is our *internal* state. Over this we have full control. Indeed, it is only this over which we truly have any control at all, and it is only this that determines our freedom.

Thus, we should discipline ourselves away from this attachment to the external through acting *in devotion* consistently with our *dharma*. It is not action consistent with *dharma* alone that leads to liberation from suffering, although such action is certainly involved. How, that is, does one eliminate attachment to the fruits of actions? It might be easy to say or even agree to the view that one should relinquish such attachment, but it it possible to actually do it? There are strong biological impulses to certain activities. How can we sever the link between hunger, pain, and suffering? Eating and satiety? Sex and pleasure? We intrinsically take joy in certain actions, and there are certain evolutionary facts that explain this. We enjoy sexual activity, for example, because such enjoyment helped to perpetuate the human species. Had our ancestors not enjoyed this act, we would not be here, and the asexual variants of humans would have died out long ago due to failure to produce progeny. The same goes with our attachment to other pleasurable acts, like eating and being social, and for our distress at unpleasurable things like pain, hunger, strife, etc.

There are a couple of responses that can be made to this. First, we have to distinguish between *pleasure* and *joy*. One can have various pleasures and pains, yet not be *attached to* or psychically "weighed down" by these pleasures and pains through attachment. The person who has relinquished attachment to the fruits of action still feels pain when he or she is cut or hit, still feels pleasure when he or she eats or has sex. The difference between this person and one attached to the fruits of action, however, is that this person is not disrupted by pleasure and pain. This person is not captivated by it such that he or she aims at attaining pleasure or avoiding pain. Such a person is equanimous concerning the two. It is only such a person who can truly endure pain and truly enjoy pleasure. He or she possess a calm joy that comes from liberation from the concern with pleasure and pain. He or she still feels it, but is not attached to it. This is true joy, as opposed to pleasure. Second, one might say that the reason that we tend to have such attachment to these states is not due to any biological necessity, but simply due to the lack of mental and meditative constraint through action via sacrifice that Krishna recommends. The fact that most people *do* in fact have certain attachments does not show that it is the natural state for humans, any more than the fact that most actual bodies of water on earth have some dirt in them show that dirt is a natural part of water (it isn't, as $H_2O$).

But, if it is possible to bring ourselves to a state of equanimity and relinquish our attachment to the fruits of action, how do we do this? It certainly can't be as easy as just accepting that such relinquishing is beneficial and then doing it. These attachments are strong and built up over many years, perhaps even many generations. Krishna proposes that the way to do this is through *devotion*, and acting as sacrifice to the divine.

Focus your mind on me, let your understanding enter me; then you will dwell in me without doubt. If you cannot concentrate your thought firmly on me, then seek to reach me, Arjuna, by discipline in practice. Even if you fail in practice, dedicate yourself to action; performing actions for my sake, you will achieve success. If you are powerless to do even this, rely on my discipline, be self-controlled, and reject all fruit of action. Knowledge is better than practice, meditation better than knowledge, rejecting fruits of action is better still—it brings peace. One who bears hate for no creature is friendly, compassionate, unselfish, free of individuality, patient, the same in suffering and joy. Content always, disciplined, self-controlled, firm in his resolve, his mind and understanding dedicated to me, devoted to me, he is dear to me. *Bhagavad Gita*, 12.8–12.14, (trans. Miller)

Why do we do the things that we do? We aim at the production of certain actions, so we can enjoy the results. But what if we act for a different reason? Given the complete physical determination of all acts, we can act with a sense of responsibility, of performing our role in the universal drama as a way of devoting ourselves to the divine intention. We can see Krishna's action, the action of *Brahman*, as that of the entire cosmos. *Brahman* is the *universal* spirit. The realization that brings the person full liberation is that *atman* is ultimately *the same as Brahman*—that the individual is literally part of the eternal and universal action of Krishna. Devotion to Krishna, then, is an inner acceptance of what one truly is. It is a recognition and appreciation of one's role as part or identified with the divine universal spirit that moves and controls, and in part *is*, all things.

# The living universe—Krishna's revelation and its impact

It was a multiform, wondrous vision, with countless mouths and eyes and celestial ornaments, brandishing many divine weapons. Everywhere was boundless divinity containing all astonishing things, wearing divine garlands and garments, anointed with divine perfume. If the light of a thousand suns were to rise in the sky at once, it would be like the light of that great spirit. *Bhagavad Gita* 11.10–11.12, (trans. Miller)

In chapter 11 of the *Gita* Krishna reveals himself in his true form, as this universal spirit, *Brahman*, which comprises and consists of the entire cosmos. What happens in this revelation, which can be seen as the climactic event of the entire *Gita*, is instructive for our understanding of the *Gita*'s view of self-cultivation.

The view of the divine presented in the *Gita* is very much unlike what we see in much of western (including Islamic) religion. "God" here, if this is a proper word for the universal spirit, *Brahman*, is unlike the benevolent and loving father figure we see in Christianity or the just and merciful master we see in Islam and Judaism. *Brahman*, first, is not a father or a mother at all. The Indian tradition has tended to understand the divine in a non-paternal way, differing from the western religious traditions who fairly uniformly see God as father, ruler, master, or head of household. In the *Gita*, God, or the universal spirit, is represented in the form of Krishna, who serves as Arjuna's charioteer. Krishna is conventionally just a warrior-ruler of the distant kingdom of Dvaraka, who on the basis of his skill and wisdom becomes an advisor to the Pandavas and Arjuna's chariot driver in the battle of Kurukshetra. Krishna is also, however, an incarnation of Vishnu, according to the tradition (and the *Mahabharata*), who is a manifestation of God as *preserver*. In the Hindu tradition consolidating around this time, there are three major deities, who some argue represent three Gods (polytheism), and others argue are representative of manifestations of a single divine entity in different forms (henotheism). I will not take a stand on that issue here. What is clear and uncontroversial enough is that the tradition holds that there are incarnations, or *avatars*, of the various Gods, gods represented in human form for some divine purpose on earth. This view of incarnation is shared with the Christian tradition, which takes there to have been a single *avatar* (of a single God), Jesus Christ.

The three major gods (or aspects of God) in the tradition are Brahma, who is called "the creator," Shiva, "the destroyer," and Vishnu, "the preserver." If we think of the three as related to the events of the world, we see that these forces appear to be the basic components of the entire cosmos. All change, motion, growth, and decay happen on the basis of creation, preservation, and destruction. Even relatively ordinary actions like the movement of an arm involve these three aspects. Creation of motion, which is caused by intention, preservation of motion, and destruction, when the arm stops, caused by a distinct intention. These three forces, according to the tradition, are present and necessary in all aspects of the life of the universe.

Krishna is an avatar of Vishnu, the preserver, and his divine purpose on earth is related to the events of the *Mahabharata* and the *Gita*. As preserver, he instructs Arjuna to fulfill his sacred duty, to preserve the integrity of the kingdom of Bharata. More generally, through the *Gita* Krishna instructs *all of us* in the way of correctly adhering to our sacred duty such that we can achieve liberation from the kind of existential distress Arjuna finds himself in at the beginning of the *Gita*.

The understanding of God, or the divine, we see throughout the Hindu tradition, then, differs from that of the father or ruler figure of the western traditions. God is represented in the *Gita* as *teacher*, friend, and ultimate *guru*. The idea of the *guru* itself is of central importance in the Hindu tradition, and God is often represented as the *guru* of all *gurus*. So what is a *guru*? The term in Sanskrit translates literally to "teacher," but a *guru* is more than simply a teacher in the way most of us in the west understand it. A guru is not one who gives lectures or drills a classroom of students in the alphabet, calculus, or history. Rather, a guru is a close spiritual confidante, who understands one's character, identity, and most importantly *dharma*, and who guides a person to try to understand the divine truth and his or her own *dharma*. As Arjuna's case shows us, we do not always *know* our own sacred duty, either because we are ignorant, or because (as in Arjuna's case), our minds are too clouded by emotion, attachment, or some other psychological barrier. The *guru*, as ideally one who is realized and understands the cosmos in the way Krishna explains it in the *Gita*, can guide us to proper understanding and self-realization through his or her own experience.

We can see, therefore, it is critical for the *guru* to him or herself be liberated, to possess the experiential knowledge and realization that he or she guides us to seek. In the Indian tradition, there is a strong focus on the realization of the spiritual teacher that can sometimes seem odd for those not familiar with the tradition. One might think, when first confronted with this view, "why does one need to be liberated in order to be a spiritual teacher? Can't one understand *how* to gain liberation without actually being liberated him or herself?" That is, to require that a *guru* be liberated might seem like requiring that a football coach be himself a top-level player. There are plenty of coaches who were never (and certainly not while they are a coach) players of that level, yet are fantastic coaches who lead their teams to championship after championship. Doesn't this undermine the Indian view of the *guru* as necessarily being liberated?

This objection, however, misses a key feature of the notion of the *guru/* student relationship. The *guru* is not like a coach, who tells the players what to do and urges them on when they are on the field. Rather, the *guru* works more as an *exemplar*. The student models his or her own activity in mind and body on that of the *guru*, and in this way gains an understanding that cannot be fully explained through words. Think of learning to play an instrument. The music instructor is a better analogy to the *guru* than is the coach. In order to learn my instrument well, I not only have to be *told* what to do, how to play it, where to put my fingers, but I have to see how a person who *knows* how to play the instrument does it, and model their action. If my music instructor understands what one needs to do to play the flute, for example, but cannot herself play the flute, she will be of no help to me. I need an exemplar to model—someone to show me the movements and the postures so that I might try to duplicate them and eventually make the right sound and discover how to produce the sought sound. The music instructor is not doing it *for* me, but in order to be able to accurately guide me, she needs herself to be able to play (and to be good at playing!) her instrument.

The *guru* works similarly. This person, as liberated, can help guide us to the state of liberation ourselves. And Krishna, as *avatar* of the universal spirit itself, is the ultimate *guru*—he is not only realized, but *is realization itself*.

In chapter 11 of the *Gita* Krishna reveals himself in his full form, as the universal spirit. And what he reveals is not what one might expect. In the western religious tradition, God is often represented as having the fullest of the *positive* qualities, such that God is all *powerful*, all *loving*, all, *just*, etc. God only represents the "good" things. This, of course, creates a couple of difficult problems in these traditions. First, if God is only identified with good things and qualities, where does evil come from? Since God is all just, injustice must be completely separate from his nature. Since God is all loving, hatred must be completely separate from his nature. In some corners of the western tradition, this consideration led thinkers to posit another deity in nature, who creates and represents *negative* qualities. The Manichaeans, Zoroastrians, and many Christian sects, for example, take this route, positing a "demon" anti-God who actively works against God. In some Christian sects, this entity is called the "Devil," and has (as it *must* have to solve the problem) a negative power of its own. If God is the source of only the good and positive, the source of the evil and negative must be the Devil. Such a view, however, presumably violates the monotheistic nature of Christianity, and these forms of Christianity might be more accurately called polytheistic.

In addition, such a view of God as only possessing and responsible for good and positive qualities creates a problem commonly referred to as the "problem of evil." We observe that evil and negative things, obviously, exist. Evil actions happen with regularity, perhaps even more often than good acts, and bad things abound in our world. If God has the property of being all-powerful and the property of being completely good, however, then it seems inconsistent with his nature that evil and negative things exist at all. And if we claim, as the western theistic traditions do, that God is solely responsible for the creation of the universe and all of the things in it, we have to conclude that not only does God exist inconsistently with things of evil nature in the universe, but that God *created* these evil things in the universe. But why would an all good and loving God create evil and horrible things? This is a contradiction. If God created such things, this shows that his nature cannot be all good and loving. Alternatively, if God truly does have a nature all good and loving, it cannot be the case that things that appear to be evil are actually so. That is, there is a fundamental inconsistency between the idea of God being all good and loving and the sole agent of the universe's creation and the existence of evil. This problem has endured throughout the history of the western religious traditions, even to today, with many theologians, philosophers, and others spending vast intellectual resources to try to solve it.

The God represented in the *Gita* does not have either of these problems. There is no problem of evil or need for an "anti-God" in the *Gita*. Krishna's revelation in chapter 11 shows why.

> I see your boundless form everywhere, the countless arms, bellies, mouths, and eyes; Lord of all, I see no end, or middle or beginning to your totality. I see you blazing through the fiery rays of your crown, mace, and discus, hard to behold in the burning light of fire and sun that surrounds your measureless presence. You are to be known as supreme eternity, the deepest treasure of all that is, the immutable guardian of enduring sacred duty; I think you are man's timeless spirit. I see no beginning or middle or end to you; only boundless strength in your endless arms, the moon and sun in your eyes, your mouths of consuming flames, your own brilliance scorching this universe. You alone fill the space between heaven and earth and all the directions; seeing this awesome, terrible form of yours, Great Soul, the three worlds tremble. *Bhagavad Gita* 11.16-11.20 (trans. Miller)

The universal spirit is, *literally*, the universal spirit. And what Arjuna finds when Krishna reveals himself in his true form is that although this form is wondrous and beautiful, it is at the same time horrific and terrifying. The *Gita* does not flinch in the face of the horrors of the world. Indeed, it is these horrors, as much as the pleasures and joys, that we must transcend to achieve liberation. The world is a harsh and often vicious place as much as it is a benevolent and supportive one. The sun gives us warmth and life, making it possible for plants to grow, for our skin to get enough vitamin D, etc. The sun can also be a killer, poisoning us with UV rays, sapping us of precious water in the desert, and exacerbating the effects of drought. Water nourishes us and gives us life, but can also drown us or ruin our crops through flooding. No aspect of nature, let alone nature itself, is either fully good or fully evil, but *both*. How much less could the universal spirit itself exemplify only one of the two? The universal spirit creates, preserves, and destroys all things. It represents the entire cosmos, good and bad, right and wrong. It is the *essence* of all things—that which makes them what they are.

> Listen, Arjuna, as I recount for you in essence the divine powers of my self; endless is my extent. I am the self abiding in the heart of all creatures; I am their beginning, their middle, and their end ... Among trees, I am the sacred fig tree; I am chief of the divine sages, leader of the celestial musicians, the recluse philosopher among saints ...

> I am the thunderbolt among weapons, among cattle, the magical wish-granting cow; I am the procreative god of love, the king of the snakes ... I am the scepter of rulers, the morality of ambitious men; I am the silence of mysteries, what men of knowledge know. Arjuna, I am the seed of all creatures; nothing animate or inanimate could exist without me. *Bhagavad Gita* 10.1–10.39 (trans. Miller)

Krishna's revelation in Chapter 11 is of such evocative poetic power it has often captured the imagination of its readers. A famous instance of reference to part of Chapter 11 is that (reportedly) of J. Robert Oppenheimer when the first atomic bomb was detonated in a test in the desert of New Mexico. He reportedly spoke from a passage that has always been one of my favorites as well, for its expression of the universal spirit as destruction as well as creation: "Now, I am become death, destroyer of worlds."

The passage Oppenheimer is referring to is 11.32, which is useful to look at in its entirety, and in context.

> I am time, the agent of the world's destruction, now grown old and set in motion to destroy the worlds. Even without you, all of these warriors arrayed in opposing battle-formation will cease to exist! *Bhagavad Gita* 11.32 (trans. Miller)

God ultimately is our destroyer as well as our creator, Krishna says. If we attribute our generation and existence to God, how much more should we also attribute our inevitable demise to God? We can try to escape this basic truth of nature by denying that we die, instead positing that we live on in some holding area of heaven, but this is to stubbornly refuse to admit something we see in every moment, and which the Buddhists also understood: *everything that arises decays. Everything that comes to be ceases.* Every animal we observe dies, plants grow and then decay, events begin and end. Our entire experience teaches us that all things in nature eventually die. Science has taught us that even the things we previously thought most permanent in life, the stars in the heavens, themselves are born and die. It may even turn out that our universe itself will eventually come to an end. If God is responsible for the universe, then certainly God is responsible for this. God gives us life, and God takes life away. God is

our friend and our enemy. God helps us and harms us. God supports us and kills us.

Part of what the realization Krishna offers can do is to wake us to the truth of destruction, to the basic yet unrecognized truth that the universal spirit includes the horrific, and that we need to look directly at death, destruction, and evil, understanding them as manifestations of the universal spirit as well. It is only in this way we can overcome our attachment to the world and the fruits of our actions. The *Gita* is not offering us an easy, sentimental path, as some interpreters claim. Its vision is bold, tough, jarring, and magnificent. It is not for the faint of heart.

# The *yogi*, the realized soul

When he strives with great effort, the *yogi* becomes purified of his faults, and over the course of many births he becomes perfected. Then finally he takes the highest path. The *yogi* is considered superior to ascetics who practice austerity, superior to men of knowledge, and superior also to men of action. Therefore, Arjuna, become a *yogi*! But among all *yogis*, the one who places his faith in me, who devotes himself to me, who has gone to me with his inmost self—I judge him to be the most disciplined of all!" *Bhagavad Gita* 6.45–6.47 (trans. Thompson)

Now that we have some understanding of how one gains liberation, through action as sacrifice in devotion to Krishna, or *Brahman*, the universal spirit, through adherence to *dharma*, or sacred duty, we can consider what such a realized person, the end goal of self-cultivation in the thought of the *Gita*, is like.

The person who has attained liberation we might call a realized or liberated *yogi*, one who has engaged in *yoga* (discipline), and through it has gained freedom from attachment and the pleasure and pain, ups and downs, suffering attached to action. Such a person, as mentioned above, will certainly still have normal human experiences, and will feel pleasure and pain, excitement and boredom. Liberation is not a matter of having intrinsically different physical and mental experiences; rather, it is a matter of a spiritual awareness and existential distance not possessed by the unliberated.

So what is such a person, a liberated *yogi* like? If they feel pain on being stabbed, pleasure on quenching thirst, aversion to disagreeable things and attraction to the beautiful, just like the rest of us do, in what sense can we say they are different? It will be helpful here to think about specific cases. Imagine the case of a liberated parent, and also Arjuna's own case, that of a liberated warrior/defender.

In the first case, we might imagine there will be a very great difference between the liberated and the unliberated person. An unliberated parent, in his or her attachment to a child, will perform duties of parenting with an underlying dread and worry of his or her child being harmed, which sometimes might even get in the way of the ability to do his or her duty. Sometimes, the duty of a parent calls for solidity in the face of terrifying possibilities—one may have to help one's child through a potentially fatal surgery or other procedure, for example. This kind of thing will be almost impossible for the attached parent to do.

But what are we saying? Isn't it part of being a good parent to have the kind of attachment to one's child that would make it nearly impossible to do such things? Thinking back to Confucius, we can imagine that he would say (and most of us might also be inclined to say) that a person who could liberate themselves from attachment to his or her child would not be a good parent at all. If one can remain with an equianimous mind in the midst of the suffering of his or her child, something has gone horribly wrong. This brings up the crucial question: is it *inhuman* to be liberated? How can this be the ideal state for a person if this makes one ethically abominable?

The *Gita* will answer that the liberated person in this case should not be seen as one who does not care or have some sense of attachment to his or her child: rather, it is a person who understands who and what his or her child *truly is*, and acts accordingly. The parent in the first case is distressed because of the possibility that the child might be harmed or even die. But the realized person understands the essence of what his or her child is cannot truly be harmed, and cannot die. Thus, while this person does care for the child and tries to prevent its death (as part of their *dharma*), his or her attachment to the child does not create such existential strife, because this person understands that the *atman* is neither born nor can it die.

There is, undoubtedly, some sense of impersonality to this system of thought. We might find it cold and distant, compared to some other systems, and rightly so. Ultimately, the liberated person *is* unattached to the world. But the price to pay for attachment to the world, as the Buddhists also point out, is the suffering inherent to this attachment, which recurs not only throughout one's life, but even into future lives. The classical Indian system, to a large degree, *is* anti-worldly. They propose not a different way of connecting with and understanding the world, but a way of *transcending* the world even while remaining within it—inaction within action, liberation from attachment, ultimate freedom of the *atman* from the physically determined jail of the world. It is, in sharp distinction from the thought of Confucius and Zhuangzi, other-wordly, making a distinction between and putting the focus on *spirit* rather than matter, a distinction that will be very familiar to readers of this book, and that is a dominant distinction throughout western thought, even down to the modern day (although the distinction is beginning to collapse in our society).

## Later Hindu thought on the *Gita*

The number of philosophical and religious schools who take the *Bhagavad Gita* as an authoritative text or who accept or otherwise adhere to the teachings of the *Gita* is enormous. Almost all Hindu sects and schools today accord a high position to the text, and many of these take the text to be the *most* important text of their tradition, as discussed above. This was not always the case, however. Historically there have been a number of different views on the text and interpretations of the text. These divisions remain down to the current day. Understandings of the *Gita* vary widely—some reading it as a full throated rallying cry for the conservative hierarchy in ancient India, some as primarily concerning warrior duty, some as a devotional text, and some even as a psychological treatise. Like the *Daodejing*, the *Bhagavad Gita* seems to be one of those texts that inspires almost as many divergent interpretations as it has readers. Indeed, this keeps with the spirit of the *Gita*, as an attempt to unite many paths to liberation into one.

## Advaita and Dvaita

One of the major differences between interpretive camps on the Gita was that between the *advaita* and the *dvaita* schools concerning the relationship between the self (*atman*) and the infinite spirit (*Brahman*). According to Advaita, which we considered above, *atman* and *Brahman* are ultimately identical, and the key to liberation is to come to realize this (understanding through experience). One thing that this entails, if the two are identical to one another, is that it is also the case that each *atman* is ultimately identical to all the other *atmans*. We believe that there is a distinction between our own selves and those of others—I am *me*, and she is *her*. But in actuality, such a distinction is only illusory. While we might have different conventional selves (*jiva*), including individuating features, our particular traits, etc., the *atman* that is the true self at the core of any person is ultimately the *same* as the one at the core of every other person, and which is also the infinite spirit itself.

Part of the difficulty with the Advaita picture of the relationship between individuals, *atman*, and the infinite spirit, is that their position engenders a host of logical problems. First, what does it mean to call individuals distinct, if the *atman* of each individual is identical? One cannot avoid the problem by attributing distinct features to the individual *jiva* of each person, because each of these *jiva* belong ultimately to the same *atman*. How do we distinguish the set of characteristics of one *jiva* from that of another, without resorting to arbitrary stipulation? If it is the *atman* that determines personhood, as the thing that remains through the various changes a person undergoes during life, then I should not be able to distinguish the connection between the current state of *my jiva* characteristics and the past or present state of *another's* from the connection between the current state of my *jiva* and the past state of my *jiva*. Absent an already present method of distinguishing *me* from *another*, we shouldn't be able to do this. But we can and do, and referring to the *atman* ought to be a way to make such distinctions, as it is supposed to be the sameness *atman* that explains how I can be considered the same person today I was as a one year old, even though every one of my physical and mental states today is distinct from those of the one-year-old years ago.

For these and other reasons, the Dvaita school rejected the Advaita position on the relationship between *atman* and *Brahman*. They maintained that each *atman* is distinct, that each individual has his or her own *atman*, thus avoiding the above problem. In addition, it is not the case, according to Dvaita, that the *atman* of the individual is identical to *Brahman*, although there is an important relationship between the two, and we can even say that *Brahman* is the basis or substance of each individual *atman*. *Brahman* comprises the essence of each *atman*. We might draw a similarity between the relationship between *atman* and *Brahman* and that between water and a wave. A wave is identical neither to the water in the sea nor the particular water that comprises it. When the wave dissipates, we can't point to the same collection of water and call this the same wave. The wave is thus something distinct from the water comprising it. Yet all there is to a wave is water—it is a certain water-event, a function of water. In this case, *atman* is like the wave, and *Brahman* like the water. Of course, the analogy is not perfect—a wave comes into and goes out of existence, whereas the *atman* is eternal, for example. But this does express how *atman* and *Brahman* are distinct, while it still being the case that *Brahman* is the ultimate nature of and basis of each *atman*.

We might ask: what is the relevance of this seemingly metaphysical speculation for the ethical questions with which we are concerned? Does one's view about the relationship between *atman* and *Brahman*, whether following Advaita or Dvaita, make a difference concerning one's position on the ideal life and how to attain such a life? It seems that it would. Think of the situation that would obtain if one accepts the Advaita position. This would entail that in realizing one's own *atman*, one thereby realizes the *atman* of everyone else who exists, and thus the *yogi*, the liberated person, gains a crucial insight into the workings of the entire universe. On the other hand, the Dvaita adherent might counter, if the Advaita view is correct, it should follow from this that if *I* gain liberation through realization of the *atman*, then *everyone* gains liberation. That is, the single *atman* that is the same in each person has gained liberation—so why does this liberation attach only to *me* as just one of the bearers of this *atman*? The Advaita response to this will have to be that it is not the *atman* that gains liberation—in a sense, the *atman* already *is* liberated. Rather, it is the person, the *jiva*, that can gain liberation through the realization of the facts about *atman* and *Brahman*, and the *jiva* is something that individuals have for themselves.

# Devotional schools; Vaishnava

The Dvaita school is connected to another very influential strain of thought that developed well after the time of the *Gita*, but is linked closely with one of the strands of the *Gita*. One understanding of the *Gita* took it to be primarily a devotional text, with Krishna teaching that the best and ultimately only way to liberation was through devotion to him. On the surface, devotion is clearly one of the ways Krishna discusses to achieve liberation in the *Gita*, but the proponents of the devotional interpretation also read the other ways as ultimately concerning devotion as well. The Hindu sect known as *Vaishnavism* represents the major strand of this devotionalist interpretation. Vaishnavas focus on devotion to and worship of the god Vishnu, who, according to their doctrine, is the preeminent and supreme deity of all the gods. As devotees of Vishnu, Vaishnavas also revere the incarnations of Vishnu, including his most famous incarnation, Krishna. There are some groups, however, who take Krishna to be an even more preeminent form of the deity than Vishnu, with Vishnu and other gods only representing aspects or forms of Krishna. One form of Krishnaist Vaishnavism well known in the west is the "Hare Krishna" movement, the International Society for Krishna Consciousness founded by Srila Prabhupada, whose nickname is derived from the refrain they chant, sing in devotional music, and repeat throughout their days. This is done, according to this school, as a part of devotion to Krishna. They believe that there is spiritual power in the recitation of Krishna's name, and that the highest act of devotion is to speak, sing, or otherwise voice the holy name in a heart of love for Krishna.

Groups like this read Krishna's discussion of sacrifice, *dharma*, action, and knowledge as all referring to aspects of devotion. The highest, purest kind of action is devotion to Krishna, and ultimately liberation is only possible through devotion. This is one way of understanding Krishna's discussion in later books of the *Gita* surrounding the differences between the way of renunciation and the way of action. Both of these ways can lead ultimately to liberation, but the way of action is more direct, as the realization that comes as part of sacrifice is the effective cause either way, but the way of action attains this much more directly. The advocate of devotion will make a similar claim concerning devotion. Liberation is ultimately caused by the state created by devotion, and all other ways to liberation work only insofar as they are able to generate the mind of devotion. What this entails is that, in order to become the ideal person Krishna discusses in the *Gita*, we must aim in all our actions at a mind of devotion to Krishna. What will make Arjuna's acts in the coming battle proper is not for them to adhere with external norms, but for them to be done as devotion.

# Gandhi's allegorical reading

Another group of interpretations of the *Gita* gives us a very different reading of the central aim of the text. Although Gandhi's interpretation is the most famous of this kind, a number of smaller schools and modern Hindu movements have adopted similar readings. Perhaps surprisingly, Mohandas (Mahatma) Gandhi, the early twentieth-century Indian leader and campaigner for human rights and the end of British rule in India, read the *Bhagavad Gita* as advocating pacifism. It is not surprising that Gandhi, perhaps best known in the west for his philosophical position of non-violent struggle, which he referred to as "*satyagraha*" ("commitment to truth"), would be committed to pacifism. But to hold that the *Gita* advocates pacifism, a text in which God himself commands Arjuna not only to fight and kill the enemy, but fight and kill his own relatives, seems rather farfetched at first. Certainly we require a good explanation for this seeming inconsistency.

According to Gandhi and other proponents of this reading, the claimed historical situation of the *Gita* is simply allegorical. The authors of the *Gita* did not intend to make a point about *dharma* as it pertains to fighting and killing the enemies of a state. Instead, we should understand the "enemy" Arjuna must fight as the negative tendencies in himself, delusion, hatred, and even violence. Thus, the Kauravas are a symbol of the negative spiritual and mental traits of humans, and Krishna's message to Arjuna is an exhortation for him to struggle against and ultimately overcome these negative traits. This interpretation thus psychologizes the message of the *Gita*. Rather than having to do with action in the world in any sense, the *Gita* should be taken as a treatise completely about the mind, and our encounters with and control over our own minds.

So what are these negative tendencies, and how do we rid ourselves of them by following the method recommended by Krishna in the *Gita*? He speaks there about *dharma*, action, devotion, etc. How does this translate into psychological terms? Some interpreters who offer the psychological reading take disciplined action to be a symbol for *meditation*. Through meditation and proper action, we can undermine the negative mental states that keep us from realization of the truth about *atman*, and thus ultimately from liberation. This reading brings the message of the *Gita* very close to that of some schools of Buddhism, especially those that stress the meditative and contemplative aspects of the path. In Gandhi's view, immoral and violent external action was caused by disharmony within the self, and the *Gita* taught the solution to this problem of disharmony. Through cultivation of dispassionate action as Krishna teaches, we can overcome this disharmony and truly thrive.

# Further resources on the *Gita* and self-cultivation

## Translations of the Gita

- Barbara Stoler Miller, *Bhagavad Gita*
- George Thompson, *Bhagavad Gita*
- Srila Prabhupada, *Bhagavad Gita As It Is*
- Buitinen, *Mahabharata*

## Secondary work on the Gita

## Films

- Mahabharata, dir. Peter Brooks

# A short biography of Vyasa and Shankara

It is impossible to link the *Bhagavad Gita* to a single author, given that we don't know the identity of the author(s) of the text, and given that the Gita, like the rest of the collected material that makes up the Mahabharata, cannot be justifiably attributed to a single person. Tradition has it that the sage Vyasa (sometimes also called Veda Vyasa) is responsible for the authorship of the entire Mahabharata, including the Gita, but this story is almost certainly mythical, as is Vyasa himself. The ancient Indian attribution of the Mahabharata to Vyasa is similar to the ancient Greek attribution of the epics *Iliad* and *Odyssey* to "Homer," another semi-mythical figure. All of these texts were likely the result of many decades and centuries of accretion of stories, passages, and styles, and are most properly attributed to the traditions themselves, the work of many authors in many periods, rather than a single figure like Vyasa or Homer.

Vyasa himself appears as a character in the Mahabharata. The text claims that Vyasa is an ancestor of both warring clans, and that he advises all parties to the war. The text claims that he witnessed the entire thing, and possessed special mystical insight which allowed him to chronicle the entirety of the Kurukshetra War and the surrounding events. Vyasa is said to be the father of both Dhritarashtra and Pandu (the heads of the two opposing clans in the *Mahabharata*), by two different women. Legend has it that Vyasa narrated the entirety of the *Mahabharata* (including the *Gita*) to Lord Ganesha (a popular Hindu deity), who transcribed his words into writing. This story seems to be of later origin than the rest of the *Mahabharata*, however. It is fairly clear that Vyasa himself is a legendary figure. In addition to the *Mahabharata*, some attribute authorship of the *Vedas*, the *Upanishads*, and the *Puranas* to Vyasa (the *Vedas* obviously present the most problematic case for adherents of certain schools, such as *Mimamsa*, as they are said to be eternal and authorless). Needless to say, any individual who could have authored all of the above mentioned texts would had a lifespan stretching more than a millennium.

We move to more stable historical ground when considering the life of the philosopher Shankara. Shankara was likely born in or around 788 CE, in the town of Kalady (in the modern day southern Indian state of Kerala). Apparently even since youth, Shankara had an interest in and talent for scholarship. Eventually, Shankara became a renunciant monk—a way of life long practiced and respected in India (see Chapter 3 on the Buddha)—and became the disciple of a teacher of the Advaita Vedanta philosophy, which Shankara would go on to popularize. Shankara's work on Advaita would become the definitive expression of Advaita philosophy throughout the rest of the history of Indian thought down to modern times, the most influential interpretation of the most influential school (Vedanta) in later Indian thought.

Shankara's demonstration of uncommon philosophical skill led his teacher to instruct him to write commentaries on the canonical texts and to teach Advaita doctrine and philosophy more broadly. During this period, Shankara wrote a number of commentaries, including his famous commentary on the *Bhagavad Gita*, which heavily informs contemporary understanding of the text. Most interpretations of the *Gita*, including the one I offer in chapter 4 above, are heavily influenced by Shankara's reading of the text. The Advaita principle of the ultimate unity and identity of *atman* and *brahman* (as opposed to the Dvaita view of their relationship) enjoys enormous influence mainly due to Shankara's work. Shankara continued to travel, teach, and engage in philosophical debates with representatives of rival schools, including famous exchanges with representatives of the rival *Mimamsa* school (scholars of duty and ritual), and the Jain school (a "heterodox" [i.e. non-Vedic] religious sect somewhat similar in their doctrines to the Buddhists).

After a life of teaching and philosophical debate, Shankara is said to have achieved final liberation and freedom of the soul from the body at Kedarnath, in the Himalaya mountains, around 820 CE.

## RELEVANT QUESTIONS

1   Is there moral value in the ability to choose one's own lifestyle as opposed to simply following a normatively specified role as suggested in the *Bhagavad Gita*? What reason is there to accept either of these views?

2   If the *atman* (the self) is something distinct from every individuating feature of a given human being, then why accept that it exists at all? How is it any more my self than your self? What could it possibly be if it has no individuating features? Why not just accept the Buddhist view that there *is no self*?

3   Is it possible to completely disengage the fruits of action while still engaging in an action? The Buddhists thought this was impossible, which is why they enjoined us to avoid certain actions. The *Gita* seems to accept the possibility of this. But could one really eat an amazing meal without feeling pleasure, or get into a fight without feeling anger or rage? Is it psychologically possible to be so removed from our actions?

4   Is it really *morally* proper to disengage from the fruits of action and concern for results in all cases? Might there not be certain roles that we could not adequately perform without attachment? Think of the role of a *parent*, for example. Is it really the case that a good parent should not be attached to his or her child, and should be unconcerned with the fruits of his or her parenting (ensuring the child remains and grows into a well-adjusted and healthy person), instead simply being satisfied with doing his or her duties regardless of the outcome?

5   If we are physically determined, why think that our *selves* and our capacity for choice are not so determined? And how can the *Gita* possibly defer to the *atman* to explain this indeterminacy, given that the *atman* seems to be completely generic and distinct from the world?

6   How can one know whether a *guru* is authentic, without oneself being liberated or enlightened? Do you think the notion of the *guru* might be morally helpful?

7   What is the *moral* significance of the negative theism (that is, the view that God is responsible for both good and evil) of the *Gita*?

# Notes

1 It may be clear from what is said here I accept the "Enlightenment" view on the efficacy of "reason" for guiding us to truth, being up front about my own commitments!

2 Despite the fact that the contemporary nation of India uses this name, most of the length of the Indus river rests in current day Pakistan, with small pieces in India and China [Tibet].

3 University of Chicago press series—see suggested texts list at the end of this chapter.

4 Barbara Stoler Miller, whose excellent and poetic translation of the *Gita* is my own favorite, translates it as "infinite spirit."

# Conclusion: New Directions in Scholarship

**W**hile the main focus of this book has been to give an overview of four major texts and traditions in ancient Chinese and Indian philosophy, the areas of Classical Chinese, Indian, and comparative philosophy are today active research areas for an increasing number of specialists and other interested scholars in academia, both within philosophy departments and in other fields (most specifically departments of East or South Asian Studies, Religious Studies, History, and Political Science). There are a number of areas and issues in Chinese and Indian philosophy that are currently the subjects of intense focus by philosophers in particular. In this section, I give a brief overview of some of the work being done by scholars in the field.

## Chinese philosophy

Currently, most of the philosophical interest in Chinese philosophy centers on issues in Warring States thought, with forays into Song-Ming Neo-Confucianism as well. Chinese Buddhism has been an area of continuing scholarly and philosophical interest, although philosophical interest in this area seems to have waned in recent years, giving way to greater focus on later (post-*Analects*) Confucianism, Mohism, and Daoism (specifically Zhuangzi). Philosopher Eric Schwitzgebel has compiled a chart comparing the number of times the names of various Pre-Qin Chinese philosophers have been mentioned in philosophical scholarship since the 1940s. While in 1940 mentions of Confucius far outranked any of the others, today mentions of Confucius have fallen to a close second place behind Mencius, and attention to Zhuangzi has climbed from almost none to strong third place (you can see the chart and Schwitzgebel's discussion at http://schwitzsplinters.blogspot.com/2012/07/chinese-philosophy-discussion-arcs.html).

While the interest in Warring States philosophy continues to grow among specialists in Chinese philosophy as well as those working in other areas of philosophy, who are increasingly coming to see the importance and value of classical Chinese philosophy, there are a number of periods and thinkers within the tradition that are relatively neglected by western scholars. The rich philosophy of the Western and Eastern Han dynasties (206 BCE–220 CE) has long been overlooked by western scholars, for example. Work by recent scholars, including some of my own work, aims at enhancing the visibility of Han philosophy and demonstrating its importance and value.

The frontier of the field seems to be consideration of comparative issues, consideration of new periods and texts in Chinese thought, and also in a movement for cross-traditional comparison with other non-western traditions. New work on Chinese–Indian comparative philosophy has come to the fore in recent years, although, as with the increasing focus on non-Warring States philosophy, this project is still in its infancy.

In addition, an overarching attempt of most philosophers working in the area is to "mainstream" Chinese philosophy within the history of philosophy in general. In previous years and even through today, Chinese philosophy was seen as something external to the history of philosophy proper, an "alternative" and inessential tradition that may be of some interest for the curious, but nothing that any serious philosopher would need to know something about. Philosophical education in our graduate schools, for example, where new generations of academic philosophers receive their "formation," has never (and still does not) require instruction in any Asian philosophical tradition, text, or thinker. At the same time, much of the European/Western tradition is required learning, such as the classical Greek philosophical tradition (including Plato and Aristotle), Medieval European philosophy (although less so in recent years, perhaps due to the ineliminable "religious" quality of this tradition, not currently fashionable in philosophical circles), Modern European philosophy (including stalwart inclusions like Descartes, Locke, Hume, Mill, Kant, etc.), and contemporary western philosophy (both in the "analytic" and "continental" traditions).

Much of the work of "mainstreaming" Chinese philosophical thought is currently done by comparativists, who attempt to put classical Chinese philosophical thought in "dialogue" with contemporary western philosophy. Such comparativists are increasingly coming from all corners of the academic philosophy world. Although the project was started mainly by specialists in Chinese philosophy, an increasing number of specialists in other areas of philosophy are contributing to the comparative project in learning and then writing about Chinese philosophy in a comparative way, engaging with the ideas of the classical Chinese thinkers and developing their ideas in ways making them relevant to contemporary philosophical debates.

# Indian philosophy

For many years, and still today, a primary interest of philosophers engaging with classical Indian philosophical thought has been the philosophy of language and logic. A number of contemporary logicians, including Graham Priest and Jay Garfield, have written on issues in Buddhist, Jain, and Hindu logic and metaphysics, with an eye to importing the concepts of these traditions for use in contemporary thought. Indeed, recent developments in the philosophy of logic surrounding "non-classical" logics (such as many-valued logics, intuitionistic logics, etc.) have been inspired and assisted by the study of classical Indian thought on logic and language.

In addition to the "heterodox" schools of Buddhist and Jain logic, scholars are also looking to the schools of the "orthodox" darshanas, especially the Nyaya school and the Mimamsa school, for unique and interesting positions concerning language, especially the issues of meaning and truth, about which the Indian traditions have lots to say, and much that has been neglected in the western traditions.

Most contemporary work on classical Indian philosophy has surrounded issues in the philosophy of language, metaphysics, and epistemology, but more attention has been brought in recent years to ethics and political philosophy in the classical Indian tradition, an easily overlooked area but an important one stressed in the work of the Vedantins (as we saw in the examination of the Bhagavad Gita) and some of the other orthodox schools, such as the Mimamsa. Buddhist ethics has also seen a rise in interest in recent years, as attention to philosophical movements such as the Madhyamaka school of the Mahayana Indian tradition have shown that metaphysical quietism was often the aim of Buddhist philosophers, and that ethical cultivation should be seen as near the center of the Buddhist worldview.

# Comparative philosophy

Much of the scholarly interest (especially within philosophy departments) in Asian philosophy has surrounded the project of "comparative philosophy" generally. Although there are probably as many different conceptions of what comparative philosophy is as there are comparative philosophers, in general scholars who engage in work in comparative philosophy see themselves as bringing Asian thought (generally either classical Chinese, Indian, or Japanese) into dialogue with western thought, either contemporary or historical. The form this dialogue takes differs according to the particular project pursued. One popular recent comparative project has been to read the classical Confucians through the lenses of classical Greek philosophy, especially

Aristotle. This generally entails using the concepts and positions of Aristotle's philosophy to explain or illuminate features of Confucianism. In recent years it has become popular to think of Confucianism as a "virtue ethics," for example, where the conceptual basis and the vocabulary of virtue ethics originates with Aristotle's Nicomachean Ethics and Eudemian Ethics. These scholars for the most part see the central theme of classical Confucian texts (including the *Analects, Mengzi,* and *Xunzi*) as cultivation of virtues, understood roughly as states of character with positive moral value. Generally, those who read the early Confucians in this way (see the works by Sim, Yu, Angle, Van Norden in the bibliography) justify the project by referring to the ends. By understanding Confucianism in terms of virtue ethics, we might effectively use the insights of the Confucian tradition to enliven and contribute to the development of contemporary virtue ethics. The influence and benefit can run in the other direction as well—contemporary Confucianism, generally practiced and taken seriously as philosophical commitment in China, can benefit from the influence of Aristotelian and contemporary virtue ethics. Thus, "dialogue" between these two traditions, sometimes based on linking the two via what Aaron Stalnaker has called "bridge concepts" such as "virtue", which may be thought of as thinly specified concepts that might be filled out with thick descriptions by either tradition, the *arête* of Aristotle and the de of Confucius in the case of Confucian and Aristotelian ethics.

Part of the difficulty of reading the classical Confucians in this way is their seeming divergence from Aristotelian (and other) virtue ethics concerning crucial concepts like *phronesis* (practical wisdom). In their attempts to find a Confucian equivalent to this concept, some have turned to the idea of *yi,* but it is unclear that this will work, as the concept of yi has to be stretched almost out of recognition to make it fit effectively with Aristotle's account of practical wisdom. This leads some to suggest that, although in Confucianism we see a type of virtue ethics being presented, it is a virtue ethics very different from that of Aristotle. In contemporary ethics, there are a number of different non-Aristotelian virtue ethical theories, such as Michael Slote's "agent-based" virtue ethics. A number of comparative philosophers, including Steve Angle, draw on what they think are salient similarities between Confucian (or Neo-Confucian) ethics and Slote's virtue ethics to make the case for Confucianism as a virtue ethics.

There are a number of alternative views concerning Confucian ethics and its possible western counterparts. Perhaps the most famous alternative to the virtue ethical approach is Roger Ames' reading of Confucian ethics as what he calls a "role ethics." Ames has held such a view of Confucian ethics for many years, but the view is made most explicit and worked out in most detail in his recent work *Confucian Role Ethics: A Vocabulary.* There are also a number of philosophers, including Chenyang Li, who see a parallel between

Confucian ethics and the ethics of care formulated by thinkers in the feminist tradition of western philosophy, mainly in response to the dominance of "principle-based" ethics throughout much of modern and contemporary philosophical history.

The comparative project in terms of Chinese-western thought has been dealt most often with ethics and political philosophy, but there are also projects dealing with epistemology (normally the Zhuangzi, read in dialogue with western views of knowledge, including skepticism), metaphysics, and in more recent years philosophy of logic and language. Much of the recent work focusing on Later Mohist thought as well as the issues of language in Xunzi has imported the conceptual vocabulary of western philosophy of language and logic to understand early Chinese conceptions of meaning, truth, and other important concepts in logic and the philosophy of language. The students of Chad Hansen, an important contemporary philosopher dealing with issues of logic and language in early Chinese thought, including Chris Fraser and Dan Robins, have been most consistent in development of this project, although in recent years others have contributed to the development of this area of comparative research as well.

Comparative Indian-Western philosophy has also been a fruitful area in recent years, with scholars of the logical systems of the orthodox and heterodox systems making contributions to contemporary philosophy of language and logic, as mentioned above.

One new and very fruitful area for future development, suggested by this very book, is the area of Chinese–Indian comparative philosophy. As you have likely noticed, there are a number of key similarities between the central texts of the Chinese and Indian philosophical traditions. Just as the concepts and terms of contemporary western philosophy can be (and are) used to put this tradition into dialogue with the ancient Chinese or Indian traditions, the Chinese and Indian traditions can and should be brought into dialogue with one another, in order to further develop the concepts and ideas in each tradition. There is a rich history of engagement between the two traditions, most obviously through the link of Buddhism, which developed in India and became very influential on its transmission to China, mainly through the Mahayana schools. In later Buddhism, Chinese and Indian thought directly engaged one another, and the resulting philosophical systems, including those of Huayan, Chan (Zen), and Tiantai Buddhism, as well as the heavily Buddhist-influenced Daoxue (Neo-Confucian) movement of the Tang and Song dynasties, became the major influential philosophical systems of later Chinese history until the modern day. Given the deep links between Chinese and Indian philosophy (and culture in general), more attention should be paid to comparative Chinese–Indian philosophy, and more scholars are beginning to realize this in recent years. The comparative project here is not and should not be limited to Buddhism and Chinese thought, however. Buddhism itself grew from a rich tradition in Indian thought wholly independent of the Buddhist religion. Anyone with a knowledge of Buddhism will immediately recognize the concepts and ideas of Brahmanistic texts like the Upanishads, the epics including the *Bhagavad Gita*, and even the ancient Vedas. Insofar as Buddhist philosophy influenced Chinese thought, so did Brahmanist philosophy.

It is in the area of Chinese-Indian comparative philosophy that I expect much of the scholarship of the next half-century to develop, especially with the economic rise of China and India, and a growing consideration of people in both the west and east of their relationship with one another. It is an area where doubtless many surprises and treasure awaits. One of my hopes is that this book can help in some (however small) way to contribute to this important project.

# An Annotated Bibliography

## Confucianism

### *Primary sources*

There are a number of excellent translations of the *Analects* in print, but my three favorite, for their ease of use, philosophical sophistication, and fidelity to the Chinese text, are Ames and Rosemont's *The Analects of Confucius: A Philosophical Translation*, D. C. Lau's *Analects*, and Chichung Huang's *The Analects of Confucius*.

Good translations of Warring States Confucian works include Bryan Van Norden's *Mengzi: With Selections from Traditional Commentaries* and D. C. Lau's *Mencius*, as well as John Knoblock's *Xunzi: A Translation and Study of the Complete Works* (in three volumes), the only complete translation of the *Xunzi* in English. Selections can be found in Burton Watson's *Hsun Tzu: Basic Writings*.

### *Secondary material*

S. Angle, *Sagehood*
A consideration of the ideal of the *sheng ren* (sage) in Neo-Confucianism, and comparative study seeking to position the Neo-Confucian view as a viable alternative for contemporary philosophy.

S. Angle and M. Slote (eds), *Virtue Ethics and Confucianism*
New collection of essays by Western and Chinese scholars on the dialogue and similarities between the two ethical traditions.

R. Ames, *Confucian Role Ethics: A Vocabulary*
A concise and thorough statement of Ames' interpretation of Confucian ethics, as developed throughout his other works. For those interested in Ames' views, this is the best place to start, even though it is a more recent work.

H. G. Creel, *Confucius: The Man and the Myth*
Another oldie but goodie. Creel discusses the life and thought of Confucius, as well as evaluates his thought from a modern perspective.

M. Csikszentmihalyi, *Readings in Han Chinese Thought*
Excerpts from a number of Han dynasty texts, including philosophical texts.

H. Fingarette, *Confucius: The Secular as Sacred*
Originally published in 1972, this short book is still one of the best philosophical overviews of Confucius' thought, particularly for those with a background in the field.

P. R. Goldin, *Rituals of the Way*
Overview of Xunzi's thought. Especially insightful concerning *li* (ritual), its purposes and its source.

A. C. Graham, *Disputers of the Tao*
Benjamin Schwartz, *The World of Thought in Ancient China*
Two of the best one-volume histories of Pre-Qin Chinese philosophy available in English. Both a bit dated, but still very useful.

Y. Huang, *Confucius: A Guide for the Perplexed*
An up-to-date and excellent overview of Confucius' thought, drawing on developments in contemporary philosophy and comparative thought.

P. J. Ivanhoe, *Confucian Moral Self-Cultivation*
Short but excellent overview of the thought of the early Confucians and the Neo-Confucians on the issue of self-cultivation.

M. Sim, *Remastering Morals with Confucius and Aristotle* and J. Yu, *Confucius and Aristotle: Mirrors of Virtue*
Two works comparing the ethics of Confucius with Aristotelian virtue ethics, as found in the *Nicomachean Ethics* and *Eudemian Ethics*. Both read Confucius as an *Aristotelian* virtue ethicist, while others, such as Angle, see Confucianism as offering a virtue ethics more along the lines of that developed by Michael Slote.

K. Shun, *Mencius and Early Chinese Thought*
Scholarly overview of the thought of Mencius.

K. Shun and D. B. Wong (eds), *Confucian Ethics:*
Similar to Van Norden's collection, recent scholarly essays on the issue of Confucian ethical thought.

A. Stalnaker, *Overcoming Our Evil: Xunzi and Augustine*
Comparative study of Xunzi and the medieval Christian philosopher Augustine, surrounding the issue of the moral value of human nature. Stalnaker develops the comparative tool of the "bridge concept" here.

B. Van Norden, ed., *Confucius and the Analects: New Essays*
Excellent collection of essays featuring relatively recent scholarship on the *Analects*, and an extremely valuable annotated bibliography of work on the *Analects* through 1998.
—*Virtue Ethics and Consequentialism in Early Chinese Philosophy*
A study of early Confucianism and Mohism through the comparative lenses

of western "virtue ethics" (beginning with Aristotle) and consequentialist theories of right action.

# Daoism

## *Primary sources*

The two best translations of the *Zhuangzi* in English available are, in my opinion, A. C. Graham's classic *Chuang-tzu: The Inner Chapters* (for which Harold Roth has also written a companion volume: *A Companion to A. C. Graham's Chuang-tzu*), and Brook Ziporyn's more recent translation *Zhuangzi: The Esssential Writings with Selections from Traditional Commentaries*. For a complete translation of the *Zhuangzi*, see Burton Watson's *The Complete Works of Chuang Tzu*. In order to fully appreciate the thought of Zhuangzi, it is necessary also to have some understanding of the *Daodejing*. Good translations of this work include Ames and Hall's *Daodejing: A Philosophical Translation*, and D. C. Lau's *Tao Te Ching*. A later Han dynasty work that will also be of important in aiding one's understanding of Daoism, especially as it concerns political philosophy, is the *Huainanzi*, recently translated in full by John Major, Sarah Queen, Andrew Meyer, and Harold Roth.

## *Secondary material*

R. E. Allinson, *Chuang-tzu for Spiritual Transformation*

S. Coutinho, *Zhuangzi and Early Chinese Philosophy: Vagueness, Transformation, and Paradox*
Scholarly interpretation of Zhuangzi's thought, focusing on issues in metaphysics and the philosophy of language.

C. Hansen, *A Daoist Theory of Chinese Thought*
A still controversial interpretation of Early Chinese philosophy through the lenses of Hansen's unique view about the operation of the Classical Chinese language.

P. Kjellberg et al., *Essays on Skepticism, Relativism, and Ethics in the Zhuangzi*

L. Komjathy, The Daoist Tradition: An Introduction
An overview of Daoism dealing with concepts developed throughout its history, down to the current day. It ties together the philosophical and religious aspects of Daoism rather than presenting them as features of distinct movements.

X. Liu, *Classifying the Zhuangzi Chapters*
Very useful textual study of the *Zhuangzi*, arguing for the historicity of certain arrangements and dates of the various parts of the text.

V. H. Mair, ed., *Experimental Essays on the Zhuangzi*

H.-G. Moeller, *The Moral Fool: A Case for Amorality*
A study of the issue of the dangers of morality in general, but with some interesting focus on what Moeller thinks is Zhuangzi's argument against the value of morality.

H. D. Roth, *Companion to A. C. Graham's Chuang Tzu: The Inner Chapters*

E. Slingerland, *Effortless Action: Wu-wei as Conceptual Metaphor*
Not limited to Daoism, this study nonetheless tracks the historical development of the concept of *wu-wei* (non-action or "effortless action") so central to the Daoist thinkers.

# Buddhism

## *Primary sources*

The little text *Dhammapada* still has a strong following, and there are a number of good translations. My own favorite of these is that of the American monk Thanissaro Bhikkhu (made available free of charge through his Metta Forest Monastery, or online at www.accesstoinsight.org, where many other excellent translations of early Buddhist material can be found). Juan Mascaro's translation of the *Dhammapada* is also very good. There are two major series of English translations of the *suttas* of the Pali Canon. The most recent (and best, in my opinion) is the Wisdom Publications *Teachings of the Buddha* series. The Pali Text Society versions are also available, though somewhat harder to find. An excellent translation of a very good classical overview of Abhidharma thought, although one that will likely be difficult for newcomers to Buddhist thought, is Bhikkhu Bodhi (ed.), *A Comprehensive Manual of Abhidhamma* (a translation of *Abhidhammatha Sangaha*). Those interested in philosophy in the early Buddhist tradition will find indispensable the *Questions of King Milinda* (*Milindapanha*), the best and most recent translation of which is that of the English monk Bhikkhu Pesala. This version includes a historical and philosophical introduction, and can be found online free of charge, at www.buddhanet.net.

## *Secondary material*

K. Chen, *Buddhism in China: A Historical Survey*
An excellent and thorough history of the development of Mahayana Buddhist schools in China.

S. Collins, *Selfless Persons*
A study of the early (Pali) Buddhist view of *anatta* ("no-self") and its role in the Buddhist project.

J. L. Garfield, *The Fundamental Wisdom of the Middle Way: Nagarjuna's Mulamadhyamakakarika*
Translation and Study of the essential work of the Madhyamaka Buddhist philosopher Nagarjuna

R. Gombrich and W. Rahula, *What the Buddha Taught*
A concise overview of Buddhist doctrine and thought, by a Theravada monk.

D. J. Kalupahana, *Buddhist Philosophy, A Historical Analysis*
One of the best philosophical considerations of Buddhism prior to the new crop of texts focusing on the topic. Stronger on early Buddhism.

M. Siderits, *Buddhism as Philosophy*
Excellent overview and analysis of a number of debates and arguments in Buddhist philosophical thought, especially focusing on Abhidharma and later Mahayana philosophy, as well as engagement with Hindu philosophy.

A. Sumedho, *The Way it Is*
Collection of talks by the Theravada monk Ajahn Sumedho, aiming at application of Buddhist teachings to everyday life, rather than a scholarly account.

A. W. Watts, *The Way of Zen*
A unique and creative look at the Zen tradition and its relationship to Daoism

# The Bhagavad Gita, Vedanta, and Hinduism

## *Primary sources*

My favorite translation of the *Gita* is Barbara Stoler Miller's *The Bhagavad Gita: Krishna's Counsel in Time of War*. Not only is it faithful to the original Sanskrit text, but it is a beautiful piece of poetry in its own right. Another very good and more recent translation is George Thompson's *Bhagavad Gita: A New Translation*. Another volume that will offer an alternative view of the *Gita* is Srila Prabhupada's *The Bhagavad Gita As It Is*. Another very useful volume and translation of the Gita is Winthrop Sergeant's *The Bhagavad Gita*, which includes Sanskrit, transliteration, and word-by-word translation, in addition to

his full English translation. A number of translations of various Indian philosophical materials are collected in *A Sourcebook in Indian Philosophy*, edited
by Charles Moore and Sarvepalli Radhakrishnan. A more recent collection of
translations, specifically in Vedanta philosophy, is the collection *The Essential
Vedanta: A New Sourcebook of Advaita Vedanta*, edited by Eliot Deutsch
and Rohit Dalvi. An excellent collection of translations from the *Upanishads*
is Patrick Olivelle's *Upanishads*, and an older but still useful collection is
Radhakrishnan's *The Principal Upanishads*.

## *Secondary material*

E. D. Deutsch, *Advaita Vedanta: A Philosophical Reconstruction*
   Scholarly overview and interpretation of Advaita philosophy.

S. Kriyananda, *The Essence of the Bhagavad Gita*
   An interesting interpretation of the *Gita* from the perspective of religious
   practitioner and devotee rather than a scholarly treatment.

S. Radhakrishnan, *Indian Philosophy, Vol. 1 and 2*
   Excellent but dated focused scholarly overview of Indian philosophical
   thought. Volume one is on the "heterodox" schools, particularly Buddhist
   and Jain philosophy, while Volume two covers the six "orthodox" schools,
   including Vedanta.

E. Sharpe, *The Universal Gita: Western Images of the Bhagavad Gita*
   Study of a number of interpretations of the *Gita* by western thinkers.

# Index